ROGET'S THESAU

OF

ENGLISH WORDS AND PHRASES

CLASS I

WORDS EXPRESSING ABSTRACT RELATIONS

SECTION I.

EXISTENCE

1. BEING, IN THE ABSTRACT

1. Existence -- **N.** existence, being, entity, ens *[Lat.]*, esse *[Lat.]*, subsistence.

reality, actuality; positiveness &c *adj.;* fact, matter of fact, sober reality; truth &c 494; actual existence.

presence &c *(existence in space)* 186; coexistence &c 120.

stubborn fact, hard fact; not a dream &c 515; no joke.

center of life, essence, inmost nature, inner reality, vital principle.

[Science of existence], ontology.

V. exist, be; have being &c *n.;* subsist, live, breathe, stand, obtain, be the case; occur &c *(event)* 151; have place, prevail; find oneself, pass the time, vegetate.

consist in, lie in; be comprised in, be contained in, be constituted by.

come into existence &c *n.;* arise &c *(begin)* 66; come forth &c *(appear)* 446.

become &c *(be converted)* 144; bring into existence &c 161.

3. Substantiality -- **N.** substantiality, hypostasis; person, being, thing, object, article, item; something, a being, an existence; creature, body, substance, flesh and blood, stuff, substratum; matter &c 316; corporeity†, element, essential nature, groundwork, materiality, substantialness, vital part.

[Totality of existences], world &c 318; plenum.

Adj. substantive, substantial; hypostatic; personal, bodily, tangible &c *(material)* 316; corporeal.

Adv. substantially &c *adj.;* bodily, essentially.

4. Unsubstantiality -- **N.** unsubstantiality†, insubstantiality; nothingness, nihility†; no degree, no part, no quantity, no thing.

nothing, naught, nil, nullity, zero, cipher, no one, nobody; never a one, ne'er a one *[Contr.]*; no such thing, none in the world; nothing whatever, nothing at all, nothing on earth; not a particle &c *(smallness)* 32; all talk, moonshine, stuff and nonsense; matter of no importance, matter of no consequence.

thing of naught, man of straw, John Doe and Richard Roe, faggot voter; nominis umbra *[Lat.]*, nonentity; flash in the pan, vox et praeterea nihil *[Lat.]*.

blood; ingenerate†, ingenite†; indigenous; in the grain &c *n.;* bred in the bone, instinctive; inward, internal &c 221; to the manner born; virtual.

characteristic &c *(special)* 79, *(indicative)* 550; invariable, incurable, incorrigible, ineradicable, fixed.

Adv. intrinsically &c *adj.;* at bottom, in the main, in effect, practically, virtually, substantially, au fond; fairly.

Phr. character is higher than intellect [Emerson]; come give us a taste of your quality [Hamlet]; magnos homines virtute metimur non fortuna *[Lat.]* [Nepos]; non numero haec judicantur sed pondere *[Lat.]* [Cicero]; vital spark of heavenly flame [Pope].

External conditions

6. Extrinsicality -- **N.** extrinsicality†, objectiveness, non ego; extraneousness &c 57; accident; appearance, phenomenon &c 448.

Adj. derived from without; objective; extrinsic, extrinsical†; extraneous &c *(foreign)* 57; modal, adventitious; ascititious†, adscititious†; incidental, accidental, nonessential; contingent, fortuitous.

implanted, ingrafted†; inculcated, infused.

outward, apparent &c *(external)* 220.

Adv. extrinsically &c *adj.*.

4. MODAL EXISTENCE

Absolute

7. State -- **N.** state, condition, category, estate, lot, ease, trim, mood, pickle, plight, temper; aspect &c *(appearance)* 448, dilemma, pass, predicament.

constitution, habitude, diathesis†; frame, fabric &c 329; stamp, set, fit, mold, mould.

mode, modality, schesis†; form &c *(shape)* 240.

tone, tenor, turn; trim, guise, fashion, light, complexion, style, character.

V. be in a state, possess a state, enjoy a state, labor under a state &c *n.;* be on a footing, do, fare; come to pass.

Adj. conditional, modal, formal; structural, organic.

Adv. conditionally &c *adj.;* as the matter stands, as things are; such being the case &c 8.

Relative

8. Circumstance -- N. circumstance, situation, phase, position, posture, attitude, place, point; terms; regime; footing, standing, status.

occasion, juncture, conjunctive; contingency &c *(event)* 151.

predicament; emergence, emergency; exigency, crisis, pinch, pass, push; occurrence; turning point.

bearings, how the land lies.

surroundings, context, environment 232; location 184.

contingency, dependence *(uncertainty)* 475; causation 153, attribution 155.

Adj. circumstantial; given, conditional, provisional; critical; modal; contingent, incidental; adventitious &c *(extrinsic)* 6; limitative[†].

Adv. in the circumstances, under the circumstances &c *n.,* the circumstances, conditions &c 7; thus, in such wise.

accordingly; that being the case, such being the case, in view of the circumstances; that being so, sith[†], since, seeing that.

as matters stand; as things go, as times go.

conditionally, provided, if, in case; if so, if so be, if it be so; depending on circumstances, in certain circumstances, under certain conditions; if it so happen, if it so turn out; in the event of; in such a contingency, in such a case, in such an event; provisionally, unless, without.

according to circumstances, according to the occasion; as it may happen, as it may turn out, as it may be; as the case may be, as the wind blows; pro re nata *[Lat.]*.

Phr. yet are my sins not those of circumstance [Lytton].

SECTION II.

RELATION

1. ABSOLUTE RELATION

9. Relation -- **N.** relation, bearing, reference, connection, concern, cognation; correlation &c 12; analogy; similarity &c 17; affinity, homology, alliance, homogeneity, association; approximation &c *(nearness)* 197; filiation &c *(consanguinity)* 11; interest; relevancy &c 23; dependency, relationship, relative position.

comparison &c 464; ratio, proportion.

link, tie, bond of union.

V. be related &c *adj.;* have a relation &c *n.;* relate to, refer to; bear upon, regard, concern, touch, affect, have to do with; pertain to, belong to, appertain to; answer to; interest.

bring into relation with, bring to bear upon; connect, associate, draw a parallel; link &c 43.

Adj. relative; correlative &c 12; cognate; relating to &c *v.;* relative to, in relation with, referable or referrible to†; belonging to &c *v.;* appurtenant to, in common with.

related, connected; implicated, associated, affiliated, allied to; en rapport, in touch with.

approximative†, approximating; proportional, proportionate, proportionable; allusive, comparable.

in the same category &c 75; like &c 17; relevant &c *(apt)* 23; applicable, equiparant†.

Adv. relatively &c *adj.;* pertinently &c 23.

thereof; as to, as for, as respects, as regards; about; concerning &c *v.;* anent; relating to, as relates to; with relation, with reference to, with respect to, with regard to; in respect of; while speaking of, a propos of *[Fr.]*; in connection with; by the way, by the by; whereas; for as much as, in as much as; in point of, as far as; on the part of, on the score of; quoad hoc *[Lat.]*; pro re nata *[Lat.]*; under the head of &c *(class)* 75, of; in the matter of, in re.

Phr. thereby hangs a tale [Taming of the Shrew].

10. *[Want, or absence of relation.]* **Irrelation** --
 N. irrelation†, dissociation; misrelation†; inapplicability; inconnection†; multifariousness; disconnection &c *(disjunction)* 44; inconsequence, independence; incommensurability; irreconcilableness &c *(disagreement)* 24; heterogeneity; unconformity &c 83; irrelevancy, impertinence, nihil ad rem *[Lat.]*; intrusion &c 24; non-pertinence.

V. have no relation to &c 9; have no bearing upon, have no concern with &c 9, have no business with; not concern &c 9; have no business there, have nothing to do with, intrude &c 24.

bring in head and shoulders, drag in head and shoulders, lug in head and shoulders.

Adj. irrelative†, irrespective, unrelated; arbitrary; independent, unallied; unconnected, disconnected; adrift, isolated, insular; extraneous, strange, alien, foreign, outlandish, exotic.

not comparable, incommensurable, heterogeneous; unconformable &c 83.

irrelevant, inapplicable; not pertinent, not to the, purpose; impertinent, inapposite, beside the mark, a propos de bottes *[Fr.]*; aside from the purpose, away from the purpose, foreign to the purpose, beside the purpose, beside the question, beside the transaction, beside the point; misplaced &c *(intrusive)* 24; traveling out of the record.

remote, far-fetched, out of the way, forced, neither here nor there, quite another thing; detached, segregate; disquiparant†.

multifarious; discordant &c 24.

incidental, parenthetical, obiter dicta, episodic.

Adv. parenthetically &c *adj.;* by the way, by the by; en passant *[Fr.]*, incidentally; irrespectively &c *adj.;* without reference to, without regard to; in the abstract &c 87; a se.

11. *[Relations of kindred.]* **Consanguinity** --

N. consanguinity, relationship, kindred, blood; parentage &c *(paternity)* 166; filiation†, affiliation; lineage, agnation†, connection, alliance; family connection, family tie; ties of blood; nepotism.

kinsman, kinfolk; kith and kin; relation, relative; connection; sibling, sib; next of kin; uncle, aunt, nephew, niece; cousin, cousin-german†; first cousin, second cousin; cousin once removed, cousin twice removed; &c near relation, distant relation; brother, sister, one's own flesh and blood.

family, fraternity; brotherhood, sisterhood, cousinhood†.

race, stock, generation; sept &c 166; stirps, side; strain; breed, clan, tribe, nation.

V. be related to &c *adj..* claim relationship with &c *n..* with.

Adj. related, akin, consanguineous, of the blood, family, allied, collateral; cognate, agnate, connate; kindred; affiliated; fraternal.

intimately related, nearly related, closely related, remotely related, distantly related, allied; german.

12. *[Double or reciprocal relation.]* **Correlation** -- **N.** reciprocalness &c *adj.*[†]; reciprocity, reciprocation; mutuality, correlation, interdependence, interrelation, connection, link, association; interchange &c 148; exchange, barter.

reciprocator, reprocitist.

V. reciprocate, alternate; interchange &c 148; exchange; counterchange[†].

Adj. reciprocal, mutual, commutual[†], correlative, reciprocative, interrelated, closely related; alternate; interchangeable; interdependent; international; complemental, complementary.

Adv. mutually, mutatis mutandis *[Lat.]*; vice versa; each other, one another; by turns &c 148; reciprocally &c *adj.*.

Phr. happy in our mutual help [Milton].

13. Identity -- **N.** identity, sameness; coincidence, coalescence; convertibility; equality &c 27; selfness[†], self, oneself; identification.

monotony, tautology &c *(repetition)* 104.

facsimile &c *(copy)* 21; homoousia: alter ego &c *(similar)* 17; ipsissima verba &c *(exactness)* 494 [Lat.]; same; self, very, one and the same; very thing, actual thing; real McCoy; no other; one and only; in the flesh.

V. be identical &c *adj.;* coincide, coalesce, merge.

treat as the same, render the same, identical; identify; recognize the identity of.

Adj. identical; self, ilk; the same &c *n..* selfsame, one and the same, homoousian†.

coincide, coalescent, coalescing; indistinguishable; one; equivalent &c *(equal)* 27; tweedle dee and tweedle dum *[Lat.]*; much the same, of a muchness†; unaltered.

Adv. identically &c *adj.;* on all fours.

14. *[Noncoincidence.]* **Contrariety** -- **N.** contrariety, contrast, foil, antithesis, oppositeness; contradiction; antagonism &c *(opposition)* 708; clashing, repugnance.

inversion &c 218; the opposite, the reverse, the inverse, the converse, the antipodes, the antithesis, the other extreme.

V. be contrary &c *adj.;* contrast with, oppose; diller toto coelo *[Lat.]*.

invert, reverse, turn the tables; turn topsy-turvy, turn end for end, turn upside down, turn inside out.

contradict, contravene; antagonize &c 708.

Adj. contrary, contrarious[†], contrariant[†]; opposite, counter, dead against; converse, reverse; opposed, antithetical, contrasted, antipodean, antagonistic, opposing; conflicting, inconsistent, contradictory, at cross purposes; negative; hostile &c 703.

differing toto coelo *[Lat.]*; diametrically opposite; diametrically opposed; as opposite as black and white, as opposite as light and darkness, as opposite as fire and water, as opposite as the poles; as different as night and day; Hyperion to a satyr [Hamlet]; quite the contrary, quite the reverse; no such thing, just the other way, tout au contraire *[Fr.]*.

Adv. contrarily &c *adj.;* contra, contrariwise, per contra, on the contrary, nay rather; vice versa; on the other hand &c *(in compensation)* 30.

Phr. all concord's born of contraries [B. Jonson].

Thesis, antithesis, synthesis [Marx].

15. Difference -- **N.** difference; variance, variation, variety; diversity, dissimilarity &c 18; disagreement &c 24; disparity &c *(inequality)* 28; distinction, contradistinction; alteration.

modification, permutation, moods and tenses.

nice distinction, fine distinction, delicate distinction, subtle distinction; shade of difference, nuance; discrimination &c 465; differentia.

different thing, something else, apple off another tree, another pair of shoes; horse of a different color; this that or the other.

V. be different &c *adj.;* differ, vary, ablude†, mismatch, contrast; divaricate; differ toto coelo *[Lat.]*, differ longo intervallo *[It]*.

vary, modify &c *(change)* 140.

discriminate &c 465.

Adj. differing &c *v.;* different, diverse, heterogeneous, multifarious, polyglot; distinguishable, dissimilar; varied, modified; diversified, various, divers, all manner of, all kinds of; variform &c 81; daedal†.

other, another, not the same; unequal &c 28.

unmatched; widely apart, poles apart, distinctive; characteristic, discriminative, distinguishing.

incommensurable, incommensurate.

Adv. differently &c *adj.*.

Phr. il y a fagots et fagots.

2. CONTINUOUS RELATION

16. Uniformity -- **N.** uniformity; homogeneity, homogeneousness; consistency; connaturality[†], connaturalness[†]; homology; accordance; conformity &c 82; agreement &c 23; consonance, uniformness.

regularity, constancy, even tenor, routine; monotony.

V. be uniform &c *adj.*; accord with &c 23; run through.

become uniform &c *adj.*; conform to &c 82.

render uniform, homogenize &c *adj.*; assimilate, level, smooth, dress.

Adj. uniform; homogeneous, homologous; of a piece *[Fr.]*, consistent, connatural[†]; monotonous, even, invariable; regular, unchanged, undeviating, unvaried, unvarying.

unsegmented.

Adv. uniformly &c *adj.;* uniformly with &c *(conformably)* 82; in harmony with &c *(agreeing)* 23.

always, invariably, without exception, without fail, unfailingly, never otherwise; by clockwork.

Phr. ab uno disce omnes *[Lat.]*.

16a. *[Absence or want of uniformity.]* **Nonuniformity** -- **N.** diversity, irregularity, unevenness; multiformity &c 81; unconformity &c 83; roughness &c 256; dissimilarity, dissimilitude, divarication, divergence.

Adj. diversified varied, irregular, uneven, rough &c 256; multifarious; multiform &c 81; of various kinds; all manner of, all sorts of, all kinds of.

Adv. variously, in all manner of ways, here there and everywhere.

3. PARTIAL RELATION

17. Similarity -- **N.** similarity, resemblance, likeness, similitude, semblance; affinity, approximation, parallelism; agreement &c 23; analogy, analogicalness†; correspondence, homoiousia†, parity.

connaturalness†, connaturality†; brotherhood, family likeness.

alliteration, rhyme, pun.

repetition &c 104; sameness &c *(identity)* 13; uniformity &c 16; isogamy†.

analogue; the like; match, pendant, fellow companion, pair, mate, twin, double, counterpart, brother, sister; one's second self, alter ego, chip of the old block, par nobile fratrum *[Lat.]*, Arcades ambo†, birds of a feather, et hoc genus omne *[Lat.]*; gens de meme famille *[Fr.]*.

parallel; simile; type &c *(metaphor)* 521; image &c *(representation)* 554; photograph; close resemblance, striking resemblance, speaking resemblance, faithful likeness, faithful resemblance.

V. be similar &c *adj.;* look like, resemble, bear resemblance; smack of, savor of, approximate; parallel, match, rhyme with; take after; imitate &c 19; favor, span *[U.S.]*.

render similar &c *adj.;* assimilate, approximate, bring near; connaturalize†, make alike; rhyme, pun.

Adj. similar; resembling &c *v.;* like, alike; twin.

analogous, analogical; parallel, of a piece *[Fr.]*; such as, so; homoiousian†.

connatural†, congener, allied to; akin to &c *(consanguineous)* 11.

approximate, much the same, near, close, something like, sort of, in the ballpark, such like; a show of; mock, pseudo, simulating, representing.

exact &c *(true)* 494; lifelike, faithful; true to nature, true to life, the very image, the very picture of; for all the world like, comme deux gouttes d'eau *[Fr.]*; as like as two peas in a pod, as like as it can stare; instar omnium *[Lat.]*, cast in the same mold, ridiculously like.

Adv. as if, so to speak; as it were, as if it were; quasi, just as, veluti in speculum *[Lat.]*.

Phr. et sic de similibus *[Lat.]*; tel maitre tel valet *[Fr.]*; tel pere tel fils *[Fr.]*; like master, like servant; like father, like son; the fruit doesn't fall far from the tree; a chip off the old block

18. Dissimilarity -- **N.** dissimilarity, dissimilaritude†; unlikeness, diversity, disparity, dissemblance†; divergence, variation.; difference &c 15; novelty, originality; creativeness; oogamy†.

V. be unlike &c *adj.;* vary &c *(differ)* 15; bear no resemblance to, differ toto coelo *[Lat.]*.

render unlike &c *adj.;* vary &c *(diversify)* 140.

Adj. dissimilar, unlike, disparate; divergent; of a different kind; &c *(class)* 75 unmatched, unique; new, novel; unprecedented &c 83; original.

nothing of the kind; no such thing, quite another thing; far from it, cast in a different mold, tertium quid *[Lat.]*, as like a dock as a daisy, very like a whale [Hamlet]; as different as chalk from cheese, as different as Macedon and Monmouth; lucus a non lucendo *[Lat.]*.

diversified &c 16.1.

Adv. otherwise.

Phr. diis aliter visum *[Lat.]*; no more like my father than I to Hercules [Hamlet].

19. Imitation -- **N.** imitation; copying &c *v.;* transcription; repetition, duplication, reduplication; quotation; reproduction; mimeograph, xerox, facsimile; reprint, offprint.

mockery, mimicry; simulation, impersonation, personation; representation &c 554; semblance; copy &c 21; assimilation.

paraphrase, parody, take-off, lampoon, caricature &c 21.

plagiarism; forgery, counterfeit &c *(falsehood)* 544; celluloid.

imitator, echo, cuckoo[†], parrot, ape, monkey, mocking bird, mime; copyist, copycat; plagiarist, pirate.

V. imitate, copy, mirror, reflect, reproduce, repeat; do like, echo, reecho, catch; transcribe; match, parallel.

mock, take off, mimic, ape, simulate, impersonate, personate; act &c *(drama)* 599; represent &c 554; counterfeit, parody, travesty, caricature, lampoon, burlesque.

follow in the steps of, tread in the steps, follow in the footsteps of, follow in the wake of; take pattern by; follow suit, follow the example of; walk in the shoes of, take a leaf out of another's book, strike in with, follow suit; take after, model after; emulate.

Adj. imitated &c v.; mock, mimic; modelled after, molded on.

paraphrastic; literal; imitative; secondhand; imitable; aping, apish, mimicking.

Adv. literally, to the letter, verbatim, literatim *[Lat.]*, sic, totidem verbis *[Lat.]*, word for word, mot a mot *[Fr.]*; exactly, precisely.

Phr. like master like man; like - but oh! how different! [Wordsworth]; genius borrows nobly [Emerson]; pursuing echoes calling 'mong the rocks [A.

Coles]; quotation confesses inferiority [Emerson]; Imitation is the sincerest form of flattery.

20. Nonimitation -- **N.** no imitation; originality; creativeness.

invention, creation.

Adj. unimitated[†], uncopied[†]; unmatched, unparalleled; inimitable &c 13; unique, original; creative, inventive, untranslated; exceptional, rare, sui generis uncommon *[Lat.]*, unexampled.

20a. Variation -- **N.** variation; alteration &c *(change)* 140.

modification, moods and tenses; discrepance[†], discrepancy.

divergency &c 291; deviation &c 279; aberration; innovation.

V. vary &c *(change)* 140; deviate &c 279; diverge &c 291; alternate, swerve.

Adj. varied &c *v.;* modified; diversified &c 16.1.

21. *[Result of imitation.]* **Copy** -- **N.** copy, facsimile, counterpart, effigies, effigy, form, likeness.

image, picture, photo, xerox, similitude, semblance, ectype[†], photo offset, electrotype; imitation &c 19; model, representation, adumbration, study; portrait &c *(representation)* 554; resemblance.

duplicate, reproduction; cast, tracing; reflex, reflexion *[Brit.]*, reflection; shadow, echo.

transcript *[copy into a non-visual form]*, transcription; recording, scan.

chip off the old block; reprint, new printing; rechauffe *[Fr.]*; apograph[†], fair copy.

parody, caricature, burlesque, travesty, travestie†, paraphrase.

[copy with some differences] derivative, derivation, modification, expansion, extension, revision; second edition &c *(repetition)* 104.

servile copy, servile imitation; plagiarism, counterfeit, fake &c *(deception)* 545; pasticcio†.

Adj. faithful; lifelike &c *(similar)* 17; close, conscientious.

unoriginal, imitative, derivative.

22. *[Thing copied.]* **Prototype** -- **N.** prototype, original, model, pattern, precedent, standard, ideal, reference, scantling, type; archetype, antitype†; protoplast, module, exemplar, example, ensample†, paradigm; lay-figure.

text, copy, design; fugleman†, keynote.

die, mold; matrix, last, plasm†; proplasm†, protoplasm; mint; seal, punch, intaglio, negative; stamp.

V. be an example, be a role model, set an example; set a copy.

Phr. a precedent embalms a principle *[Lat.Tran]* [Disraeli]; exempla sunt odiosa *[Lat.]*.

4. GENERAL RELATION

23. Agreement -- **N.** agreement; accord, accordance; unison, harmony; concord &c 714; concordance, concert; understanding, mutual understanding.

conformity &c 82; conformance; uniformity &c 16; consonance, consentaneousness†, consistency; congruity, congruence; keeping; congeniality; correspondence, parallelism, apposition, union.

fitness, aptness &c *adj.;* relevancy; pertinence, pertinencey†; sortance†; case in point; aptitude, coaptation†, propriety, applicability, admissibility, commensurability, compatibility; cognation &c *(relation)* 9.

adaption†, adjustment, graduation, accommodation; reconciliation, reconcilement; assimilation.

consent &c *(assent)* 488; concurrence &c 178; cooperation &c 709.

right man in the right place, very thing; quite the thing, just the thing.

V. be accordant &c *adj.;* agree, accord, harmonize; correspond, tally, respond; meet, suit, fit, befit, do, adapt itself to; fall in with, chime in with, square with, quadrate with, consort with, comport with; dovetail, assimilate; fit like a glove, fit to a tittle, fit to a T; match &c 17; become one; homologate[†].

consent &c *(assent)* 488.

render accordant &c *adj.;* fit, suit, adapt, accommodate; graduate; adjust &c *(render equal)* 27; dress, regulate, readjust; accord, harmonize, reconcile; fadge[†], dovetail, square.

Adj. agreeing, suiting &c *v.;* in accord, accordant, concordant, consonant, congruous, consentaneous[†], correspondent, congenial; coherent; becoming; harmonious reconcilable, conformable; in accordance with, in harmony with, in keeping with, in unison with, &c *n.;* at one with, of one mind, of a piece *[Fr.]*; consistent, compatible, proportionate; commensurate; on all fours.

apt, apposite, pertinent, pat; to the point, to the purpose; happy, felicitous, germane, ad rem *[Lat.]*, in point, on point, directly on point, bearing upon, applicable, relevant, admissible.

fit adapted, in loco, a propos *[Fr.]*, appropriate, seasonable, sortable, suitable, idoneous[†], deft; meet &c *(expedient)* 646.

at home, in one's proper element.

Adv. a propos of *[Fr.]*; pertinently &c *adj.*.

Phr. rem acu tetigisti *[Lat.]*; if the shoe fits, wear it; the cap fits; auxilia humilia firma consensus facit *[Lat.]* [Syrus]; discers concordia *[Lat.]* [Ovid].

24. Disagreement -- **N.** disagreement; discord, discordance; dissonance, dissidence, discrepancy; unconformity &c 83; incongruity, incongruence†; discongruity†, mesalliance; jarring &c *v.;* dissension &c 713; conflict &c *(opposition)* 708; bickering, clashing, misunderstanding, wrangle.

disparity, mismatch, disproportion; dissimilitude, inequality; disproportionateness &c *adj.*†*;* variance, divergence, repugnance.

unfitness &c *adj.;* inaptitude, impropriety; inapplicability &c *adj.;* inconsistency, inconcinnity†; irrelevancy &c *(irrelation)* 10.

misjoining†, misjoinder†; syncretism†, intrusion, interference; concordia discors *[Lat.]*.

fish out of water.

V. disagree; clash, jar &c *(discord)* 713; interfere, intrude, come amiss; not concern &c 10; mismatch; humano capiti cervicem jungere equinam *[Lat.]*.

Adj. disagreeing &c *v.;* discordant, discrepant; at variance, at war; hostile, antagonistic, repugnant, incompatible, irreconcilable, inconsistent with; unconformable, exceptional &c 83; intrusive, incongruous; disproportionate, disproportionated†; inharmonious, unharmonious†; inconsonant, unconsonant†; divergent, repugnant to.

inapt, unapt, inappropriate, improper; unsuited, unsuitable; inapplicable, not to the point; unfit, unfitting, unbefitting; unbecoming; illtimed, unseasonable, mal a propos *[Fr.]*, inadmissible; inapposite &c *(irrelevant)* 10.

uncongenial; ill-assorted, ill-sorted; mismatched, misjoined†, misplaced, misclassified; unaccommodating, irreducible, incommensurable, uncommensurable†; unsympathetic.

out of character, out of keeping, out of proportion, out of joint, out of tune, out of place, out of season, out of its element; at odds with, at variance with.

Adv. in defiance, in contempt, in spite of; discordantly &c *adj.;* a tort et a travers†.

Phr. asinus ad lyram *[Lat.]*.

SECTION III.

QUANTITY

1. SIMPLE QUANTITY

25. *[Absolute quantity.]* **Quantity** -- **N.** quantity, magnitude; size &c *(dimensions)* 192; amplitude, magnitude, mass, amount, sum, quantum, measure, substance, strength, force.

[Science of quantity.] mathematics, mathesis[†].

[Logic.] category, general conception, universal predicament.

[Definite or finite quantity.] armful, handful, mouthful, spoonful, capful; stock, batch, lot, dose; yaffle[†].

V. quantify, measure, fix, estimate, determine, quantitate, enumerate.

Adj. quantitative, some, any, aught, more or less, a few.

Adv. to the tune of, all of, a full, the sum of, fully, exactly, precisely.

26. *[Relative quantity.]* **Degree** -- **N.** degree, grade, extent, measure, amount, ratio, stint, standard, height, pitch; reach, amplitude, range, scope, caliber; gradation, shade; tenor, compass; sphere, station, rank, standing; rate, way, sort.

point, mark, stage &c *(term)* 71; intensity, strength &c *(greatness)* 31.

Adj. comparative; gradual, shading off; within the bounds &c *(limit)* 233.

Adv. by degrees, gradually, inasmuch, pro tanto *[It]*; however, howsoever; step by step, bit by bit, little by little, inch by inch, drop by drop; a little at a time, by inches, by slow degrees, by degrees, by little and little; in some degree, in some measure; to some extent; di grado in grado *[Lat.]*.

2. COMPARATIVE QUANTITY

27. *[Sameness of quantity or degree.]* **Equality** --
 N. equality, parity, coextension†, symmetry, balance, poise; evenness, monotony, level.

equivalence; equipollence†, equipoise, equilibrium, equiponderance†; par, quits, a wash; not a pin to choose; distinction without a difference, six of one and half a dozen of the other; tweedle dee and tweedle dum *[Lat.]*; identity &c 13; similarity &c 17.

equalization, equation; equilibration, co-ordination, adjustment, readjustment.

drawn game, drawn battle; neck and neck race; tie, draw, standoff, dead heat.

match, peer, compeer, equal, mate, fellow, brother; equivalent.

V. be equal &c *adj.;* equal, match, reach, keep pace with, run abreast; come to, amount to, come up to; be on a level with, lie on a level with; balance; cope with; come to the same thing.

render equal &c *adj.;* equalize level, dress, balance, equate, handicap, give points, spot points, handicap, trim, adjust, poise; fit, accommodate; adapt &c *(render accordant)* 23; strike a balance; establish equality, restore equality, restore equilibrium; readjust; stretch on the bed of Procrustes.

Adj. equal, even, level, monotonous, coequal, symmetrical, coordinate; on a par with, on a level with, on a footing with; up to the mark; equiparant[†].

equivalent, tantamount; indistinguishable; quits; homologous; synonymous &c 522; resolvable into, convertible, much at one, as broad as long, neither more nor less.; much the same as, the same thing as, as good as; all one, all the same; equipollent, equiponderant[†], equiponderous[†], equibalanced[†]; equalized &c *v.;* drawn; half and half; isochronal, isochronous isoperimetric†, isoperimetrical†; isobath *[Ocean.]*, isobathic *[Ocean.]*.

Adv. equally &c *adj.;* pari passu *[Lat.]*, ad eundum *[Lat.]*, caeteris paribus *[Lat.]*; in equilibrio *[Lat.]*; to all intents and purposes.

Phr. it comes to the same thing, it amounts to the same thing; what is sauce for the goose is sauce for the gander.

28. *[Difference of quantity or degree.]* **Inequality** -- **N.** inequality; disparity, imparity; odds; difference &c 15; unevenness; inclination of the balance, partiality, bias, weight; shortcoming; casting weight, make-weight; superiority &c 33; inferiority &c 34; inequation†.

V. be unequal &c *adj.;* countervail; have the advantage, give the advantage; turn the scale; kick the beam; topple, topple over; overmatch &c 33; not come up to &c 34.

Adj. unequal, uneven, disparate, partial; unbalanced, overbalanced; top-heavy, lopsided, biased, skewed; disquiparant†.

Adv. haud passibus aequis *[Lat.]* [Vergil].

29. Mean -- **N.** mean, average; median, mode; balance, medium, mediocrity, generality; golden mean &c *(mid-course)* 628; middle &c 68; compromise &c 774; middle course, middle state; neutrality.

mediocrity, least common denominator.

V. split the difference; take the average &c *n.;* reduce to a mean &c *n.;* strike a balance, pair off.

Adj. mean, intermediate; middle &c 68; average; neutral.

mediocre, middle-class; commonplace &c *(unimportant)* 643.

Adv. on an average, in the long run; taking one with another, taking all things together, taking it for all in all; communibus annis *[Lat.]*, in round numbers.

Phr. medium tenuere beati *[Lat.]*.

30. Compensation -- **N.** compensation, equation; commutation; indemnification; compromise; &c 774 neutralization, nullification; counteraction &c 179; reaction; measure for measure, retaliation, &c 718 equalization; &c 27; robbing Peter to pay Paul.

set-off, offset; make-weight, casting-weight; counterpoise, ballast; indemnity, equivalent, quid pro quo; bribe, hush money; amends &c *(atonement)* 952; counterbalance, counterclaim; cross-debt, cross-demand.

V. make compensation; compensate, compense†; indemnify; counteract, countervail, counterpoise; balance; outbalance†, overbalance, counterbalance; set off; hedge, square, give and take; make up for, lee way; cover, fill up, neutralize, nullify; equalize &c 27; make good; redeem &c *(atone)* 952.

Adj. compensating, compensatory; countervailing &c *v.;* in the opposite scale; equivalent &c *(equal)* 27.

Adv. in return, in consideration; but, however, yet, still, notwithstanding; nevertheless, nathless†, none the less; although, though; albeit, howbeit; mauger†; at all events, at any rate; be that as it may, for all that, even so, on the other, hand, at the same time, quoad minus *[Lat.]*, quand meme *[Fr.]*, however that may be; after all is said and done; taking one thing with another &c *(average)* 29.

Phr. light is mingled with the gloom [Whittier]; every dark cloud has a silver lining; primo avulso non deficit alter [Vergil]; saepe creat molles aspera spina rosas *[Lat.]* [Ovid].

1 QUANTITY BY COMPARISON WITH A STANDARD

31. Greatness -- **N.** greatness &c *adj.;* magnitude; size &c *(dimensions)* 192; multitude &c *(number)* 102; immensity; enormity; infinity &c 105; might, strength, intensity, fullness; importance &c 642.

great quantity, quantity, deal, power, sight, pot, volume, world; mass, heap &c *(assemblage)* 72; stock &c *(store)* 636; peck, bushel, load, cargo; cartload[†], wagonload, shipload; flood, spring tide; abundance &c *(sufficiency)* 639.

principal part, chief part, main part, greater part, major part, best part, essential part; bulk, mass &c *(whole)* 50.

V. be great &c *adj.;* run high, soar, tower, transcend; rise to a great height, carry to a great height; know no bounds; ascend, mount.

enlarge &c *(increase)* 35, *(expand)* 194.

Adj. great; greater &c 33; large, considerable, fair, above par; big, huge &c *(large in size)* 192; Herculean, cyclopean; ample; abundant; &c *(enough)* 639 full, intense, strong, sound, passing, heavy, plenary, deep, high; signal, at its height, in the zenith.

world-wide, widespread, far-famed, extensive; wholesale; many &c 102.

goodly, noble, precious, mighty; sad, grave, heavy, serious; far gone, arrant, downright; utter, uttermost; crass, gross, arch, profound, intense, consummate; rank, uninitiated, red-hot, desperate; glaring, flagrant, stark staring; thorough-paced, thoroughgoing; roaring, thumping; extraordinary.; important &c 642; unsurpassed &c *(supreme)* 33; complete &c 52.

august, grand, dignified, sublime, majestic &c *(repute)* 873.

vast, immense, enormous, extreme; inordinate, excessive, extravagant, exorbitant, outrageous, preposterous, unconscionable, swinging, monstrous, overgrown; towering, stupendous, prodigious, astonishing, incredible; marvelous &c 870.

unlimited &c *(infinite)* 105; unapproachable, unutterable, indescribable, ineffable, unspeakable, inexpressible, beyond expression, fabulous.

undiminished, unabated, unreduced[†], unrestricted.

absolute, positive, stark, decided, unequivocal, essential, perfect, finished.

remarkable, of mark, marked, pointed, veriest; noteworthy; renowned.

Adv. truly &c *(truth)* 494 *[in a positive degree];* decidedly, unequivocally, purely, absolutely, seriously, essentially, fundamentally, radically, downright, in all conscience; for the most part, in the main.

[in a complete degree] entirely &c *(completely)* 52; abundantly &c *(sufficiently)* 639; widely, far and wide.

[in a great or high degree] greatly &c *adj.;* much, muckle†, well, indeed, very, very much, a deal, no end of, most, not a little; pretty, pretty well; enough, in a great measure, richly; to a large extent, to a great extent, to a gigantic extent; on a large scale; so; never so, ever so; ever so dole; scrap, shred, tag, splinter, rag, much; by wholesale; mighty, powerfully; with a witness, ultra *[Lat.]*, in the extreme, extremely, exceedingly, intensely, exquisitely, acutely, indefinitely, immeasurably; beyond compare, beyond comparison, beyond measure, beyond all bounds; incalculably, infinitely.

[in a supreme degree] preeminently, superlatively &c *(superiority)* 33.

[in a too great degree] immoderately, monstrously, preposterously, inordinately, exorbitantly, excessively, enormously, out of all proportion, with a vengeance.

[in a marked degree] particularly, remarkably, singularly, curiously, uncommonly, unusually, peculiarly, notably, signally, strikingly, pointedly, mainly, chiefly; famously, egregiously, prominently, glaringly, emphatically, kat exochin *[Gr.]*, strangely, wonderfully, amazingly, surprisingly, astonishingly, incredibly, marvelously, awfully, stupendously.

[in an exceptional degree] peculiarly &c *(unconformity)* 83.

[in a violent degree] furiously &c *(violence)* 173; severely, desperately, tremendously, extravagantly, confoundedly, deucedly, devilishly, with a vengeance; a outrance†, a toute outrance*[Fr.]*.

[in a painful degree] painfully, sadly, grossly, sorely, bitterly, piteously, grievously, miserably, cruelly, woefully, lamentably, shockingly, frightfully, dreadfully, fearfully, terribly, horribly.

Phr. a maximis ad minima *[Lat.]*; greatness knows itself [Henry IV]; mightiest powers by deepest calms are fed [B.

Cornwall]; minimum decet libere cui multum licet *[Lat.]* [Seneca]; some are born great, some achieve greatness, and some have greatness thrust upon them [Twelfth Night].

32. Smallness -- N. smallness &c *adj.;* littleness &c *(small size)* 193; tenuity; paucity; fewness &c *(small number)* 103; meanness, insignificance *(unimportance)* 643; mediocrity, moderation.

small quantity, modicum, trace, hint, minimum; vanishing point; material point, atom, particle, molecule, corpuscle, point, speck, dot, mote, jot, iota, ace; minutiae, details; look, thought, idea, soupcon, dab, dight[†], whit, tittle, shade, shadow; spark, scintilla, gleam; touch, cast; grain, scruple, granule, globule, minim, sup, sip, sop, spice, drop, droplet, sprinkling, dash, morceau[†], screed, smack, tinge, tincture; inch, patch, scantling, tatter, cantlet[†], flitter, gobbet[†], mite, bit, morsel, crumb, seed, fritter, shive[†]; snip, snippet; snick[†], snack, snatch, slip, scrag[†]; chip, chipping; shiver, sliver, driblet, clipping, paring, shaving, hair.

nutshell; thimbleful, spoonful, handful, capful, mouthful; fragment; fraction &c *(part)* 51; drop in the ocean.

animalcule &c 193.

trifle &c *(unimportant thing)* 643; mere nothing, next to nothing; hardly anything; just enough to swear by; the shadow of a shade.

finiteness, finite quantity.

V. be small &c *adj.;* lie in a nutshell.

diminish &c *(decrease)* 36; *(contract)* 195.

Adj. small, little; diminutive &c *(small in size)* 193; minute; fine; inconsiderable, paltry &c *(unimportant)* 643; faint &c *(weak)* 160; slender, light, slight, scanty, scant, limited; meager &c *(insufficient)* 640; sparing; few &c 103; low, so-so, middling, tolerable, no great shakes; below par, under par, below the mark; at a low ebb; halfway; moderate, modest; tender, subtle.

inappreciable, evanescent, infinitesimal, homeopathic, very small; atomic, corpuscular, microscopic, molecular, subatomic.

mere, simple, sheer, stark, bare; near run.

dull, petty, shallow, stolid, ungifted, unintelligent.

Adv. to a small extent *[in a small degree],* on a small scale; a little bit, a wee bit; slightly &c *adj.;* imperceptibly; miserably, wretchedly; insufficiently &c 640; imperfectly; faintly &c 160; passably, pretty well, well enough.

[in a certain or limited degree] partially, in part; in a certain degree, to a certain degree; to a certain extent; comparatively; some, rather in some degree, in some measure; something, somewhat; simply, only, purely, merely; at least, at the least, at most, at the most; ever so little, as little as may be, tant soit peu *[Fr.]*, in ever so small a degree; thus far, pro

tanto *[It]*, within bounds, in a manner, after a fashion, so to speak.

almost, nearly, well-nigh, short of, not quite, all but; near upon, close upon; peu s'en faut *[Fr.]*, near the mark; within an ace of, within an inch of; on the brink of; scarcely, hardly, barely, only just, no more than.

about *[in an uncertain degree]*, thereabouts, somewhere about, nearly, say; be the same, be little more or less.

no ways *[in no degree]*, no way, no wise; not at all, not in the least, not a bit, not a bit of it, not a whit, not a jot, not a shadow; in no wise, in no respect; by no means, by no manner of means; on no account, at no hand.

Phr. dare pondus idonea fumo *[Lat.]* [Persius]; magno conatu magnas nugas *[Lat.]* [Terence]; small sands the mountain, moments make the year [Young].

2 QUANTITY BY COMPARISON WITH A SIMILAR OBJECT

33. *[Supremacy.]* **Superiority** -- **N.** superiority, majority; greatness &c 31; advantage; pull; preponderance, preponderation; vantage ground, prevalence, partiality; personal superiority; nobility

&c *(rank)* 875; Triton among the minnows, primus inter pares *[Lat.]*, nulli secundus *[Lat.]*, captain; crackajack *[U.S.]*.

supremacy, preeminence; lead; maximum; record; trikumia *[Gr.]*, climax; culmination &c *(summit)* 210; transcendence; ne plus ultra *[Lat.]*; lion's share, Benjamin's mess; excess, surplus &c *(remainder)* 40; *(redundancy)* 641.

V. be superior &c *adj.;* exceed, excel, transcend; outdo, outbalance†, outweigh, outrank, outrival, out-Herod; pass, surpass, get ahead of; over-top, override, overpass, overbalance, overweigh, overmatch; top, o'ertop, cap, beat, cut out; beat hollow; outstrip &c 303; eclipse, throw into the shade, take the shine out of, outshine, put one's nose out of joint; have the upper hand, have the whip hand of, have the advantage; turn the scale, kick the beam; play first fiddle &c *(importance)* 642; preponderate, predominate, prevail; precede, take precedence, come first; come to a head, culminate; beat all others, &c bear the palm; break the record; take the cake *[U.S.]*.

become larger, render larger &c *(increase)* 35, *(expand)* 194.

Adj. superior, greater, major, higher; exceeding &c *v.;* great &c 31; distinguished, ultra *[Lat.]*; vaulting; more than a match for.

supreme, greatest, utmost, paramount, preeminent, foremost, crowning; first-rate
&c *(important)* 642, *(excellent)* 648; unrivaled peerless, matchless; none such, second to none, sans pareil*[Fr.]*; unparagoned†, unparalleled, unequalled, unapproached†, unsurpassed; superlative, inimitable facile princeps *[Lat.]*, incomparable, sovereign, without parallel, nulli secundus *[Lat.]*, ne plus ultra *[Lat.]*; beyond compare, beyond comparison; culminating &c *(topmost)* 210; transcendent, transcendental; plus royaliste que le Roi *[Fr.]*, more catholic than the Pope increased &c *(added to)* 35; enlarged &c *(expanded)* 194.

Adv. beyond, more, over; over the mark, above the mark; above par; upwards of, in advance of; over and above; at the top of the scale, at its height.

[in a superior or supreme degree] eminently, egregiously, preeminently, surpassing, prominently, superlatively, supremely, above all, of all things, the most, to crown all, kat exochin *[Gr.]*, par excellence, principally, especially, particularly, peculiarly, a fortiori, even, yea, still more.

Phr. I shall not look upon his like again [Hamlet]; deos fortioribus addesse *[Lat.]* [Tacitus].

34. Inferiority -- **N.** inferiority, minority, subordinacy; shortcoming, deficiency; minimum;

smallness &c 32; imperfection; lower quality, lower worth.

[personal inferiority] commonalty &c 876.

V. be inferior &c *adj.;* fall short of, come short of; not pass, not come up to; want.

become smaller, render smaller &c *(decrease)* 36, *(contract)* 195; hide its diminished head, retire into the shade, yield the palm, play second fiddle, be upstaged, take a back seat.

Adj. inferior, smaller; small &c 32; minor, less, lesser, deficient, minus, lower, subordinate, secondary; secondrate &c *(imperfect)* 651; sub, subaltern; thrown into the shade; weighed in the balance and found wanting; not fit to hold a candle to, can't hold a candle to.

least, smallest &c *(little) (small)* &c 193; lowest.

diminished &c *(decreased)* 36; reduced &c *(contracted)* 195; unimportant &c 643.

Adv. less; under the mark, below the mark, below par; at the bottom of the scale, at a low ebb, at a disadvantage; short of, under.

3 CHANGES IN QUANTITY

35. Increase -- **N.** increase, augmentation, enlargement, extension; dilatation &c *(expansion)* 194; increment, accretion; accession &c 37; development, growth; aggrandizement, aggravation; rise; ascent &c 305; exaggeration exacerbation; spread &c *(dispersion)* 73; flood tide; gain, produce, product, profit.

V. increase, augment, add to, enlarge; dilate &c *(expand)* 194; grow, wax, get ahead.

gain strength; advance; run up, shoot up; rise; ascend &c 305; sprout &c 194.

aggrandize; raise, exalt; deepen, heighten; strengthen; intensify, enhance, magnify, redouble; aggravate, exaggerate; exasperate, exacerbate; add fuel to the flame, oleum addere camino*[Lat.]*, superadd &c *(add)* 37; spread &c *(disperse)* 73.

Adj. increased &c *v.;* on the increase, undiminished; additional &c *(added)* 37.

Adv. crescendo.

Phr. vires acquirit eundo *[Lat.]* [Vergil].

36. Nonincrease, Decrease -- **N.** decrease, diminution; lessening &c *v.;* subtraction &c 38; reduction, abatement, declension; shrinking

&c *(contraction.)* 195; coarctation†; abridgment &c *(shortening)* 201; extenuation.

subsidence, wane, ebb, decline; ebbing; descent &c 306; decrement, reflux, depreciation; deterioration &c 659; anticlimax; mitigation &c *(moderation)* 174.

V. decrease, diminish, lessen; abridge &c *(shorten)* 201; shrink &c *(contract)* 195; drop off, fall off, tail off; fall away, waste, wear; wane, ebb, decline; descend &c 306; subside; melt away, die away; retire into the shade, hide its diminished head, fall to a low ebb, run low, languish, decay, crumble.

bate, abate, dequantitate†; discount; depreciate; extenuate, lower, weaken, attenuate, fritter away; mitigate &c *(moderate)* 174; dwarf, throw into the shade; reduce &c 195; shorten &c 201; subtract &c 38.

Adj. unincreased† &c 35; decreased &c *v.;* decreasing &c *v.;* on the wane &c *n..*

Phr. a gilded halo hovering round decay [Byron]; fine by degrees and beautifully less [Prior].

3. CONJUNCTIVE QUANTITY

37. Addition -- **N.** addition, annexation, adjection†; junction &c 43; superposition, superaddition, superjunction†, superfetation; accession, reinforcement; increase &c 35; increment, supplement; accompaniment &c 88; interposition &c 228; insertion &c 300.

V. add, annex, affix, superadd†, subjoin, superpose; clap on, saddle on; tack to, append, tag; ingraft†; saddle with; sprinkle; introduce &c *(interpose)* 228; insert &c 300.

become added, accrue; advene†, supervene.

reinforce, reenforce, restrengthen†; swell the ranks of; augment &c 35.

Adj. added &c *v.;* additional; supplemental, supplementary; suppletory†, subjunctive; adjectitious†, adscititious†, ascititious†; additive, extra, accessory.

Adv. au reste *[Fr.]*, in addition, more, plus, extra; and, also, likewise, too, furthermore, further, item; and also, and eke; else, besides, to boot, et cetera; &c; and so on, and so forth; into the bargain, cum multis aliis *[Lat.]*, over and above, moreover.

with, withal; including, inclusive, as well as, not to mention, let alone; together with, along with, coupled with, in conjunction with; conjointly; jointly &c 43.

Phr. adde parvum parvo magnus acervus erit *[Lat.]*.

38. Nonaddition. Subtraction -- N. subtraction, subduction†; deduction, retrenchment; removal, withdrawal; ablation, sublation†; abstraction &c *(taking)* 789; garbling, &c *v*.. mutilation, detruncation†; amputation; abscission, excision, recision; curtailment &c 201; minuend, subtrahend; decrease &c 36; abrasion.

V. subduct, subtract; deduct, deduce; bate, retrench; remove, withdraw, take from, take away; detract.

garble, mutilate, amputate, detruncate†; cut off, cut away, cut out; abscind†, excise; pare, thin, prune, decimate; abrade, scrape, file; geld, castrate; eliminate.

diminish &c 36; curtail &c *(shorten)* 201; deprive of &c *(take)* 789; weaken.

Adj. subtracted &c *v.;* subtractive.

Adv. in deduction &c *n.;* less; short of; minus, without, except, except for, excepting, with the exception of, barring, save, exclusive of, save and except, with a reservation; not counting, if one doesn't count.

39. *[Thing added]* **Adjunct** -- **N.** adjunct; addition, additament†; additum *[Lat.]*, affix, appelidage†, annexe†, annex; augment, augmentation; increment, reinforcement, supernumerary, accessory, item; garnish, sauce; accompaniment &c 88; adjective, addendum; complement, supplement; continuation.

rider, offshoot, episode, side issue, corollary; piece *[Fr.]*; flap, lappet, skirt, embroidery, trappings, cortege; tail, suffix &c *(sequel)* 65; wing.

Adj. additional &c 37.

alate†, alated†; winged.

Adv. in addition &c 37.

40. *[Thing remaining.]* **Remainder** -- **N.** remainder, residue; remains, remanent, remnant, rest, relic; leavings, heeltap†, odds and ends, cheesepairings†, candle ends, orts†; residuum; dregs &c *(dirt)* 653; refuse &c *(useless)* 645; stubble, result, educt†; fag-end; ruins, wreck, skeleton., stump; alluvium.

surplus, overplus†, excess; balance, complement; superplus†, surplusage†; superfluity &c *(redundancy)* 641; survival, survivance†.

V. remain; be left &c *adj.;* exceed, survive; leave.

Adj. remaining, left; left behind left over; residual, residuary; over, odd; unconsumed, sedimentary; surviving; net; exceeding, over and above; outlying, outstanding; cast off &c 782; superfluous &c *(redundant)* 641.

40a. *[Thing deducted.]* **Decrement** -- **N.** decrement, discount, defect, loss, deduction; afterglow; eduction[†]; waste.

41. *[Forming a whole without coherence.]* **Mixture** -- **N.** mixture, admixture, commixture, commixtion[†]; commixion[†], intermixture, alloyage[†], matrimony; junction &c 43; combination &c 48; miscegenation.

impregnation; infusion, diffusion suffusion, transfusion; infiltration; seasoning, sprinkling, interlarding; interpolation; &c 228 adulteration, sophistication.

[Thing mixed] tinge, tincture, touch, dash, smack, sprinkling, spice, seasoning, infusion, soupcon.

[Compound resulting from mixture] alloy, amalgam; brass, chowchow[†], pewter; magma, half-and-half, melange, tertium quid *[Lat.]*, miscellany, ambigu[†], medley, mess, hotchpot[†], pasticcio[†], patchwork, odds and ends, all sorts; jumble &c *(disorder)* 59; salad,

sauce, mash, omnium gatherum *[Lat.]*, gallimaufry, olla-podrida†, olio, salmagundi, potpourri, Noah's ark, caldron texture, mingled yarn; mosaic &c *(variegation)* 440.

half-blood, half-caste.

mulatto; terceron†, quarteron†, quinteron† &c; quadroon, octoroon; griffo†, zambo†; cafuzo†; Eurasian; fustee†, fustie†; griffe, ladino†, marabou, mestee†, mestizo, quintroon, sacatra zebrule *[Lat.]*; catalo†; cross, hybrid, mongrel.

V. mix; join &c 43; combine &c 48; commix, immix†, intermix; mix up with, mingle; commingle, intermingle, bemingle†; shuffle &c *(derange)* 61; pound together; hash up, stir up; knead, brew; impregnate with; interlard &c *(interpolate)* 228; intertwine, interweave &c 219; associate with; miscegenate†.

be mixed &c; get among, be entangled with.

instill, imbue; infuse, suffuse, transfuse; infiltrate, dash, tinge, tincture, season, sprinkle, besprinkle, attemper†, medicate, blend, cross; alloy, amalgamate, compound, adulterate, sophisticate, infect.

Adj. mixed &c *v.;* implex†, composite, half-and-half, linsey-woolsey, chowchow, hybrid, mongrel, heterogeneous; motley &c *(variegated)* 440; miscellaneous, promiscuous, indiscriminate; miscible.

Adv. among, amongst, amid, amidst; with; in the midst of, in the crowd.

42. *[Freedom from mixture.]* **Simpleness** -- **N.** simpleness &c *adj.;* purity, homogeneity.

elimination; sifting &c *v.;* purification &c *(cleanness)* 652.

V. render simple &c *adj.;* simplify.

sift, winnow, bolt, eliminate; exclude, get rid of; clear; purify &c *(clean)* 652; disentangle &c *(disjoin)* 44.

Adj. simple, uniform, of a piece *[Fr.]*, homogeneous, single, pure, sheer, neat.

unmixed, unmingled†, unblended, uncombined, uncompounded; elementary, undecomposed; unadulterated, unsophisticated, unalloyed, untinged†, unfortified, pur et simple *[Fr.]*; incomplex†.

free from, exempt from; exclusive.

Adv. simple &c *adj..* only.

43. Junction -- **N.** junction; joining &c *v.;* joinder *[Law]*, union connection, conjunction, conjugation; annexion†, annexation, annexment†; astriction†, attachment, compagination†, vincture†, ligation, alligation†; accouplement†; marriage &c *(wedlock,)* 903; infibulation†, inosculation†, symphysis *[Anat.]*, anastomosis, confluence, communication, concatenation; meeting, reunion; assemblage &c 72.

coition, copulation; sex, sexual congress, sexual conjunction, sexual intercourse, love-making.

joint, joining, juncture, pivot, hinge, articulation, commissure†, seam, gore, gusset, suture, stitch; link &c 45; miter mortise.

closeness, tightness, &c *adj.;* coherence &c 46; combination &c 48.

annexationist.

V. join, unite; conjoin, connect; associate; put together, lay together, clap together, hang together, lump together, hold together, piece together *[Fr.]*, tack together, fix together, bind up together together; embody, reembody†; roll into one.

attach, fix, affix, saddle on, fasten, bind, secure, clinch, twist, make fast &c *adj.;* tie, pinion, string, strap, sew, lace, tat, stitch, tack, knit, button, buckle, hitch, lash, truss, bandage, braid, splice, swathe, gird, tether, moor, picket, harness, chain; fetter &c *(restrain)* 751; lock, latch, belay, brace, hook, grapple, leash, couple, accouple†, link, yoke, bracket; marry &c *(wed)* 903; bridge over, span.

braze; pin, nail, bolt, hasp, clasp, clamp, crimp, screw, rivet; impact, solder, set; weld together, fuse together; wedge, rabbet, mortise, miter, jam, dovetail, enchase†; graft, ingraft†, inosculate†; entwine, intwine†; interlink, interlace, intertwine, intertwist†, interweave; entangle; twine round, belay; tighten; trice up, screw up.

be joined &c; hang together, hold together; cohere &c 46.

Adj. joined &c *v.;* joint; conjoint, conjunct; corporate, compact; hand in hand.

firm, fast, close, tight, taut, taught, secure, set, intervolved†; inseparable, indissoluble, insecable†, severable.

Adv. jointly &c *adj.;* in conjunction with &c *(in addition to)* 37; fast, firmly, &c *adj.;* intimately.

Phr. tria juncta in uno *[Lat.]*.

44. Disjunction -- N. disjunction, disconnection, disunity, disunion, disassociation, disengagement; discontinuity &c 70; abjunction†; cataclasm†; inconnection†; abstraction, abstractedness; isolation; insularity, insulation; oasis; island; separateness

&c *adj.;* severalty; disjecta membra *[Lat.]*; dispersion &c 73; apportionment &c 786.

separation; parting &c *v.;* circumcision; detachment, segregation; divorce, sejunction[†], seposition[†], diduction[†], diremption[†], discerption[†]; elision; caesura, break, fracture, division, subdivision, rupture; compartition[†]; dismemberment, dislocation; luxation[†]; severance, disseverance; scission; rescission, abscission; laceration, dilaceration[†]; disruption, abruption[†]; avulsion[†], divulsion[†]; section, resection, cleavage; fission; partibility[†], separability.

fissure, breach, rent, split, rift, crack, slit, incision.

dissection anatomy; decomposition &c 49; cutting instrument &c *(sharpness)* 253; buzzsaw, circular saw, rip saw.

separatist.

V. be disjoined &c*;* come off, fall off, come to pieces, fall to pieces; peel off; get loose.

disjoin, disconnect, disengage, disunite, dissociate, dispair[†]; divorce, part, dispart[†], detach, separate, cut off, rescind, segregate; set apart, keep apart; insulate, isolate; throw out of gear; cut adrift; loose; unloose, undo, unbind, unchain, unlock &c *(fix)* 43, unpack, unravel; disentangle; set free &c *(liberate)* 750.

sunder, divide, subdivide, sever, dissever, abscind[†]; circumcise; cut; incide[†], incise; saw, snip, nib, nip, cleave, rive, rend, slit, split, splinter, chip, crack, snap, break, tear, burst; rend &c, rend asunder, rend in twain; wrench, rupture, shatter, shiver, cranch†, crunch, craunch†, chop; cut up, rip up; hack, hew, slash; whittle; haggle, hackle, discind†, lacerate, scamble†, mangle, gash, hash, slice.

cut up, carve, dissect, anatomize; dislimb†; take to pieces, pull to pieces, pick to pieces, tear to pieces; tear to tatters, tear piecemeal, tear limb from limb; divellicate†; skin &c 226; disintegrate, dismember, disbranch†, disband; disperse &c 73; dislocate, disjoint; break up; mince; comminute &c *(pulverize)* 330; apportion &c 786.

part, part company; separate, leave.

Adj. disjoined &c *v.;* discontinuous &c 70; multipartite†, abstract; disjunctive; secant; isolated &c *v.;* insular, separate, disparate, discrete, apart, asunder, far between, loose, free; unattached, unannexed, unassociated, unconnected; distinct; adrift; straggling; rift, reft†.

[capable of being cut] scissile *[Chem]*, divisible, discerptible†, partible, separable.

Adv. separately &c *adj.;* one by one, severally, apart; adrift, asunder, in twain; in the abstract, abstractedly.

45. *[Connecting medium.]* **Connection** --
N. vinculum, link; connective, connection; junction &c 43; bond of union, copula, hyphen, intermedium†; bracket; bridge, stepping-stone, isthmus.

bond, tendon, tendril; fiber; cord, cordage; riband, ribbon, rope, guy, cable, line, halser†, hawser, painter, moorings, wire, chain; string &c *(filament)* 205.

fastener, fastening, tie; ligament, ligature; strap; tackle, rigging; standing rigging, running rigging; traces, harness; yoke; band ribband, bandage; brace, roller, fillet; inkle†; with, withe, withy; thong, braid; girder, tiebeam; girth, girdle, cestus†, garter, halter, noose, lasso, surcingle, knot, running knot; cabestro *[U.S.]*, cinch *[U.S.]*, lariat, legadero†, oxreim†; suspenders.

pin, corking pin, nail, brad, tack, skewer, staple, corrugated fastener; clamp, U-clamp, C-clamp; cramp, cramp iron; ratchet, detent, larigo†, pawl; terret†, treenail, screw, button, buckle; clasp, hasp, hinge, hank, catch, latch, bolt, latchet†, tag; tooth; hook, hook and eye; lock, holdfast†, padlock, rivet; anchor, grappling iron, trennel†, stake, post.

cement, glue, gum, paste, size, wafer, solder, lute, putty, birdlime, mortar, stucco, plaster, grout; viscum†.

shackle, rein &c *(means of restraint)* 752; prop &c *(support)* 215.

V. bridge over, span; connect &c 43; hang &c 214.

46. Coherence -- **N.** coherence, adherence, adhesion, adhesiveness; concretion accretion; conglutination, agglutination, agglomeration; aggregation; consolidation, set, cementation; sticking, soldering &c *v.;* connection; dependence.

tenacity, toughness; stickiness &c 352; inseparability, inseparableness; bur, remora.

conglomerate, concrete &c *(density)* 321.

V. cohere, adhere, stick, cling, cleave, hold, take hold of, hold fast, close with, clasp, hug; grow together, hang together; twine round &c *(join)* 43.

stick like a leech, stick like wax; stick close; cling like ivy, cling like a bur; adhere like a remora, adhere like Dejanira's shirt.

glue; agglutinate, conglutinate†; cement, lute, paste, gum; solder, weld; cake, consolidate &c *(solidify)* 321; agglomerate.

Adj. cohesive, adhesive, adhering, cohering &c *v.;* tenacious, tough; sticky &c 352.

united, unseparated, unsessile†, inseparable, inextricable, infrangible†; compact &c *(dense)* 321.

47. *[Want of adhesion, nonadhesion, immiscibility.]* **Incoherence** -- **N.** nonadhesion†; immiscibility; incoherence; looseness &c *adj.;* laxity; relaxation; loosening &c *v.;* freedom; disjunction &c 44; rope of sand.

V. make loose &c *adj.;* loosen, slacken, relax; unglue &c 46; detach &c *(disjoin)* 44.

Adj. nonadhesive, immiscible; incoherent, detached, loose, baggy, slack, lax, relaxed, flapping, streaming; disheveled; segregated, like grains of sand unconsolidated &c 231, uncombined &c 48; noncohesive†.

48. Combination -- **N.** combination; mixture &c 41; junction &c 43; union, unification, synthesis, incorporation, amalgamation, embodiment, coalescence, crasis†, fusion, blending, absorption, centralization.

alloy, compound, amalgam, composition, tertium quid *[Lat.]*; resultant, impregnation.

V. combine, unite, incorporate, amalgamate, embody, absorb, reembody†, blend, merge, fuse, melt into one, consolidate, coalesce, centralize, impregnate; put together, lump together; cement a union, marry.

Adj. combined &c *v.;* impregnated with, ingrained; imbued inoculated.

49. Decomposition -- **N.** decomposition, analysis, dissection, resolution, catalysis, dissolution; corruption &c *(uncleanness)* 653; dispersion &c 73; disjunction &c 44; disintegration.

V. decompose, decompound; analyze, disembody, dissolve; resolve into its elements, separate into its elements; electrolyze *[Chem]*; dissect, decentralize, break up; disperse &c 73; unravel &c *(unroll)* 313; crumble into dust.

Adj. decomposed &c *v.;* catalytic, analytical; resolvent, separative, solvent.

4. CONCRETE QUANTITY

50. *[Principal part.]* **Whole** -- **N.** whole, totality, integrity; totalness &c *adj.*[†]; entirety, ensemble, collectiveness[†]; unity &c 87; completeness &c 52;

indivisibility, indiscerptibility†; integration, embodiment; integer.

all, the whole, total, aggregate, one and all, gross amount, sum, sum total, tout ensemble, length and breadth of, Alpha and Omega, be all and end all; complex, complexus†; lock stock and barrel.

bulk, mass, lump, tissue, staple, body, compages†; trunk, torso, bole, hull, hulk, skeleton greater part, major part, best part, principal part, main part; essential part &c *(importance)* 642; lion's share, Benjamin's mess; the long and the short; nearly, all, almost all.

V. form a whole, constitute a whole; integrate, embody, amass; aggregate &c *(assemble)* 72; amount to, come to.

Adj. whole, total, integral, entire; complete &c 52; one, individual.

unbroken, intact, uncut, undivided, unsevered†, unclipped†, uncropped, unshorn; seamless; undiminished; undemolished, undissolved, undestroyed, unbruised.

indivisible, indissoluble, indissolvable†, indiscerptible†.

wholesale, sweeping; comprehensive.

Adv. wholly, altogether; totally &c *(completely)* 52; entirely, all, all in all, as a whole, wholesale, in a body, collectively, all put together; in the aggregate, in the lump, in the mass, in the gross, in the main, in the long run; en masse, as a body, on the whole, bodily†, en bloc, in extenso *[Lat.]*, throughout, every inch; substantially.

Phr. tout bien ou rien *[Fr.]*.

51. Part -- N. part, portion; dose; item, particular; aught, any; division, ward; subdivision, section; chapter, clause, count, paragraph, verse; article, passage; sector, segment; fraction, fragment; cantle, frustum; detachment, parcel.

piece *[Fr.]*, lump, bit cut, cutting; chip, chunk, collop†, slice, scale; lamina &c 204; small part; morsel, particle &c *(smallness)* 32; installment, dividend; share &c *(allotment)* 786.

debris, odds and ends, oddments, detritus; excerpta†; member, limb, lobe, lobule, arm, wing, scion, branch, bough, joint, link, offshoot, ramification, twig, bush, spray, sprig; runner; leaf, leaflet; stump; component part &c 56; sarmentum†.

compartment; department &c *(class)* 75; county &c *(region)* 181.

V. part, divide, break &c *(disjoin)* 44; partition &c *(apportion)* 786.

Adj. fractional, fragmentary; sectional, aliquot; divided &c *v.;* in compartments, multifid†; disconnected; partial.

Adv. partly, in part, partially; piecemeal, part by part; by by installments, by snatches, by inches, by driblets; bit by bit, inch by inch, foot by foot, drop by drop; in detail, in lots.

52. Completeness -- N. completeness &c *adj.;* completion &c 729; integration; allness†.

entirety; perfection &c 650; solidity, solidarity; unity; all; ne plus ultra *[Lat.]*, ideal, limit.

complement, supplement, make-weight; filling, up &c *v..* impletion†; saturation, saturity†; high water; high tide, flood tide, spring tide; fill, load, bumper, bellyful†; brimmer†; sufficiency &c 639.

V. be complete &c *adj.;* come to a head.

render complete &c *adj.;* complete &c *(accomplish)* 729; fill, charge, load, replenish; make up, make good; piece out *[Fr.]*, eke out; supply deficiencies; fill up, fill in, fill to the brim, fill the measure of; saturate.

go the whole hog, go the whole length; go all lengths.

Adj. complete, entire; whole &c 50; perfect &c 650; full, good, absolute, thorough, plenary; solid, undivided; with all its parts; all-sided.

exhaustive, radical, sweeping, thorough-going; dead.

regular, consummate, unmitigated, sheer, unqualified, unconditional, free; abundant &c *(sufficient)* 639.

brimming; brimful, topful, topfull; chock full, choke full; as full as an egg is of meat, as full as a vetch; saturated, crammed; replete &c *(redundant)* 641; fraught, laden; full-laden, full-fraught, full-charged; heavy laden.

completing &c *v.;* supplemental, supplementary; ascititious[†].

Adv. completely &c *adj.;* altogether, outright, wholly, totally, in toto, quite; all out; over head and ears; effectually, for good and all, nicely, fully, through thick and thin, head and shoulders; neck and heel, neck and crop; in all respects, in every respect; at all points, out and out, to all intents and purposes; toto coelo *[Lat.];* utterly; clean, clean as a whistle; to the full, to the utmost, to the backbone; hollow, stark; heart and soul, root and branch, down to the ground.

to the top of one's bent, as far as possible, a outrance†.

throughout; from first to last, from beginning to end, from end to end, from one end to the other, from Dan to Beersheba, from head to foot, from top to toe, from top to bottom, de fond en comble *[Fr.]*; a fond, a capite ad calcem *[Lat.]*, ab ovo usque ad mala *[Lat.]*, fore and aft; every, whit, every inch; cap-a-pie, to the end of the chapter; up to the brim, up to the ears, up to the eyes; as a as can be.

on all accounts; sous tous les rapports *[Fr.]*; with a vengeance, with a witness.

Phr. falsus in uno falsus in omnibus *[Lat.]*, false in one thing, false in everything; omnem movere lapidem *[Lat.]*; una scopa nuova spazza bene *[It]*.

53. Incompleteness -- **N.** incompleteness &c *adj.;* deficiency, short measure; shortcoming &c 304; insufficiency &c 640; imperfection &c 651; immaturity &c *(nonpreparation)* 674; half measures.

[part wanting] defect, deficit, defalcation, omission; caret; shortage; interval &c 198; break &c *(discontinuity)* 70; noncompletion &c 730; missing link.

missing piece, missing part, gap, hole, lacuna.

V. be incomplete &c *adj.;* fall short of &c 304; lack &c *(be insufficient)* 640; neglect &c 460.

Adj. incomplete; imperfect &c 651; unfinished; uncompleted &c *(complete)* &c 729; defective, deficient, wanting, lacking, failing; in default, in arrear†; short of; hollow, meager, lame, halfand-half, perfunctory, sketchy; crude &c *(unprepared)* 674.

mutilated, garbled, docked, lopped, truncated.

in progress, in hand; going on, proceeding.

Adv. incompletely &c *adj.;* by halves.

Phr. caetera desunt *[Lat.]*; caret.

54. Composition -- **N.** composition, constitution, crasis†; combination &c 48; inclusion, admission, comprehension, reception; embodiment; formation.

V. be composed of, be made of, be formed of, be made up of; consist of, be resolved into.

include &c *(in a class)* 76; contain, hold, comprehend, take in, admit, embrace, embody; involve, implicate; drag into.

compose, constitute, form, make; make up, fill up, build up; enter into the composition of &c *(be a component)* 56.

Adj. containing, constituting &c *v..*

55. Exclusion -- **N.** exclusion, nonadmission, omission, exception, rejection, repudiation; exile &c *(seclusion)* 893; noninclusion†, preclusion, prohibition.

separation, segregation, seposition†, elimination, expulsion; cofferdam.

V. be excluded from &c; exclude, bar; leave out, shut out, bar out; reject, repudiate, blackball; lay apart, put apart, set apart, lay aside, put aside; relegate, segregate; throw overboard; strike off, strike out; neglect &c 460; banish &c *(seclude)* 893; separate &c *(disjoin)* 44.

pass over, omit; garble; eliminate, weed, winnow.

Adj. excluding &c *v.;* exclusive.

excluded &c *v.;* unrecounted†, not included in; inadmissible.

Adv. exclusive of, barring; except; with the exception of; save; bating.

56. Component -- **N.** component; component part, integral part, integrant part†; element, constituent, ingredient, leaven; part and parcel; contents; appurtenance; feature; member &c *(part)*51; personnel.

V. enter into, enter into the composition of; be a component &c *n.* be part of, form part of &c 51; merge in, be merged in; be implicated in; share in &c *(participate)* 778; belong to, appertain to; combine, inhere in, unite.

form, make, constitute, compose.

Adj. forming &c *v..* inclusive.

57. Extraneousness -- N. extraneousness &c *adj.;* extrinsicality &c 6; exteriority &c 220; alienage†, alienism.

foreign body, foreign substance, foreign element; alien, stranger, intruder, interloper, foreigner, novus homo *[Lat.]*, newcomer, immigrant, emigrant; creole, Africander†; outsider; Dago*[Slang]*, wop, mick, polak, greaser, slant, Easterner *[U.S.]*, Dutchman, tenderfoot.

Adj. extraneous, foreign, alien, ulterior; tramontane, ultramontane.

excluded &c 55; inadmissible; exceptional.

Adv. in foreign parts, in foreign lands; abroad, beyond seas; over sea on one's travels.

SECTION IV.

ORDER

1. ORDER IN GENERAL

58. Order -- **N.** order, regularity, uniformity, symmetry, lucidus ordo *[Lat.]*; music of the spheres.

gradation, progression; series &c *(continuity)* 69.

subordination; course, even tenor, routine; method, disposition, arrangement, array, system, economy, discipline orderliness &c *adj..* rank, place &c *(term)* 71.

V. be in order, become in order &c *adj.;* form, fall in, draw up; arrange itself, range itself, place itself;

fall into one's place, take one's place, take one's rank; rally round.

adjust, methodize, regulate, systematize.

Adj. orderly, regular; in order, in trim, in apple-pie order, in its proper place; neat, tidy, en regle *[Fr.]*, well regulated, correct, methodical, uniform, symmetrical, shipshape, businesslike, systematic; unconfused &c *(confuse)* &c 61; arranged &c 60.

Adv. in order; methodically &c *adj.;* in turn, in its turn; by steps, step by step; by regular steps, by regular gradations, by regular stages, by regular intervals; seriatim, systematically, by clockwork, gradatim *[Lat.]*; at stated periods &c *(periodically)* 138.

Phr. natura non facit saltum *[Lat.]*; order is heaven's first law [Pope]; order from disorder sprung [Paradise Lost]; ordo est parium dispariumque rerum sua loca tribuens dispositio *[Lat.]*[St.

Augustine].

59. *[Absence, or want of Order, &c]* **Disorder** --
 N. disorder; derangement &c 61; irregularity; anomaly &c *(unconformity)* 83; anarchy, anarchism; want of method; untidiness &c *adj.;*disunion; discord &c 24.

confusion; confusedness &c *adj.;* mishmash, mix; disarray, jumble, huddle, litter, lumber; cahotage†; farrago; mess, mash, muddle, muss *[U.S.]*, hash, hodgepodge; hotch-potch†, hotch-pot†; imbroglio, chaos, omnium gatherum *[Lat.]*, medley; mere mixture &c 41; fortuitous concourse of atoms, disjecta membra *[Lat.]*, rudis indigestaque moles *[Lat.]* [Ovid].

complexity &c 59.1.

turmoil; ferment &c *(agitation)* 315; to-do, trouble, pudder†, pother, row, rumble, disturbance, hubbub, convulsion, tumult, uproar, revolution, riot, rumpus, stour†, scramble, brawl, fracas, rhubarb, fight, free-for-all, row, ruction, rumpus, embroilment, melee, spill and pelt, rough and tumble; whirlwind &c 349; bear garden, Babel, Saturnalia, donnybrook, Donnybrook Fair, confusion worse confounded, most admired disorder, concordia discors *[Lat.]*; Bedlam, all hell broke loose; bull in a china shop; all the fat in the fire, diable a' quatre *[Fr.]*, Devil to pay; pretty kettle of fish; pretty piece of work *[Fr.]*, pretty piece of business *[Fr.]*.

[legal terms] disorderly person; disorderly persons offence; misdemeanor.

[moral disorder] slattern, slut *(libertine)* 962.

V. be disorderly &c *adj.;* ferment, play at cross-purposes.

put out of order; derange &c 61; ravel &c 219; ruffle, rumple.

Adj. disorderly, orderless; out of order, out of place, out of gear; irregular, desultory; anomalous &c *(unconformable)* 83; acephalous[†], deranged; aimless; disorganized; straggling; unmethodical, immethodical[†]; unsymmetric[†], unsystematic; untidy, slovenly; dislocated; out of sorts; promiscuous, indiscriminate; chaotic, anarchical; unarranged &c *(arrange)* &c 60; confused; deranged &c 61; topsy-turvy &c *(inverted)* 218; shapeless &c 241; disjointed, out of joint.

troublous[†]; riotous &c *(violent)* 173.

complex &c 59.1.

Adv. irregularly &c *adj.;* by fits, by fits and snatches, by fits and starts; pellmell; higgledy-piggledy; helter-skelter, harum-scarum; in a ferment; at sixes and sevens, at cross-purposes; upside down &c 218.

Phr. the cart before the horse; hysteron proteron *[Gr.]*; chaos is come again; the wreck of matter and the crush of worlds [Addison].

59a. Complexity -- **N.** complexity; complexness &c *adj.;* complexus[†]; complication, implication; intricacy, intrication[†]; perplexity; network, labyrinth;

wilderness, jungle; involution, raveling, entanglement; coil &c *(convolution)* 248; sleave†, tangled skein, knot, Gordian knot, wheels within wheels; kink, gnarl, knarl†; webwork†.

[complexity if a task or action] difficulty &c 704.

V. complexify†, complicate.

Adj. gnarled, knarled†.

complex, complexed; intricate, complicated, perplexed, involved, raveled, entangled, knotted, tangled, inextricable; irreducible.

60. *[Reduction to Order.]* **Arrangement** --
 N. arrangement; plan &c 626; preparation &c 673; disposal, disposition; collocation, allocation; distribution; sorting &c *v.;* assortment, allotment, apportionment, taxis, taxonomy, syntaxis†, graduation, organization; grouping; tabulation.

analysis, classification, clustering, division, digestion.

[Result of arrangement] digest; synopsis &c *(compendium)* 596; syntagma *[Gramm.]*, table, atlas; file, database; register.

&c *(record)* 551; organism, architecture.

[Instrument for sorting] sieve, riddle, screen, sorter.

V. reduce to order, bring into order; introduce order into; rally.

arrange, dispose, place, form; put in order, set in order, place in order; set out, collocate, pack, marshal, range, size, rank, group, parcel out, allot, distribute, deal; cast the parts, assign the parts; dispose of, assign places to; assort, sort; sift, riddle; put to rights, set to rights, put into shape, put in trim, put in array; apportion.

class, classify; divide; file, string together, thread; register &c *(record)* 551; catalogue, tabulate, index, graduate, digest, grade.

methodize, regulate, systematize, coordinate, organize, settle, fix.

unravel, disentangle, ravel, card; disembroil[†]; feaze[†].

Adj. arranged &c *v.;* embattled, in battle array; cut and dried; methodical, orderly, regular, systematic.

Phr. In vast cumbrous array [Churchill].

61. *[Subversion of Order; bringing into disorder.]* **Derangement** -- **N.** derangement &c *v.;* disorder &c 59; evection[†], discomposure, disturbance; disorganization, deorganization[†];

dislocation; perturbation, interruption; shuffling &c *v.;* inversion &c 218; corrugation &c *(fold)* 258; involvement.

interchange &c 148.

V. derange; disarrange, misarrange†; displace, misplace; mislay, discompose, disorder; deorganize†, discombobulate, disorganize; embroil, unsettle, disturb, confuse, trouble, perturb, jumble, tumble; shuffle, randomize; huddle, muddle, toss, hustle, fumble, riot; bring into disorder, put into disorder, throw into disorder &c 59; muss *[U.S.]*; break the ranks, disconcert, convulse; break in upon.

unhinge, dislocate, put out of joint, throw out of gear.

turn topsy-turvy &c *(invert)* 218; bedevil; complicate, involve, perplex, confound; imbrangle†, embrangle†, tangle, entangle, ravel, tousle, towzle†, dishevel, ruffle; rumple &c *(fold)* 258.

litter, scatter; mix &c 41.

rearrange &c 148.

Adj. deranged &c *v.;* syncretic, syncretistic†; mussy, messy; flaky; random, unordered *[U.S.]*.

2. CONSECUTIVE ORDER

62. Precedence -- **N.** precedence; coming before &c *v.;* the lead, le pas; superiority &c 33; importance &c 642; antecedence, antecedency†; anteriority &c *(front)* 234; precursor &c 64; priority &c 116; precession &c 280; anteposition†; epacme†; preference.

V. precede; come before, come first; head, lead, take the lead; lead the way, lead the dance; be in the vanguard; introduce, usher in; have the pas; set the fashion &c *(influence)* 175; open the ball; take precedence, have precedence; have the start &c *(get before)* 280.

place before; prefix; premise, prelude, preface.

Adj. preceding &c *v.;* precedent, antecedent; anterior; prior &c 116; before; former; foregoing; beforementioned†, abovementioned†, aforementioned; aforesaid, said; precursory, precursive†; prevenient†, preliminary, prefatory, introductory; prelusive, prelusory; proemial†, preparatory.

Adv. before; in advance &c *(precession)* 280.

Phr. seniores priores *[Lat.]*; prior tempore prior jure *[Lat.]*.

63. Sequence -- **N.** sequence, coming after; going after &c *(following)* 281; consecution, succession; posteriority &c 117.

continuation; order of succession; successiveness; paracme[†].

secondariness[†]; subordinancy &c *(inferiority)* 34.

afterbirth, afterburden[†]; placenta, secundines *[Med.]*.

V. succeed; come after, come on, come next; follow, ensue, step into the shoes of; alternate.

place after, suffix, append.

Adj. succeeding &c; *v.;* sequent[†]; subsequent, consequent, sequacious[†], proximate, next; consecutive &c *(continuity)* 69; alternate, amoebean[†].

latter; posterior &c 117.

Adv. after, subsequently; behind &c *(rear)* 235.

64. Precursor -- **N.** precursor, antecedent, precedent, predecessor; forerunner, vancourier[†], avant-coureur *[Fr.]*, pioneer, prodrome[†], prodromos[†], prodromus[†], outrider; leader, bellwether; herald, harbinger; foreboding; dawn; avant-courier, avant-garde, bellmare[†], forelooper[†], foreloper†, stalking-horse, voorlooper *[Afrik.]*, voortrekker *[Afrik.]*.

prelude, preamble, preface, prologue, foreword, avant-propos *[Fr.]*, protasis†, proemium†, prolusion†, proem, prolepsis *[Gramm.]*, prolegomena, prefix, introduction; heading, frontispiece, groundwork; preparation &c 673; overture, exordium *[Lat.]*, symphony; premises.

prefigurement &c 511; omen &c 512.

Adj. precursory; prelusive, prelusory, preludious†; proemial†, introductory, prefatory, prodromous†, inaugural, preliminary; precedent &c *(prior)* 116.

Phr. a precedent embalms a principle [Disraeli].

65. Sequel -- N. sequel, suffix, successor; tail, queue, train, wake, trail, rear; retinue, suite; appendix, postscript; epilogue; peroration; codicil; continuation, sequela†; appendage; tail piece*[Fr.]*, heelpiece†; tag, more last words; colophon.

aftercome†, aftergrowth†, afterpart†, afterpiece†, aftercourse†, afterthought, aftergame†; arriere pensee *[Fr.]*, second thoughts; outgrowth.

66. Beginning -- **N.** beginning, commencement, opening, outset, incipience, inception, inchoation†; introduction &c *(precursor)* 64; alpha, initial; inauguration, debut, le premier pas, embarcation *[Fr.]*, rising of the curtain; maiden speech; outbreak, onset, brunt; initiative, move, first move; narrow end of the wedge, thin end of the wedge; fresh start, new departure.

origin &c *(cause)* 153; source, rise; bud, germ &c 153; egg, rudiment; genesis, primogenesis†, birth, nativity, cradle, infancy; start, inception, creation, starting point &c 293; dawn &c *(morning)* 125; evolution.

title-page; head, heading; van &c *(front)* 234; caption, fatihah†.

entrance, entry; inlet, orifice, mouth, chops, lips, porch, portal, portico, propylon†, door; gate, gateway; postern, wicket, threshold, vestibule; propylaeum†; skirts, border &c *(edge)* 231.

first stage, first blush, first glance, first impression, first sight.

rudiments, elements, outlines, grammar, alphabet, ABC.

V. begin, start, commence; conceive, open, dawn, set in, take its rise, enter upon, enter; set out &c *(depart)* 293; embark in; incept†.

initiate, launch, inaugurate.

inchoate, rise, arise, originate.

usher in; lead off, lead the way; take the lead, take the initiative; head; stand at the head, stand first, stand for; lay the foundations &c *(prepare)* 673; found &c *(cause)* 153; set up, set on foot, agoing†, set abroach†, set the ball in motion; apply the match to a train; broach; open up, open the door to.

get underway, set about, get to work, set to work, set to; make a beginning, make a start.

handsel; take the first step, lay the first stone, cut the first turf; break ground, break the ice, break cover; pass the Rubicon, cross the Rubicon; open fire, open the ball; ventilate, air; undertake &c 676.

come into existence, come into the world; make one's debut, take birth; burst forth, break out; spring up, spring forth, crop up, pop up, appear, materialize.

begin at the beginning, begin ab ovo *[Lat.]*.

begin again, begin de novo; start afresh, make a fresh start, take it from the top, shuffle the cards, reshuffle the cards, resume, recommence.

Adj. beginning &c *v.;* initial, initiatory, initiative; inceptive, introductory, incipient; proemial†, inaugural; inchoate, inchoative†; embryonic, rudimental; primogenial†; primeval, primitive, primordial &c *(old)* 124; aboriginal; natal, nascent.

first, foremost, leading; maiden.

begun &c *v.;* just begun &c *v..*

Adv. at the beginning, in the beginning, &c *n.;* first, in the first place, imprimis *[Lat.]*, first and foremost; in limine *[Lat.]*; in the bud, in embryo, in its infancy; from the beginning, from its birth; ab initio *[Lat.]*, ab ovo *[Lat.]*, ab incunabilis *[Lat.]*, ab origine *[Lat.]*.

Phr. let's get going!, let's get this show on the road!, up and at 'em!; aller Anfang ist schwer *[G.]*, dimidium facti qui coepit habet *[Lat.]* [Cicero]; omnium rerum principia parva sunt *[Lat.]*[Cicero].

67. End -- **N.** end, close, termination; desinence†, conclusion, finis, finale, period, term, terminus, endpoint, last, omega; extreme, extremity; gable end, butt end, fag-end; tip, nib, point; tail &c *(rear)* 235; verge &c *(edge)* 231; tag, peroration; bonne bouche *[Fr.]*; bottom dollar, tail end, rear guard.

consummation, denouement; finish &c *(completion)* 729; fate; doom, doomsday; crack of doom, day of Judgment, dies irae, fall of the curtain; goal, destination; limit, determination; expiration, expiry†, extinction, extermination; death &c 360; end of all things; finality; eschatology.

break up, commencement de la fin, last stage, turning point; coup de grace, deathblow; knock-out-blow; sockdolager *[U.S.]*.

V. end, close, finish, terminate, conclude, be all over; expire; die &c 360; come-, draw-to-a-close &c *n.;* have run its course; run out, pass away.

bring to an end &c *n.;* put an end to, make an end of; determine; get through; achieve &c *(complete)* 729; stop &c *(make to cease)* 142; shut up shop; hang up one's fiddle.

Adj. ending &c *v.;* final, terminal, definitive; crowning &c *(completing)* 729; last, ultimate; hindermost†; rear &c 235; caudal; vergent†.

conterminate†, conterminous, conterminable†.

ended &c *v.;* at an end; settled, decided, over, played out, set at rest; conclusive.

penultimate; last but one, last but two, &c unbegun, uncommenced†; fresh.

Adv. finally &c *adj.;* in fine; at the last; once for all.

Phr. as high as Heaven and as deep as hell [Beaumont and Fletcher]; deficit omne quod nascitur *[Lat.]* [Quintilian]; en toute chose il faut considerer la fin *[Fr.]*; finem respice *[Lat.]*; ultimus Romanorum *[Lat.]*.

68. Middle -- **N.** middle, midst, mediety†, mean &c 29; medium, middle term; center &c 222, mid-course &c 628; mezzo termine *[It]*; juste milieu &c 628 [Fr.]; halfway house, nave, navel, omphalos†; nucleus, nucleolus.

equidistance†, bisection, half distance; equator, diaphragm, midriff; intermediate &c 228.

Adj. middle, medial, mesial *[Med.]*, mean, mid, median, average; middlemost, midmost; mediate; intermediate &c *(interjacent)* 228; equidistant; central &c 222; mediterranean, equatorial; homocentric.

Adv. in the middle; midway, halfway; midships†, amidships, in medias res.

69. *[Uninterrupted sequence.]* **Continuity** -- **N.** continuity; consecution, consecutiveness &c *adj.;* succession, round, suite, progression, series, train chain; catenation, concatenation; scale; gradation, course; ceaselessness, constant flow, unbroken extent.

procession, column; retinue, cortege, cavalcade, rank and file, line of battle, array.

pedigree, genealogy, lineage, race; ancestry, descent, family, house; line, line of ancestors; strain.

rank, file, line, row, range, tier, string, thread, team; suit; colonnade.

V. follow in a series, form a series &c *n.;* fall in.

arrange in a series, collate &c *n.;* string together, file, thread, graduate, organize, sort, tabulate.

Adj. continuous, continued; consecutive; progressive, gradual; serial, successive; immediate, unbroken, entire; linear; in a line, in a row &c *n.;* uninterrupted, unintermitting[†]; unremitting, unrelenting *(perseverence)* 604.1; perennial, evergreen; constant.

Adv. continuously &c *adj.;* seriatim; in a line &c *n.;* in succession, in turn; running, gradually, step by step, gradatim *[Lat.]*, at a stretch; in file, in column, in single file, in Indian file.

70. *[Interrupted sequence.]* **Discontinuity** --
 N. discontinuity; disjunction &c 44; anacoluthon[†]; interruption, break, fracture, flaw, fault, crack, cut; gap &c *(interval)* 198; solution of continuity, caesura; broken thread; parenthesis, episode, rhapsody, patchwork; intermission; alternation &c *(periodicity)* 138; dropping fire.

V. be discontinuous &c *adj.;* alternate, intermit, sputter, stop and start, hesitate.

discontinue, pause, interrupt; intervene; break, break in upon, break off; interpose &c 228; break the thread, snap the thread; disconnect &c *(disjoin)* 44; dissever.

Adj. discontinuous, unsuccessive[†], broken, interrupted, dicousu *[Fr.]*; disconnected, unconnected; discrete, disjunctive; fitful &c *(irregular)* 139; spasmodic, desultory; intermitting, occasional &c *v.,* intermittent; alternate; recurrent &c *(periodic)* 138.

Adv. at intervals; by snatches, by jerks, by skips, by catches, by fits and starts; skippingly[†], per saltum *[Lat.]*; longo intervallo *[It]*.

Phr. like 'angel visits few and far between' [Campbell].

71. Term -- **N.** term, rank, station, stage, step; degree &c 26; scale, remove, grade, link, peg, round of the ladder, status, position, place, point, mark, pas, period, pitch; stand, standing; footing, range.

V. hold a place, occupy a place, find a place, fall into a place &c *n..*

3. COLLECTIVE ORDER

72. Assemblage -- N. {opp.

73} assemblage; collection, collocation, colligation†; compilation, levy, gathering, ingathering, muster, attroupement†; team; concourse, conflux†, congregation, contesseration†, convergence &c 290; meeting, levee, reunion, drawing room, at home; conversazione *[It]* &c *(social gathering)* 892; assembly, congress; convention, conventicle; gemote†; conclave &c *(council)* 696; posse, posse comitatus *[Lat.]*; Noah's ark.

miscellany, collectanea†; museum, menagerie &c *(store)* 636; museology†.

crowd, throng, group; flood, rush, deluge; rabble, mob, press, crush, cohue†, horde, body, tribe; crew, gang, knot, squad, band, party; swarm, shoal, school, covey, flock, herd, drove; atajo†; bunch, drive, force, mulada *[U.S.]*; remuda†; roundup *[U.S.]*; array, bevy, galaxy; corps, company, troop, troupe, task force; army, regiment &c *(combatants)* 726; host &c *(multitude)* 102; populousness.

clan, brotherhood, fraternity, sorority, association &c *(party)* 712.

volley, shower, storm, cloud.

group, cluster, Pleiades, clump, pencil; set, batch, lot, pack; budget, assortment, bunch; parcel; packet, package; bundle, fascine†, fasces†, bale; seron†, seroon†; fagot, wisp, truss, tuft; shock, rick, fardel†, stack, sheaf, haycock†; fascicle, fascicule†, fasciculus *[Lat.]*, gavel, hattock†, stook†.

accumulation &c *(store)* 636; congeries, heap, lump, pile, rouleau†, tissue, mass, pyramid; bing†; drift; snowball, snowdrift; acervation†, cumulation; glomeration†, agglomeration; conglobation†; conglomeration, conglomerate; coacervate *[Chem]*, coacervation *[Chem]*, coagmentation†, aggregation, concentration, congestion, omnium gaterum *[Lat.]*, spicilegium†, black hole of Calcutta; quantity &c *(greatness)* 31.

collector, gatherer; whip, whipper in.

V. assemble *[be or come together]*, collect, muster; meet, unite, join, rejoin; cluster, flock, swarm, surge, stream, herd, crowd, throng, associate; congregate, conglomerate, concentrate; precipitate; center round, rendezvous, resort; come together, flock get together, pig together; forgather; huddle; reassemble.

[get or bring together] assemble, muster; bring together, get together, put together, draw together, scrape together, lump together; collect, collocate, colligate†; get, whip in; gather; hold a meeting; convene, convoke, convocate†; rake up, dredge; heap, mass, pile; pack, put up, truss, cram; acervate†;

agglomerate, aggregate; compile; group, aggroup†, concentrate, unite; collect into a focus, bring into a focus; amass, accumulate &c *(store)* 636; collect in a dragnet; heap Ossa upon Pelion.

Adj. assembled &c *v.;* closely packed, dense, serried, crowded to suffocation, teeming, swarming, populous; as thick as hops; all of a heap, fasciculated cumulative.

Phr. the plot thickens; acervatim *[Lat.]*; tibi seris tibi metis *[Lat.]*.

73. Nonassemblage. Dispersion -- N. {opp. 72}

dispersion; disjunction &c 44; divergence &c 291; aspersion; scattering &c *v.;* dissemination, diffusion, dissipation, distribution; apportionment &c 786; spread, respersion†, circumfusion†, interspersion, spargefaction†; affusion†.

waifs and estrays†, flotsam and jetsam, disjecta membra *[Lat.]*, [Horace]; waveson†.

V. disperse, scatter, sow, broadcast, disseminate, diffuse, shed, spread, bestrew, overspread, dispense, disband, disembody, dismember, distribute; apportion &c 786; blow off, let out, dispel, cast forth, draught off; strew, straw, strow†; ted; spirtle†, cast, sprinkle; issue, deal out, retail, utter; resperse†, intersperse; set abroach†, circumfuse†.

turn adrift, cast adrift; scatter to the winds; spread like wildfire, disperse themselves.

Adj. unassembled &c *(assemble)* &c 72; dispersed &c *v.;* sparse, dispread, broadcast, sporadic, widespread; epidemic &c *(general)* 78; adrift, stray; disheveled, streaming.

Adv. sparsim[†], here and there, passim.

74. *[Place of meeting.]* **Focus** -- **N.** focus; point of convergence &c 290; corradiation[†]; center &c 222; gathering place, resort haunt retreat; venue; rendezvous; rallying point, headquarters, home, club; depot &c *(store)* 636; trysting place; place of meeting, place of resort, place of assignation; point de reunion; issue.

V. bring to a point, bring to a focus, bring to an issue.

4. DISTRIBUTIVE ORDER

75. Class -- **N.** class, division, category, categorema[†], head, order, section; department, subdepartment, province, domain.

kind, sort, genus, species, variety, family, order, kingdom, race, tribe, caste, sept, clan, breed, type, subtype, kit, sect, set, subset; assortment; feather, kidney; suit; range; gender, sex, kin.

manner, description, denomination, designation, rubric, character, stamp predicament; indication, particularization, selection, specification.

similarity &c 17.

76. *[Comprehension under, or reference to a class.]* **Inclusion** -- **N.** {opp. 77} inclusion, admission, comprehension, reception.

composition &c *(inclusion in a compound)* 54.

V. be included in &c*;* come under, fall under, range under; belong to, pertain to; range with; merge in.

include, comprise, comprehend, contain, admit, embrace, receive; inclose &c *(circumscribe)* 229; embody, encircle.

reckon among, enumerate among, number among; refer to; place with, arrange with, place under; take into account.

Adj. included, including &c *v.;* inclusive; congener, congenerous; of the same class &c 75; encircling.

Phr. a maximis ad minima *[Lat.]*, et hoc genus omne *[Lat.]*, &c etc.; et coetera *[Lat.]*.

77. Exclusion -- N. {opp.

76} exclusion &c 55.

78. Generality -- N. {opp.

79} generality, generalization; universality; catholicity, catholicism; miscellany, miscellaneousness†; dragnet; common run; worldwideness†.

everyone, everybody; all hands, all the world and his wife; anybody, N or M, all sorts.

prevalence, run.

V. be general &c *adj.;* prevail, be going about, stalk abroad.

render general &c *adj.;* generalize.

Adj. general, generic, collective; broad, comprehensive, sweeping; encyclopedical†, widespread &c *(dispersed)* 73.

universal; catholic, catholical†; common, worldwide; ecumenical, oecumenical†; transcendental; prevalent, prevailing, rife, epidemic, besetting; all over, covered with.

Pan-American, Anglican†, Pan-Hellenic, Pan-Germanic, slavic; panharmonic†.

every, all; unspecified, impersonal.

customary &c *(habitual)* 613.

Adv. whatever, whatsoever; to a man, one and all.

generally &c *adj.;* always, for better for worse; in general, generally speaking; speaking generally; for the most part; in the long run &c *(on an average)* 29.

79. Speciality -- N. {opp. 78} speciality, specialite†; individuality, individuity†; particularity, peculiarity; idiocrasy &c *(tendency)* 176; personality, characteristic, mannerism, idiosyncrasy; specificness &c *adj.*†*;* singularity &c *(unconformity)* 83; reading, version, lection; state; trait; distinctive feature; technicality; differentia.

particulars, details, items, counts; minutiae.

I, self, I myself; myself, himself, herself, itself.

V. specify, particularize, individualize, realize, specialize, designate, determine; denote, indicate, point out, select.

descend to particulars, enter into detail, go into detail, come to the point.

Adj. special, particular, individual, specific, proper, personal, original, private, respective, definite, determinate, especial, certain, esoteric, endemic, partial, party, peculiar, appropriate, several, characteristic, diagnostic, exclusive; singular &c *(exceptional)* 83; idiomatic; idiotypical; typical.

this, that; yon, yonder.

Adv. specially, especially, particularly &c *adj.;* in particular, in propria persona *[Lat.]*; ad hominem *[Lat.]*; for my part.

each, apiece, one by one, one at a time; severally, respectively, each to each; seriatim, in detail, in great detail, in excruciating detail, in mind-numbing detail; bit by bit; pro hac vice *[Lat.]*, pro re nata *[Lat.]*.

namely, that is to say, for example, id est, exemplia gratia *[Lat.]*, e.g., i.e., videlicet, viz.; to wit.

Phr. le style est l'homme meme *[Fr.]*.

5. ORDER AS REGARDS CATEGORIES

80. Normality -- **N.** normality, normalcy, normalness†; familiarity, naturalness; commonness *(frequency)* 136; rule, standard *(conformity)* 82; customary *(habit)* 613; standard, pattern *(prototype)* 22.

V. normalize, standardize.

Adj. normal, natural, unexceptional; common, usual *(frequency)* 136;

81. Multiformity -- **N.** multiformity, omniformity†; variety, diversity; multifariousness &c *adj.;* varied assortment.

dissimilarity &c 18.

Adj. polymorphous, multiform, multifold, multifarious, multigenerous†, multiplex; heterogeneous, diversified, dissimilar, various, varied, variform†; manifold, many-sided; variegated, motley, mosaic; epicene, indiscriminate, desultory, irregular; mixed, different, assorted, mingled, odd, diverse, divers; all manner of; of every description, of all sorts and kinds; et hoc genus omne *[Lat.]*; and what not? de omnibus rebus et quibusdam aliis *[Lat.]*.

jumbled, confused, mixed up, discordant; inharmonious, unmatched, unrelated, nonuniform.

omniform†, omnigenous†, omnifarious†; protean *(form)* 240.

Phr. harmoniously confused [Pope]; variety's the very spice of life [Cowper].

82. Conformity -- N. {opp.

83} conformity, conformance; observance; habituation.

naturalization; conventionality &c *(custom)* 613; agreement &c 23.

example, instance, specimen, sample, quotation; exemplification, illustration, case in point; object lesson; elucidation.

standard, model, pattern &c *(prototype)* 22.

rule, nature, principle; law; order of things; normal state, natural state, ordinary state, model state, normal condition, natural condition, ordinary condition, model condition; standing dish, standing order; Procrustean law; law of the Medes and Persians; hard and fast rule.

V. conform to, conform to rule; accommodate oneself to, adapt oneself to; rub off corners.

be regular &c *adj.;* move in a groove; follow observe the rules, go by the rules, bend to the rules, obey the rules, obey the precedents; comply with, tally with, chime in with, fall in with; be guided by, be regulated by; fall into a custom, fall into a usage; follow the fashion, follow the crowd, follow the multitude; pass muster, do as others do, hurler avec les loups *[Fr.]*; stand on ceremony; when in Rome do as the Romans do; go with the stream, go with the flow, swim with the stream, swim with the current, swim with the tide, blow with the wind; stick to the beaten track &c *(habit)* 613; keep one in countenance.

exemplify, illustrate, cite, quote, quote precedent, quote authority, appeal to authority, put a case; produce an instance &c *n.;* elucidate, explain.

Adj. conformable to rule; regular &c 136; according to regulation, according to rule, according to Hoyle, according to Cocker, according to Gunter; en regle *[Fr.]*, selon les regles *[Fr.]*, well regulated, orderly; symmetric &c 242.

conventional &c *(customary)* 613; of daily occurrence, of everyday occurrence; in the natural order of things; ordinary, common, habitual, usual, everyday, workaday.

in the order of the day; naturalized.

typical, normal, nominal, formal; canonical, orthodox, sound, strict, rigid, positive, uncompromising, Procrustean.

secundum artem *[Lat.]*, shipshape, technical.

exemple *[Fr.]*.

illustrative, in point.

Adv. conformably &c *adj.;* by rule; agreeably to; in conformity with, in accordance with, in keeping with; according to; consistently with; as usual, ad instar *[Lat.]*, instar omnium *[Lat.]*; more solito *[Lat.]*, more-majorum.

for the sake of conformity; as a matter of course, of course; pro forma *[Lat.]*, for form's sake, by the card.

invariably, &c *(uniformly)* 16.

for example, exempli gratia *[Lat.]*, e.g.; inter alia *[Lat.]*, among other things; for instance.

Phr. cela va sans dire *[Fr.]*; ex pede Herculem *[Lat.]*; noscitur a sociis *[Lat.]*; ne e quovis ligno Mercurius fiat *[Lat.]* [Erasmus]; they are happy men whose natures sort with their vocations [Bacon].

The nail that sticks up hammered down *[Jap.Tr.]*; Tall poppy syndrome; Stick your neck out and it may get cut off.

83. Unconformity -- N. {opp.

82} nonconformity &c 82; unconformity, disconformity; unconventionality, informality, abnormity†, abnormality, anomaly; anomalousness &c *adj.*†; exception, peculiarity; infraction of law, breach, of law, violation of law, violation of custom, violation of usage, infringement of law, infringement of custom, infringement of usage; teratism†, eccentricity, bizarrerie†, oddity, je ne sais quoi *[Fr.]*, monster, monstrosity, rarity; freak, freak of Nature, weirdo, mutant; rouser, snorter *[U.S.]*.

individuality, idiosyncrasy, originality, mannerism.

aberration; irregularity; variety; singularity; exemption; salvo &c *(qualification)* 469.

nonconformist; nondescript, character, original, nonesuch, nonsuch†, monster, prodigy, wonder, miracle, curiosity, flying fish, black sheep, black swan, lusus naturae *[Lat.]*, rara avis *[Lat.]*, queer fish; mongrel, random breed; half-caste, half-blood, half-breed; metis *[Lat.]*, crossbreed, hybrid, mule, hinny, mulatto; tertium quid *[Lat.]*, hermaphrodite.

[Mythical animals] phoenix, chimera, hydra, sphinx, minotaur; griffin, griffon; centaur; saggittary†; kraken, cockatrice, wyvern, roc, dragon, sea serpent; mermaid, merman, merfolk†; unicorn; Cyclops, men whose heads do grow beneath their shoulders [Othello]; teratology.

[unconformable to the surroundings] fish out of water; neither one thing nor another, neither fish nor fowl, neither fish flesh nor fowl nor good red herring; one in a million, one in a way, one in a thousand; outcast, outlaw; off the beaten track; oasis.

V. be uncomformable &c *adj.;* abnormalize†; leave the beaten track, leave the beaten path; infringe a law, infringe a habit, infringe a usage, infringe a custom, break a law, break a habit, break a usage, break a custom, violate a law, violate a habit, violate a usage, violate a custom; drive a coach and six through; stretch a point; have no business there; baffle all description, beggar all description.

Adj. uncomformable, exceptional; abnormal, abnormous†; anomalous, anomalistic; out of order, out of place, out of keeping, out of tune, out of one's element; irregular, arbitrary; teratogenic; lawless, informal, aberrant, stray, wandering, wanton; peculiar, exclusive, unnatural, eccentric, egregious; out of the beaten track, off the beaten track, out of the common, out of the common run; beyond the pale of, out of the pale of; misplaced; funny.

unusual, unaccustomed, uncustomary, unwonted, uncommon; rare, curious, odd, extraordinary, out of the ordinary; strange, monstrous; wonderful &c 870; unexpected, unaccountable; outre *[Fr.]*, out of the way, remarkable, noteworthy; queer, quaint, nondescript, none such, sui generis *[Lat.]*; unfashionable; fantastic, grotesque, bizarre; outlandish, exotic, tombe des nues *[Fr.]*, preternatural; denaturalized†.

heterogeneous, heteroclite *[Gramm.]*, amorphous, mongrel, amphibious, epicene, half blood, hybrid; androgynous, androgynal†; asymmetric &c 243; adelomorphous†, bisexual, hermaphrodite, monoclinous†.

qualified &c 469.

singular, unique, one-of-a-kind.

newfangled, novel, non-classical; original, unconventional, unheard of, unfamiliar; undescribed, unprecedented, unparalleled, unexampled.

Adv. unconformably &c *adj.;* except, unless, save barring, beside, without, save and except, let alone.

however, yet, but.

once in a blue moon, once in a million years.

Int. what on earth!, what in the world!, What the devil!, Holy cow!, Can you top that?; Sacre bleu *[Fr.]*.

Phr. never was seen the like, never was heard the like, never was known the like.

I could hardly believe it; I saw it, but I didn't believe it.

SECTION V.

NUMBER

1. NUMBER, IN THE ABSTRACT

84. Number -- **N.** number, symbol, numeral, figure, cipher, digit, integer; counter; round number; formula; function; series.

sum, difference, complement, subtrahend; product; multiplicand, multiplier, multiplicator†; coefficient, multiple; dividend, divisor, factor, quotient, submultiple *[Math.]*; fraction, rational number; surd, irrational number; transcendental number; mixed number, complex number, complex conjugate; numerator, denominator; decimal, circulating decimal, repetend; common measure, aliquot part; prime number, prime, relative prime, prime factor, prime pair; reciprocal; totient[†].

binary number, octal number, hexadecimal number *[Comp.]*.

permutation, combination, variation; election.

ratio, proportion, comparison &c 464; progression; arithmetical progression, geometrical progression, harmonical progression[†]; percentage, permilage.

figurate numbers[†], pyramidal numbers, polygonal numbers.

power, root, exponent, index, logarithm, antilogarithm; modulus, base.

differential, integral, fluxion[†], fluent.

Adj. numeral, complementary, divisible, aliquot, reciprocal, prime, relatively prime, fractional, decimal, figurate[†], incommensurable.

proportional, exponential, logarithmic, logometric[†], differential, fluxional[†], integral, totitive[†].

positive, negative; rational, irrational; surd, radical, real; complex, imaginary; finite; infinite; impossible.

Adv. numerically; modulo.

85. Numeration -- **N.** numeration; numbering &c *v.;* pagination; tale, recension†, enumeration, summation, reckoning, computation, supputation†; calculation, calculus; algorithm, algorism†, rhabdology†, dactylonomy†; measurement &c 466; statistics.

arithmetic, analysis, algebra, geometry, analytical geometry, fluxions†; differential calculus, integral calculus, infinitesimal calculus; calculus of differences.

[Statistics] dead reckoning, muster, poll, census, capitation, roll call, recapitulation; account &c *(list)* 86.

[Operations] notation,, addition, subtraction, multiplication, division, rule of three, practice, equations, extraction of roots, reduction, involution, evolution, estimation, approximation, interpolation, differentiation, integration.

[Instruments] abacus, logometer†, slide rule, slipstick *[Coll.]*, tallies, Napier's bones, calculating machine, difference engine, suan-pan†; adding machine; cash register; electronic calculator, calculator, computer; *[people who calculate]* arithmetician, calculator, abacist†, algebraist, mathematician; statistician, geometer; programmer; accountant, auditor.

V. number, count, tally, tell; call over, run over; take an account of, enumerate, muster, poll, recite, recapitulate; sum; sum up, cast up; tell off, score, cipher, compute, calculate, suppute†, add, subtract, multiply, divide, extract roots.

algebraize†.

check, prove, demonstrate, balance, audit, overhaul, take stock; affix numbers to, page.

amount to, add up to, come to.

Adj. numeral, numerical; arithmetical, analytic, algebraic, statistical, numerable, computable, calculable; commensurable, commensurate; incommensurable, incommensurate, innumerable, unfathomable, infinite.

Adv. quantitatively; arithmetically; measurably; in numbers.

86. List -- **N.** list, catalog, catalogue, inventory; register &c *(record)* 551.

account; bill, bill of costs; terrier; tally, listing, itemization; atlas; book, ledger; catalogue raisonne *[Fr.]*; tableau; invoice, bill of lading; prospectus; bill of fare, menu, carte *[Fr.]*; score, census, statistics, returns.

[list of topics in a document] contents, table of contents, outline; synopsis.

[written list used as an aid to memory] checklist.

table, chart, database; index, inverted file, word list, concordance.

dictionary, lexicon; vocabulary, glossary; thesaurus.

file, card index, card file, rolodex, address book.

Red book, Blue book, Domesday book; cadastre *[Fr.]*; directory, gazetter[†].

almanac; army list, clergy list, civil service list, navy list; Almanach de Gotha[†], cadaster; Lloyd's register, nautical almanac; who's who; Guiness's Book of World Records.

roll; check roll, checker roll, bead roll; muster roll, muster book; roster, panel, jury list; cartulary, diptych.

V. list, itemize; sort, collate; enumerate, tabulate, catalog, tally.

Adj. cadastral[†].

2. DETERMINATE NUMBER

87. Unity -- **N.** unity; oneness &c *adj.;* individuality; solitude &c *(seclusion)* 893; isolation &c *(disjunction)* 44; unification &c 48.

one, unit, ace; individual; none else, no other.

V. be one, be alone &c *adj.;* dine with Duke Humphrey[†].

isolate &c *(disjoin)* 44.

render one; unite &c *(join)* 43, *(combine)* 48.

Adj. one, sole, single, solitary, unitary; individual, apart, alone; kithless[†].

unaccompanied, unattended; solus *[Lat.]*, single-handed; singular, odd, unique, unrepeated[†], azygous, first and last; isolated &c *(disjoined)* 44; insular.

monospermous[†]; unific[†], uniflorous[†], unifoliate[†], unigenital[†], uniliteral[†], unijocular[†], unimodal *[Math.]*, unimodular[†].

lone, lonely, lonesome; desolate, dreary.

insecable[†], inseverable[†], indiscerptible[†]; compact, indivisible, atomic, irresolvable[†].

Adv. singly &c *adj.;* alone, by itself, per se, only, apart, in the singular number, in the abstract; one by one, one at a time; simply; one and a half, sesqui-†.

Phr. natura il fece *[It]*, e poi roppe la stampa *[It]*; du fort au faible *[Fr.]*; two souls with but a single thought, two hearts that beat as one.

88. Accompaniment -- **N.** accompaniment; adjunct &c 39; context; appendage, appurtenance.

coexistence, concomitance, company, association, companionship; partnership, copartnership; coefficiency†.

concomitant, accessory, coefficient; companion, buddy, attendant, fellow, associate, friend, colleague; consort, spouse, mate; partner, co-partner; satellite, hanger on, fellow-traveller, shadow; escort, cortege; attribute.

V. accompany, coexist, attend; hang on, wait on; go hand in hand with; synchronize &c 120; bear company, keep company; row in the same boat; bring in its train; associate with, couple with.

Adj. accompanying &c *v.;* concomitant, fellow, twin, joint; associated with, coupled with; accessory, attendant, obbligato.

Adv. with, withal; together with, along with, in company with; hand in hand, side by side; cheek by jowl, cheek by jole†; arm in arm; therewith, herewith; and &c *(addition)* 37.

together, in a body, collectively.

Phr. noscitur a sociis *[Lat.]*; virtutis fortuna comes *[Lat.]*.

89. Duality -- N. duality, dualism; duplicity; biplicity†, biformity†; polarity.

two, deuce, couple, duet, brace, pair, cheeks, twins, Castor and Pollux, gemini, Siamese twins; fellows; yoke, conjugation; dispermy†, doublets, dyad, span.

V. pair *[unite in pairs]*, couple, bracket, yoke; conduplicate†; mate, span *[U.S.]*.

Adj. two, twin; dual, dualistic, double; binary, binomial; twin, biparous†; dyadic *[Math.]*; conduplicate†; duplex &c 90; biduous†, binate†, diphyletic†, dispermic†, unijugate†; tete-a-tete.

coupled &c *v.;* conjugate.

both, both the one and the other.

90. Duplication -- **N.** duplication; doubling &c *v.;* gemination, ingemination†; reduplication; iteration &c *(repetition)* 104; renewal.

V. double, redouble, duplicate, reduplicate; geminate; repeat &c 104; renew &c 660.

Adj. double; doubled &c *v.;* bicipital†, bicephalous†, bidental†, bilabiate, bivalve, bivalvular†, bifold†, biform†, bilateral; bifarious†, bifacial†; twofold, two-sided; disomatous†; duplex; double-faced, double-headed; twin, duplicate, ingeminate†; second.

Adv. twice, once more; over again &c *(repeatedly)* 104; as much again, twofold.

secondly, in the second place, again.

91. *[Division into two parts.]* **bisection** -- **N.** bisection, bipartition; dichotomy, subdichotomy†; halving &c *v.;* dimidiation†.

bifurcation, forking, branching, ramification, divarication; fork, prong; fold.

half, moiety.

V. bisect, halve, divide, split, cut in two, cleave dimidiate†, dichotomize.

go halves, divide with.

separate, fork, bifurcate; branch off, out; ramify.

Adj. bisected &c *v.;* cloven, cleft; bipartite, biconjugate†, bicuspid, bifid; bifurcous†, bifurcate, bifurcated; distichous, dichotomous, furcular†; semi-, demi-, hemi†.

92. Triality -- N. Triality†, trinity; triunity†.

three, triad, triplet, trey, trio, ternion†, leash; shamrock, tierce†, spike-team *[U.S.]*, trefoil; triangle, trident, triennium†, trigon†, trinomial, trionym†, triplopia†, tripod, trireme, triseme†, triskele†, triskelion, trisula†.

third power, cube; cube root.

Adj. three; triform†, trinal†, trinomial; tertiary; ternary; triune; triarch, triadie†; triple &c 93.

tri- *[Pref.]*, tris- *[Pref.]*.

Phr. tria juncta in uno *[Lat.]*.

93. Triplication -- N. triplication, triplicity†; trebleness†, trine.

V. treble, triple; triplicate, cube.

Adj. treble, triple; tern, ternary; triplicate, threefold, trilogistic†; third; trinal†, trine.

Adv. three times, three fold; thrice, in the third place, thirdly; trebly &c *adj.*.

94. *[Division into three parts.]* **Trisection** -- **N.** trisection, tripartition†, trichotomy; third, third part.

V. trisect, divide into three parts.

Adj. trifid; trisected &c *v.;* tripartite, trichotomous†, trisulcate†.

Triadelphous†, triangular, tricuspid, tricapsular†, tridental†, tridentate, tridentiferous†, trifoliate, trifurcate, trigonal†, trigrammic†, trigrammatic†, tripetalous†, tripodal, tripodic†, triquetral†, triquetrous†.

95. Four -- **N.** quaternity†, four, tetrad, quartet, quaternion, square, quarter.

[planar form with four sides] tetract†, tetragon, quadrangle, rectangle.

[three dimensional object with four surfaces] tetrahedron.

quadrature, quadrifoil, quadriform, quadruplet; quatrefoil.

[object or animal with four legs] tetrapod.

[geographical area with four sides] quadrangle, quad *[Coll.]*.

[electromagnetic object] quadrupole.

[four fundamental studies] quadrivium.

V. reduce to a square, square.

Adj. four; quaternary, quaternal[†]; quadratic; quartile; tetract[†], tetractic[†], tetractinal[†]; tetrad, tetragonal; square, quadrate.

96. Quadruplication -- N. quadruplication.

V. multiply by four, quadruplicate, biquadrate[†].

Adj. fourfold, four times; quadrable[†], quadrumanous[†], quadruple, quadruplicate, quadrible[†]; fourth.

quadrifoliate[†], quadrifoliolate[†], quadrigeminal[†], quadrigeminate[†], quadriplanar[†], quadriserial[†].

Adv. four times; in the fourth place, fourthly.

97. *[Division into four parts.]* **Quadrisection** --
N. quadrisection, quadripartition†; quartering &c v.; fourth; quart; quarter, quartern†; farthing†, fourthing; quadrant.

V. quarter, divide into four parts.

Adj. quartered &c v.; quadrifid†, quadripartite.

rectangular.

98. Five &c -- **N.** five, cinque *[Fr.]*, quint, quincux†; six, half-a-dozen, half dozen; seven; eight; nine, three times three; dicker; ten, decade; eleven; twelve, dozen; thirteen; long dozen, baker's dozen; quintuplet; twenty, score; twenty-four, four and twenty, two dozen; twenty-five, five and twenty, quarter of a hundred; forty, two score; fifty, half a hundred; sixty, three score; seventy, three score and ten; eighty, four score; ninety, fourscore and ten; sestiad†.

hundred, centenary, hecatomb, century; hundredweight, cwt.; one hundred and forty-four, gross.

thousand, chiliad; millennium, thousand years, grand *[Coll.]*; myriad; ten thousand, ban *[Jap.]*, man *[Jap.]*; ten thousand years, banzai *[Jap.]*; lac, one hundred thousand, plum; million; thousand million, milliard, billion, trillion &c

V. centuriate†; quintuplicate.

Adj. five, quinary†, quintuple; fifth; senary†, sextuple; sixth; seventh; septuple; octuple; eighth; ninefold, ninth; tenfold, decimal, denary†, decuple†, tenth; eleventh; duodenary†, duodenal; twelfth; in one's 'teens, thirteenth.

vicesimal†, vigesimal; twentieth; twenty-fourth &c *n.;* vicenary†, vicennial†.

centuple†, centuplicate†, centennial, centenary, centurial†; secular, hundredth; thousandth, &c

99. Quinquesection &c -- **N.** division by five &c 98; quinquesection &c; decimation; fifth &c

V. decimate; quinquesect.

Adj. quinquefid, quinquelateral, quinquepartite; quinqevalent, pentavalent; quinquarticular†; octifid†; decimal, tenth, tithe; duodecimal, twelfth; sexagesimal†, sexagenary†; hundredth, centesimal; millesimal &c

100. {opp.

87} *[More than one.]* **Plurality** -- **N.** plurality; a number, a certain number; one or two, two or three &c; a few, several; multitude &c 102; majority.

[large number] multitude &c 102.

Adj. plural, more than one, upwards of; some, several, a few; certain; not alone &c 87.

Adv. et cetera, &c etc.

among other things, inter alia *[Lat.]*.

Phr. non deficit alter *[Lat.]*.

3. INDETERMINATE NUMBER

100a. *[Less than one.]* **Fraction** -- **N.** fraction, fractional part; part &c 51.

Adj. fractional, fragmentary, inconsiderable, negligible, infinitesimal.

101. Zero -- **N.** zero, nothing; null, nul, naught, nought, void; cipher, goose egg; none, nobody, no one; nichts *[G.]*, nixie *[Slang]*, nix *[Slang]*; zilch *[Slang]*, zip *[Slang]*, zippo *[Slang]*; not a soul;

ame qui vive *[Fr.]*; absence &c 187; unsubstantiality &c 4 [Obs.].

Adj. not one, not a one, not any, nary a one *[Dial.]*; not a, never a; not a whit of, not an iota of, not a drop of, not a speck of, not a jot; not a trace of, not a hint of, not a smidgen of, not a suspicion of, not a shadow of, neither hide nor hair of.

102. Multitude -- **N.** multitude; numerous &c *adj.*; numerosity, numerality; multiplicity; profusion &c *(plenty)* 639; legion, host; great number, large number, round number, enormous number; a quantity, numbers, array, sight, army, sea, galaxy; scores, peck, bushel, shoal, swarm, draught, bevy, cloud, flock, herd, drove, flight, covey, hive, brood, litter, farrow, fry, nest; crowd &c *(assemblage)* 72; lots; all in the world and his wife.

[Increase of number] greater number, majority; multiplication, multiple.

V. be numerous &c *adj.*; swarm with, teem with, creep with; crowd, swarm, come thick upon; outnumber, multiply; people; swarm like locusts, swarm like bees.

Adj. many, several, sundry, divers, various, not a few; Briarean; a hundred, a thousand, a myriad, a million, a quadrillion, a nonillion, a thousand and one; some ten or a dozen, some forty or fifty &c; half a dozen, half a hundred &c; very many, full many, ever so many; numerous; numerose[†]; profuse, in profusion; manifold, multiplied, multitudinous, multiple, multinominal, teeming, populous, peopled, crowded, thick, studded; galore.

thick coming, many more, more than one can tell, a world of; no end of, no end to; cum multis aliis *[Lat.]*; thick as hops, thick as hail; plenty as blackberries; numerous as the stars in the firmament, numerous as the sands on the seashore, numerous as the hairs on the head; and what not, and heaven knows what; endless &c *(infinite)* 105.

Phr. their name is 'legion'; acervatim *[Lat.]*; en foule *[Fr.]*; many-headed multitude [Sidney]; numerous as glittering gems of morning dew [Young]; vel prece vel pretio *[Lat.]*.

103. Fewness -- **N.** fewness &c *adj.;* paucity, small number; small quantity &c 32; rarity; infrequency &c 137; handful, maniple; minority; exiguity.

[Diminution of number] reduction; weeding &c *v.;* elimination, sarculation[†], decimation; eradication.

V. be few &c *adj..* render few &c *adj.;* reduce, diminish the number, weed, eliminate, cull, thin, decimate.

Adj. few; scant, scanty; thin, rare, scattered, thinly scattered, spotty, few and far between, exiguous; infrequent &c 137; rari nantes *[Lat.]*; hardly any, scarcely any; to be counted on one's fingers; reduced &c *v.;* unrepeated†.

Adv. rarely, here and there.

104. Repetition -- **N.** repetition, iteration, reiteration, harping, recurrence, succession, run; battology, tautology; monotony, tautophony; rhythm &c 138; diffuseness, pleonasm, redundancy.

chimes, repetend, echo, ritornello†, burden of a song, refrain; rehearsal; rechauffe *[Fr.]*, rifacimento *[It]*, recapitulation.

cuckoo &c *(imitation)* 19; reverberation &c 408; drumming &c *(roll)* 407; renewal
&c *(restoration)* 660.

twice-told tale; old story, old song; second edition, new edition; reappearance, reproduction, recursion *[Comp.]*; periodicity &c 138.

V. repeat, iterate, reiterate, reproduce, echo, reecho, drum, harp upon, battologize†, hammer, redouble.

recur, revert, return, reappear, recurse *[Comp.]*; renew &c *(restore)* 660.

rehearse; do over again, say over again; ring the changes on; harp on the same string; din in the ear, drum in the ear; conjugate in all its moods tenses and inflexions†, begin again, go over the same ground, go the same round, never hear the last of; resume, return to, recapitulate, reword.

Adj. repeated &c v.; repetitional†, repetitionary†; recurrent, recurring; ever recurring, thick coming; frequent, incessant; redundant, pleonastic.

monotonous, harping, iterative, recursive *[Comp.]*, unvaried; mocking, chiming; retold; aforesaid, aforenamed†; above-mentioned, above-said; habitual &c 613; another.

Adv. repeatedly, often, again, anew, over again, afresh, once more; ding-dong, ditto, encore, de novo, bis†, da capo *[It]*.

again and again; over and over, over and over again; recursively *[Comp.]*; many times over; time and again, time after time; year after year; day by day &c; many times, several times, a number of times; many a time, full many a time; frequently &c 136.

Phr. ecce iterum Crispinus *[Lat.]*; toujours perdrix *[Fr.]*; cut and come again [Crabbe]; tomorrow and tomorrow and tomorrow [Macbeth]; cantilenam eandem canis *[Lat.]* [Terence]; nullum est jam dictum quod non dictum sit prius *[Lat.]* [Terence].

105. Infinity -- N. infinity, infinitude, infiniteness &c *adj.;* perpetuity &c 112; boundlessness.

V. be infinite &c *adj.;* know no limits, have no limits, know no bounds, have no bounds; go on for ever.

Adj. infinite; immense; numberless, countless, sumless[†], measureless; innumerable, immeasurable, incalculable, illimitable, inexhaustible, interminable, unfathomable, unapproachable; exhaustless, indefinite; without number, without measure, without limit, without end; incomprehensible; limitless, endless, boundless, termless[†]; untold, unnumbered, unmeasured, unbounded, unlimited; illimited[†]; perpetual &c 112.

Adv. infinitely &c *adj.;* ad infinitum.

Phr. as boundless as the sea [Romeo and Juliet].

SECTION VI.

TIME

1. ABSOLUTE TIME

106. Time -- **N.** time, duration; period, term, stage, space, span, spell, season; the whole time, the whole period; space-time; course &c 109; snap.

intermediate time, while, interim, interval, pendency[†]; intervention, intermission, intermittence, interregnum, interlude; respite.

era, epoch; time of life, age, year, date; decade &c *(period)* 108; moment, &c *(instant)* 113.

glass of time, sands of time, march of time, Father Time, ravages of time; arrow of time; river of time, whirligig of time, noiseless foot of time; scythe.

V. continue last endure, go on, remain, persist; intervene; elapse &c 109; hold out.

take time, take up time, fill time, occupy time.

pass time, pass away time, spend time, while away time, consume time, talk against time; tide over; use time, employ time; seize an opportunity &c 134; waste time &c *(be inactive)* 683.

Adj. continuing &c *v.;* on foot; permanent &c *(durable)* 110.

Adv. while, whilst, during, pending; during the time, during the interval; in the course of, at that point, at that point in time; for the time being, day by day; in the time of, when; meantime, meanwhile; in the meantime, in the interim; ad interim, pendente lite *[Lat.]*; de die in diem *[Lat.]*; from day to day, from hour to hour &c; hourly, always; for a time, for a season; till, until, up to, yet, as far as, by that time, so far, hereunto, heretofore, prior to this, up to this point.

the whole time, all the time; all along; throughout &c *(completely)* 52; for good &c *(diuturnity)* 110.

hereupon, thereupon, whereupon; then; anno Domini, A.D.; ante Christum, A.C.; before Christ, B.C.; anno urbis conditae *[Lat.]*, A.U.C.; anno regni *[Lat.]*, A.R.; once upon a time, one fine morning, one fine day, one day, once.

Phr. time flies, tempus fugit *[Lat.]*; time runs out, time runs against, race against time, racing the clock, time marches on, time is of the essence, time and tide wait for no man.

ad calendas Groecas *[Lat.]*; panting Time toileth after him in vain [Johnson]; 'gainst the tooth of time and razure of oblivion *[Contr.]* [Measure for Measure]; rich with the spoils of time [Gray]; tempus edax rerum *[Lat.]* [Horace]; the long hours come and go [C.G.

Rossetti]; the time is out of joint [Hamlet]; Time rolls his ceaseless course [Scott]; Time the foe of man's dominion [Peacock]; time wasted is existence, used is life [Young]; truditur dies die *[Lat.]* [Horace]; volat hora per orbem *[Lat.]* [Lucretius]; carpe diem *[Lat.]*.

107. Neverness -- N. neverness; absence of time, no time; dies non; Tib's eve; Greek Kalends, a blue moon.

Adv. never, ne'er *[Contr.]*; at no time, at no period; on the second Tuesday of the week, when Hell freezes over; on no occasion, never in all one's born days, nevermore, sine die; in no degree.

108. *[Definite duration, or portion of time.]* **Period -- N.** period, age, era; second, minute, hour, day, week, month, quarter, year, decade, decenniumm lustrum†, quinquennium, lifetime, generation; epoch, ghurry†, lunation†, moon.

century, millennium; annus magnus *[Lat.]*.

Adj. horary†; hourly, annual &c *(periodical)* 138.

108a. Contingent Duration --

Adv. during pleasure, during good behavior; quamdiu se bene gesserit *[Lat.]*.

109. *[Indefinite duration.]* **Course** -- **N.** corridors of time, sweep of time, vesta of time†, course of time, progress of time, process of time, succession of time, lapse of time, flow of time, flux of time, stream of time, tract of time, current of time, tide of time, march of time, step of time, flight of time; duration &c 106.

[Indefinite time] aorist†.

V. elapse, lapse, flow, run, proceed, advance, pass; roll on, wear on, press on; flit, fly, slip, slide, glide; run its course.

run out, expire; go by, pass by; be past &c 122.

Adj. elapsing &c *v.;* aoristic†; progressive.

Adv. in due time, in due season; in in due course, in due process, in the fullness of time; in time.

Phr. labitur et labetur *[Lat.]* [Horace]; truditur dies die *[Lat.]* [Horace]; fugaces labuntur anni *[Lat.]* [Horace]; tomorrow and tomorrow and tomorrow creeps in this petty pace from day to day [Macbeth].

110. *[Long duration.]* **Diuturnity** -- **N.** diuturnity†; a long time, a length of time; an age, a century, an eternity; slowness &c 275; perpetuity &c 112; blue moon, coon's age *[U.S.]*, dog's age.

durableness, durability; persistence, endlessness, lastingness &c *adj.*[†]; continuance, standing; permanence &c *(stability)* 150; survival, survivance[†]; longevity &c *(age)* 128; distance of time.

protraction of time, prolongation of time, extension of time; delay &c *(lateness)* 133.

V. last, endure, stand, remain, abide, continue, brave a thousand years.

tarry &c *(be late)* 133; drag on, drag its slow length along, drag a lengthening chain; protract, prolong; spin out, eke out, draw out, lengthen out; temporize; gain time, make time, talk against time.

outlast, outlive; survive; live to fight again.

Adj. durable; lasting &c *v.;* of long duration, of long-standing; permanent, endless, chronic, long-standing; intransient[†], intransitive; intransmutable[†], persistent; lifelong, livelong; longeval[†], long-lived, macrobiotic, diuturnal[†], evergreen, perennial; sempervirent[†], sempervirid[†]; unrelenting, unintermitting[†], unremitting; perpetual &c 112.

lingering, protracted, prolonged, spun out &c *v..* long-pending, long-winded; slow &c 275.

Adv. long; for a long time, for an age, for ages, for ever so long, for many a long day; long ago &c *(in a past time)* 122; longo intervallo *[It]*.

all the day long, all the year round; the livelong day, as the day is long, morning noon and night; hour after hour, day after day, &c; for good; permanently &c *adj.*.

111. *[Short duration.]* **Transientness** --
 N. transience, transientness &c *adj.*†; evanescence, impermanence, fugacity *[Chem]*, caducity†, mortality, span; nine days' wonder, bubble, Mayfly; spurt; flash in the pan; temporary arrangement, interregnum.

velocity &c 274; suddenness &c 113; changeableness &c 149.

transient, transient boarder, transient guest *[U.S.]*.

V. be transient &c *adj.*; flit, pass away, fly, gallop, vanish, fade, evaporate; pass away like a cloud, pass away like a summer cloud, pass away like a shadow, pass away like a dream.

Adj. transient, transitory, transitive; passing, evanescent, fleeting, cursory, short-lived, ephemeral; flying &c *v.*; fugacious, fugitive; shifting, slippery; spasmodic; instantaneous, momentaneous†.

temporal, temporary; provisional, provisory; deciduous; perishable, mortal, precarious, unstable, insecure; impermanent.

brief, quick, brisk, extemporaneous, summary; pressed for time &c *(haste)* 684; sudden, momentary &c *(instantaneous)* 113.

Adv. temporarily &c *adj.;* pro tempore *[Lat.];* for the moment, for a time; awhile, en passant *[Fr.],* in transitu *[Lat.];* in a short time; soon &c *(early)* 132; briefly &c *adj.;* at short notice; on the point of, on the eve of; in articulo; between cup and lip.

Phr. one's days are numbered; the time is up; here today and gone tomorrow; non semper erit aestas *[Lat.];* eheu! fugaces labuntur anni *[Lat.];* sic transit gloria mundi *[Lat.];* a schoolboy's tale, the wonder of the hour! [Byron]; dum loquimur fugerit invidia aetas *[Lat.];* fugit hora *[Lat.];* all that is transitory is but an illusion [Goethe].

112. *[Endless duration.]* **Perpetuity -- N.** perpetuity, eternity, everness†, aye, sempiternity†, immortality, athanasia†; interminability†, agelessness†, everlastingness &c *adj.;* perpetuation; continued existence, uninterrupted existence; perennity†; permanence *(durability)* 110.

V. last forever, endure forever, go on forever; have no end.

eternize, perpetuate.

Adj. perpetual, eternal; everduring†, everlasting, ever-living, ever-flowing; continual, sempiternal†; coeternal; endless, unending; ceaseless, incessant, uninterrupted, indesinent†, unceasing; endless, unending, interminable, having no end; unfading†, evergreen, amaranthine; neverending†, never-dying, never-fading; deathless, immortal, undying, imperishable.

Adv. perpetually &c *adj.;* always, ever, evermore, aye; for ever, for aye, till the end of the universe, forevermore, forever and a day, for ever and ever; in all ages, from age to age; without end; world without end, time without end; in secula seculorum *[Lat.]*; to the end of time, to the crack of doom, to the 'last syllable of recorded time' [Macbeth]; till doomsday; constantly &c *(very frequently)* 136.

Phr. esto perpetuum *[Lat.]*; labitur et labetur in omne volubilis oevum *[Lat.]* [Horace]; but thou shall flourish in immortal youth [Addison]; Eternity! thou pleasing, dreadful thought [Addison]; her immortal part with angels lives [Romeo and Juliet]; ohne Rast *[G.]*, [Goethe's motto]; ora e sempre *[It]*.

113. *[Point of time]* **Instantaneity** --
N. instantaneity, instantaneousness, immediacy; suddenness, abruptness.

moment, instant, second, minute; twinkling, trice, flash, breath, crack, jiffy, coup, burst, flash of lightning, stroke of time.

epoch, time; time of day, time of night; hour, minute; very minute &c, very time, very hour; present time, right time, true time, exact correct time.

V. be instantaneous &c *adj.;* twinkle, flash.

Adj. instantaneous, momentary, sudden, immediate, instant, abrupt, discontinuous, precipitous, precipitant, precipitate; subitaneous†, hasty; quick as thought, quick as lightning, quick as a flash; rapid as electricity.

speedy, quick, fast, fleet, swift, lively, blitz; rapid *(velocity)* 274.

Adv. instantaneously &c *adj.;* in no time, in less than no time; presto, subito†, instanter, suddenly, at a stroke, like a shot; in a moment &c *n..* in the blink of an eye, in the twinkling of an eye, in a trice; in one's tracks; right away; toute a l'heure *[Fr.]*; at one jump, in the same breath, per saltum *[Lat.]*, uno saltu *[Lat.]*; at once, all at once; plump, slap; at one fell swoop; at the same instant &c *n.;* immediately &c *(early)* 132; extempore, on the moment, on the spot, on the spur of the moment; no sooner said than done; just then; slap-dash &c *(haste)* 684.

Phr. touch and go; no sooner said than done.

114. *[Estimation, measurement, and record of time.]* **Chronometry** -- **N.** chronometry, horometry†, horology; date, epoch; style, era.

almanac, calendar, ephemeris; register, registry; chronicle, annals, journal, diary.

[Instruments for the measurement of time] chronogram; clock, wall clock, pendulum clock, grandfather's clock, cuckoo clock, alarm clock, clock radio; watch, wristwatch, pocket watch, stopwatch, Swiss watch; atomic clock, digital clock, analog clock, quartz watch, water clock; chronometer, chronoscope†, chronograph; repeater; timekeeper, timepiece; dial, sundial, gnomon, horologe, pendulum, hourglass, clepsydra†; ghurry†.

chronographer†, chronologer, chronologist, timekeeper; annalist.

calendar year, leap year, Julian calendar, Gregorian calendar, Chinese calendar, Jewish calendar, perpetual calendar, Farmer's almanac, fiscal year.

V. fix the time, mark the time; date, register, chronicle; measure time, beat time, mark time; bear date; synchronize watches.

Adj. chronological, chronometrical†, chronogrammatical†; cinquecento *[Fr.]*, quattrocento†, trecento†.

Adv. o'clock.

115. *[False estimate of time.]* **Anachronism** --
N. anachronism, metachronism, parachronism, prochronism; prolepsis, misdate; anticipation, antichronism.

disregard of time, neglect of time, oblivion of time.

intempestivity &c 135 [Obs.].

V. misdate, antedate, postdate, backdate, overdate[†]; anticipate; take no note of time, lose track of time; anachronize[†].

Adj. misdated &c *v.;* undated; overdue, past due; out of date.

2. RELATIVE TIME
1. Time with reference to Succession

116. Priority -- **N.** priority, antecedence, anteriority, precedence, pre-existence; precession &c 280; precursor &c 64; the past &c 122; premises.

V. precede, come before; forerun; go before &c *(lead)* 280; preexist; dawn; presage &c 511; herald, usher in.

be beforehand &c *(be early)* 132; steal a march upon, anticipate, forestall; have the start, gain the start.

Adj. prior, previous; preceding, precedent; anterior, antecedent; pre-existing, pre-existent; former, foregoing; aforementioned, before-mentioned, abovementioned; aforesaid, said; introductory &c *(precursory)* 64.

Adv. before, prior to; earlier; previously &c *adj.;* afore†, aforehand†, beforehand, ere, theretofore, erewhile†; ere then, ere now, before then, before now; erewhile†, already, yet, beforehand; on the eve of.

Phr. prior tempore prior jure *[Lat.]*.

117. Posteriority -- **N.** posteriority; succession, sequence; following &c 281; subsequence, supervention; futurity &c 121; successor; sequel &c 65; remainder, reversion.

V. follow after &c 281, come after, go after; succeed, supervene; ensue, occur; step into the shoes of.

Adj. subsequent, posterior, following, after, later, succeeding, postliminious†, postnate†; postdiluvial†, postdiluvian†; puisne†; posthumous; future &c 121; afterdinner, postprandial.

Adv. subsequently, after, afterwards, since, later; at a subsequent, at a later period, at a later date; next, in the sequel, close upon, thereafter, thereupon, upon which, eftsoons†; from that time, from that moment; after a while, after a time; in process of time.

118. The Present Time -- N. the present, the present time, the present day, the present moment, the present juncture, the present occasion; the times, the existing time, the time being; today, these days, nowadays, our times, modern times, the twentieth century; nonce, crisis, epoch, day, hour.

age, time of life.

Adj. present, actual, instant, current, existing, extant, that is; present-day, up-to-date, up-to-the-moment.

Adv. at this time, at this moment &c 113; at the present time &c *n.;* now, at present; at hand.

at this time of day, today, nowadays; already; even now, but now, just now; on the present occasion; for the time being, for the nonce; pro hac vice. *[Lat.]*; on the nail, on the spot; on the spur of the moment, until now; to this day, to the present day.

Phr. the present hour alone is man's [Johnson].

119. *[Time different from the present.]* **Different time -- N.** different time, other time.

[Indefinite time] aorist.

Adj. aoristic; indefinite.

Adv. at that time, at which time, at that moment, at that instant; then, on that occasion, upon; not now, some other time.

when; whenever, whensoever; upon which, on which occasion; at another time, at a different time, at some other time, at any time; at various times; some one of these days, one of these days, one fine morning; eventually, some day, by and by, sooner or later; some time or other; once upon a time.

120. Synchronism -- N. synchronism; coexistence, coincidence; simultaneousness, simultaneity &c *adj.;* concurrence, concomitance, unity of time, interim.

[Having equal times] isochronism[†].

contemporary, coetanian[†].

V. coexist, concur, accompany, go hand in hand, keep pace with; synchronize.

Adj. synchronous, synchronal[†], synchronic, synchronical, synchronistical[†]; simultaneous, coexisting, coincident, concomitant, concurrent; coeval, coevous[†]; contemporary, contemporaneous; coetaneous[†]; coeternal; isochronous.

Adv. at the same time; simultaneously &c *adj.;* together, in concert, during the same time; in the same breath; pari passu *[Lat.]*; in the interim; as one.

at the very moment &c 113; just as, as soon as; meanwhile &c *(while)* 106.

121. *[Prospective time.]* **Futurity -- N.** futurity, futurition; future, hereafter, time to come; approaching time, coming time, subsequent time, after time, approaching age, coming age, subsequent age, after age, approaching days, coming days, subsequent days, after days, approaching hours, coming hours, subsequent hours, after hours, approaching ages, coming ages, subsequent ages, after ages, approaching life, coming life, subsequent life, after life, approaching years, coming years, subsequent years, after years; morrow; millennium, doomsday, day of judgment, crack of doom, remote future.

approach of time advent, time drawing on, womb of time; destiny &c 152; eventuality.

heritage, heirs posterity.

prospect &c *(expectation)* 507; foresight &c 510.

V. look forwards; anticipate
&c *(expect)* 507, *(foresee)* 510; forestall &c *(be early)* 132.

come on, draw on; draw near; approach, await, threaten; impend &c *(be destined)* 152.

Adj. future, to come; coming &c *(impending)* 152; next, near; close at hand; eventual, ulterior; in prospect &c *(expectation)* 507.

Adv. prospectively, hereafter, in future; kal[†], tomorrow, the day after tomorrow; in course of time, in process of time, in the fullness of time; eventually, ultimately, sooner or later; proximo *[Lat.]*; paulo post futurum *[Lat.]*; in after time; one of these days; after a time, after a while.

from this time; henceforth, henceforwards†; thence; thenceforth, thenceforward; whereupon, upon which.

soon &c *(early)* 132; on the eve of, on the point of, on the brink of; about to; close upon.

Phr. quid sit futurum cras fuge quaerere *[Lat.]* [Horace].

122. *[Retrospective time.]* **The Past** -- **N.** the past, past time; days of yore, times of yore, days of old, times of old, days past, times past, days gone by, times gone by; bygone days; old times, ancient times, former times; fore time; the good old days, the olden time, good old time; auld lang syne†; eld†.

antiquity, antiqueness†, status quo; time immemorial; distance of time; remote age, remote time; remote past; rust of antiquity.

[study of the past] paleontology, paleography, paleology†; paleozoology; palaetiology†, archaeology; paleogeography; paleoecology; paleobotany; paleoclimatoogy; archaism, antiquarianism, medievalism, Pre-Raphaelitism; paleography.

retrospect, retrospection, looking back, memory &c 505.

laudator temporis acti *[Lat.]*; medievalist, Pre-Raphaelite; antiquary, antiquarian; archmologist &c; Oldbuck, Dryasdust.

ancestry &c *(paternity)* 166.

V. be past &c *adj.*; have expired &c *adj.*, have run its course, have had its day; pass; pass by, go by, pass away, go away, pass off, go off; lapse, blow over.

look back, trace back, cast the eyes back; exhume.

Adj. past, gone, gone by, over, passed away, bygone, foregone; elapsed, lapsed, preterlapsed†, expired, no more, run out, blown over, has-been, that has been, extinct, antediluvian, antebellum, never to return, gone with the wind, exploded, forgotten, irrecoverable; obsolete &c *(old)* 124.

former, pristine, quondam, ci-devant *[Fr.]*, late; ancestral.

foregoing; last, latter; recent, over night; preterperfect†, preterpluperfect†.

looking back &c *v.*; retrospective, retroactive; archaeological &c *n.*.

Adv. paleo-; archaeo-; formerly; of old, of yore; erst *[G.]*, whilom, erewhile†, time was, ago, over; in the olden time &c *n.*; anciently, long ago, long since; a long while, a long time ago; years ago, yesteryear, ages ago; some time ago, some time since, some time back.

yesterday, the day before yesterday; last year, ultimo; lately &c *(newly)* 123.

retrospectively; ere now, before now, till now; hitherto, heretofore; no longer; once, once upon a time; from time immemorial, from prehistoric times; in the memory of man; time out of mind; already, yet, up to this time; ex post facto.

Phr. time was; the time has been, the time hath been; you can't go home again; fuimus Troes *[Lat.]* [Vergil]; fruit Ilium *[Lat.]* [Vergil]; hoc erat in more majorum *[Lat.]*; O call back yesterday, bid time return [Richard II]; tempi passati *[It]*; the eternal landscape of the past [Tennyson]; ultimus Romanorum *[Lat.]*; what's past is prologue [Tempest]; whose yesterdays look backward with a smile [Young].

   2. Time with reference to a particular period

123. Newness -- **N.** newness &c *adj.;* novelty, recency; immaturity; youth &c 127; gloss of novelty.

innovation; renovation &c *(restoration)* 660.

modernism; mushroom, parvenu; latest fashion.

V. renew &c *(restore)* 660; modernize.

Adj. new, novel, recent, fresh, green; young &c 127; evergreen; raw, immature, unsettled, yeasty; virgin; untried, unhandseled[†], untrodden, untrod, unbeaten; fire-new, span-new.

late, modern, neoteric, hypermodern, nouveau; new-born, nascent, neonatal *[Med.]*, new-fashioned, new-fangled, new-fledged; of yesterday; just out, brand-new, up to date, up to the minute, with it, fashionable, in fashion; in, hip *[Coll.]*; vernal, renovated, sempervirent[†], sempervirid[†].

fresh as a rose, fresh as a daisy, fresh as paint; spick and span.

Adv. newly &c *adj.;* afresh, anew, lately, just now, only yesterday, the other day; latterly, of late.

not long ago, a short time ago.

Phr. di novello tutto par bello *[It]*; nullum est jam dictum quod non dictum est prius *[Lat.]*; una scopa nuova spazza bene *[It]*.

124. Oldness -- N. oldness &c *adj.*[†]; age, antiquity; cobwebs of antiquity.

maturity; decline, decay; senility &c 128.

seniority, eldership, primogeniture.

archaism &c *(the past)* 122; thing of the past, relic of the past; megatherium†; Sanskrit.

tradition, prescription, custom, immemorial usage, common law.

V. be old &c *adj.;* have had its day, have seen its day; become old &c *adj.;* age, fade, senesce.

Adj. old, ancient, antique; of long standing, time-honored, venerable; elder, eldest; firstborn.

prime; primitive, primeval, primigenous†; paleolontological, paleontologic, paleoanthropological, paleoanthropic†, paleolithic, primordial, primordinate†; aboriginal &c *(beginning)* 66; diluvian†, antediluvian; protohistoric†; prehistoric; antebellum, colonial, precolumbian; patriarchal, preadamite†; paleocrystic†; fossil, paleozoolical, paleozoic, preglacial†, antemundane†; archaic, classic, medieval, Pre-Raphaelite, ancestral, black-letter.

immemorial, traditional, prescriptive, customary, whereof the memory of man runneth not to the contrary; inveterate, rooted.

antiquated, of other times, rococo, of the old school, after-age, obsolete; out of date, out of fashion, out of it; stale, old-fashioned, behind the age; old-world; exploded; gone out, gone by; passe, run out; senile

&c 128; time worn; crumbling
&c *(deteriorated)* 659; secondhand.

old as the hills, old as Methuselah, old as Adam[†], old as history.

[geological eras (list, starting at given number of years bp)] Archeozoic [5,000,000,000], Proterozoic [1,500,000,000], Paleozoic [600,000,000], Mesozoic [220,000,000], Cenozoic [70,000,000].

[geological periods] Precambrian, Cambrian [600,000,000], Ordovician [500,000,000], Silurian [440,000,000], Devonian [400,000,000], Mississippian [350,000,000], Pennsylvanian [300,000,000], Permian [270,000,000], Triassic [220,000,000], Jurassic [180,000,000], Cretaceous [135,000,000], Tertiary [70,000,000], Paleogene [70,000,000], Neocene [25,0000,000], Quaternary [1,000,000].

[geological epochs (list, starting at 70,000,000 years bp)] Paleocene, Eocene, Oligocene, Miocene, Pliocene, Pleistocene, Recent.

Adv. since the world was made, since the year one, since the days of Methuselah.

Phr. vetera extollimus recentium incuriosi *[Lat.]* [Tacitus].

125. Morning *[Noon.]* -- **N.** morning, morn, forenoon, a.m., prime, dawn, daybreak; dayspring[†], foreday[†], sunup; peep of day, break of day; aurora; first blush of the morning, first flush of the morning, prime of the morning; twilight, crepuscule, sunrise; cockcrow, cockcrowing[†]; the small hours, the wee hours of the morning.

spring; vernal equinox, first point of Aries.

noon; midday, noonday; noontide, meridian, prime; nooning, noontime.

summer, midsummer.

Adj. matin, matutinal[†]; vernal.

Adv. at sunrise &c *n.;* with the sun, with the lark, when the morning dawns.

Phr. at shut of evening flowers [Paradise Lost]; entre chien et loup *[Fr.]*; flames in the forehead of the morning sky [Milton]; the breezy call of incense-breathing morn [Gray].

126. Evening *[Midnight.]* -- **N.** evening, eve; decline of day, fall of day, close of day; candlelight, candlelighting[†]; eventide, nightfall, curfew, dusk, twilight, eleventh hour; sunset, sundown; going down of the sun, cock-shut, dewy eve, gloaming, bedtime.

afternoon, postmeridian, p.m.

autumn, fall, fall of the leaf; autumnal equinox; Indian summer, St.

Luke's summer, St.

Martin's summer.

midnight; dead of night, witching hour, witching hour of night, witching time of night; winter; killing time.

Adj. vespertine, autumnal, nocturnal.

Phr. midnight, the outpost of advancing day [Longfellow]; sable-vested Night [Milton]; this gorgeous arch with golden worlds inlay'd [Young].

127. Youth -- N. youth; juvenility, juvenescence†; juniority†; infancy; babyhood, childhood, boyhood, girlhood, youthhood†; incunabula; minority, nonage, teens, tender age, bloom.

cradle, nursery, leading strings, pupilage, puberty, pucelage†.

prime of life, flower of life, springtide of life†, seedtime of life, golden season of life; heyday of youth, school days; rising generation.

Adj. young, youthful, juvenile, green, callow, budding, sappy, puisne, beardless, under age, in one's teens; in statu pupillari *[Lat.]*; younger, junior; hebetic†, unfledged.

Phr. youth on the prow and pleasure at the helm [Gray]; youth a the glad season of life [Carlyle].

128. Age -- N. age; oldness† &c *adj.;* old age, advanced age, golden years; senility, senescence; years, anility†, gray hairs, climacteric, grand climacteric, declining years, decrepitude, hoary age, caducity†, superannuation; second childhood, second childishness; dotage; vale of years, decline of life, sear and yellow leaf [Macbeth]; threescore years and ten; green old age, ripe age; longevity; time of life.

seniority, eldership; elders &c *(veteran)* 130; firstling; doyen, father; primogeniture.

[Science of old age.] geriatrics, nostology†.

V. be aged &c *adj.;* grow old, get old &c *adj.;* age; decline, wane, dodder; senesce.

Adj. aged; old &c 124; elderly, geriatric, senile; matronly, anile†; in years; ripe, mellow, run to seed, declining, waning, past one's prime; gray, gray-headed; hoar, hoary; venerable, time-worn, antiquated, passe, effete, decrepit, superannuated; advanced in life, advanced in years; stricken in years; wrinkled, marked with the crow's foot; having one foot in the grave; doting &c *(imbecile)* 499; like the last of pea time.

older, elder, eldest; senior; firstborn.

turned of, years old; of a certain age, no chicken, old as Methuselah; ancestral, patriarchal, &c *(ancient)* 124; gerontic.

Phr. give me a staff of honor for my age [Titus Andronicus]; bis pueri senes *[Lat.]*; peu de gens savent elre vieux *[Fr.]*; plenus annis abiit plenus honoribus *[Lat.]* [Pliny the Younger]; old age is creeping on apace [Byron]; slow-consuming age [Gray]; the hoary head is a crown of glory [Proverbs xvi, 31]; the silver livery of advised age [II Henry VI]; to grow old gracefully; to vanish in the chinks that Time has made [Rogers].

129. Infant -- N. infant, babe, baby, babe in arms; nurseling, suckling, yearling, weanling; papoose, bambino; kid; vagitus.

child, bairn *[Scot.]*, little one, brat, chit, pickaninny, urchin; bantling, bratling[†]; elf.

youth, boy, lad, stripling, youngster, youngun, younker[†], callant[†], whipster[†], whippersnapper, whiffet *[U.S.]*, schoolboy, hobbledehoy, hopeful, cadet, minor, master.

scion; sap, seedling; tendril, olive branch, nestling, chicken, larva, chrysalis, tadpole, whelp, cub, pullet, fry, callow; codlin, codling; foetus, calf, colt, pup, foal, kitten; lamb, lambkin†; aurelia†, caterpillar, cocoon, nymph, nympha†, orphan, pupa, staddle†.

girl; lass, lassie; wench, miss, damsel, demoiselle; maid, maiden; virgin; hoyden.

Adj. infantine†, infantile; puerile; boyish, girlish, childish, babyish, kittenish; baby; newborn, unfledged, new-fledged, callow.

in the cradle, in swaddling clothes, in long clothes, in arms, in leading strings; at the breast; in one's teens.

130. Veteran -- N. veteran, old man, seer, patriarch, graybeard; grandfather, grandsire; grandam; gaffer, gammer; crone; pantaloon; sexagenarian, octogenarian, nonagenarian, centenarian; old stager; dotard &c 501.

preadamite†, Methuselah, Nestor, old Parr; elders; forefathers &c *(paternity)* 166.

Phr. superfluous lags the veteran on the stage [Johnson].

131. Adolescence -- **N.** adolescence, pubescence, majority; adultism; adultness &c *adj.;* manhood, virility, maturity full age, ripe age; flower of age; prime of life, meridian of life, spring of life.

man &c 373; woman &c 374; adult, no chicken.

V. come of age, come to man's estate, come to years of discretion; attain majority, assume the toga virilis *[Lat.]*; have cut one's eyeteeth, have sown one's mild oats.

Adj. adolescent, pubescent, of age; of full age, of ripe age; out of one's teens, grown up, mature, full grown, in one's prime, middle-aged, manly, virile, adult; womanly, matronly; marriageable, nubile.

3. Time with reference to an Effect or Purpose

132. Earliness -- **N.** {ant.

133} earliness &c *adj.;* morning &c 125.

punctuality; promptitude &c *(activity)* 682; haste &c *(velocity)* 274; suddenness &c *(instantaneity)* 113.

prematurity, precocity, precipitation, anticipation; a stitch in time.

V. be early &c *adj.,* be beforehand &c *adv.;* keep time, take time by the forelock, anticipate, forestall; have the start, gain the start; steal a march upon; gain time, draw on futurity; bespeak, secure, engage, preengage†.

accelerate; expedite &c *(quicken)* 274; make haste &c *(hurry)* 684.

Adj. early, prime, forward; prompt &c *(active)* 682; summary.

premature, precipitate, precocious; prevenient†, anticipatory; rath†.

sudden &c *(instantaneous)* 113; unexpected &c 508; near, near at hand; immediate.

Adv. early, soon, anon, betimes, rath†; eft, eftsoons; ere long, before long, shortly; beforehand; prematurely &c *adj.;* precipitately &c *(hastily)* 684; too soon; before its time, before one's time; in anticipation; unexpectedly &c 508.

suddenly &c *(instantaneously)* 113; before one can say 'Jack Robinson', at short notice, extempore; on the spur of the moment, on the spur of the occasion [Bacon]; at once; on the spot, on the instant; at sight; offhand, out of hand; a' vue d'oeil *[Fr.]*; straight, straightway, straightforth†; forthwith, incontinently, summarily, immediately, briefly, shortly, quickly, speedily, apace, before the ink is dry, almost immediately, presently at the first opportunity, in no long time, by and by, in a while, directly.

Phr. no sooner said than done, immediately, if not sooner; tout vicnt a temps pour qui sait attendre *[Fr.]*.

132a. Punctuality -- **N.** punctuality, promptness, immediateness.

V. be prompt, be on time, be in time; arrive on time; be in the nick of time.

Adj. timely, seasonable, in time, punctual, prompt.

Adv. on time, punctually, at the deadline, precisely, exactly; right on time, to the minute; in time; in good time, in military time, in pudding time[†], in due time; time enough; with no time to spare, by a hair's breadth.

Phr. touch and go, not a minute too soon, in the nick of time, just under the wire, get on board before the train leaves the station.

133. Lateness -- **N.** {ant.

132} lateness &c *adj.;* tardiness &c *(slowness)* 275.

delay, delation; cunctation, procrastination; deferring, deferral &c *v.;* postponement, adjournment, prorogation, retardation, respite, pause, reprieve, stay of execution; protraction, prolongation; Fabian policy, medecine expectante *[Fr.]*, chancery suit, federal case; leeway; high time; moratorium, holdover.

V. be late &c *adj.;* tarry, wait, stay, bide, take time; dawdle &c *(be inactive)* 683; linger, loiter; bide one's time, take one's time; gain time; hang fire; stand over, lie over.

put off, defer, delay, lay over, suspend; table *[Parl.]*; shift off, stave off; waive, retard, remand, postpone, adjourn; procrastinate; dally; prolong, protract; spin out, draw out, lengthen out, stretch out; prorogue; keep back; tide over; push to the last, drive to the last; let the matter stand over; reserve &c *(store)* 636; temporize; consult one's pillow, sleep on it.

lose an opportunity &c 135; be kept waiting, dance attendance; kick one's heels, cool one's heels; faire antichambre *[Fr.]*; wait impatiently; await &c *(expect)* 507; sit up, sit up at night.

Adj. late, tardy, slow, behindhand, serotine[†], belated, postliminious[†], posthumous, backward, unpunctual, untimely; delayed, postponed; dilatory &c *(slow)* 275; delayed &c *v.;* in abeyance.

Adv. late; lateward†, backward; late in the day; at sunset, at the eleventh hour, at length, at last; ultimately; after time, behind time, after the deadline; too late; too late for &c 135.

slowly, leisurely, deliberately, at one's leisure; ex post facto; sine die.

Phr. nonum prematur in annum *[Lat.]* [Horace]; against the sunbeams serotine and lucent [Longfellow]; ie meglio tardi che mai *[It]*; deliberando saepe perit occasio *[Lat.]* [Syrus].

134. Occasion -- N. {ant.

135} timeliness, occasion, opportunity, opening, room; event *(eventuality)* 151; suitable season, proper season, suitable time, proper time; high time; opportuneness &c *adj.;* tempestivity†.

crisis, turn, juncture, conjuncture; crisis, turning point, given time.

nick of time; golden opportunity, well timed opportunity, fine opportunity, favorable opportunity, opening; clear stage, fair field; mollia tempora *[Lat.]*; fata Morgana *[Lat.]*; spare time &c*(leisure)* 685.

V. seize an opportunity &c *(take)* 789, use an opportunity &c 677, give an opportunity &c 784, use an occasion; improve the occasion.

suit the occasion &c *(be expedient)* 646.

seize the occasion, strike while the iron is hot, battre le fer sur l'enclume *[Fr.]*, make hay while the sun shines, seize the present hour, take time by the forelock, prendre la balle au bond*[Fr.]*.

Adj. opportune, timely, well-timed, timeful†, seasonable.

providential, lucky, fortunate, happy, favorable, propitious, auspicious, critical; suitable &c 23; obiter dicta.

Adv. opportunely &c *adj.;* in proper course, in due course, in proper season, in due season, in proper time, in due time; for the nonce; in the nick of time, in the fullness of time; all in good time; just in time, at the eleventh hour, now or never.

by the way, by the by; en passant *[Fr.]*, a propos *[Fr.]*; pro re nata *[Lat.]*, pro hac vice *[Lat.]*; par parenthese *[Fr.]*, parenthetically, by way of parenthesis, incidentally; while speaking of, while on the subject; extempore; on the spur of the moment, on the spur of the occasion; on the spot &c *(early)* 132.

Phr. carpe diem *[Lat.]*, [Horace]; occasionem cognosce *[Lat.]*; one's hour is come, the time is up; that reminds me, now that you mention it, come to think of it; bien perdu bien connu *[Fr.]*; e sempre l'ora *[It]*; ex quovis ligno non fit Mercurius *[Lat.]*; nosce tempus *[Lat.]*; nunc aut nunquam *[Lat.]*.

135. Untimeliness -- N. {ant.

134} untimeliness, intempestivity[†], unseasonableness, inexpedience; unsuitable time, improper time; unreasonableness &c *adj.*; evil hour; contretemps; intrusion; anachronism &c 115.

bad time, wrong time, inappropriate time, not the right occasion, unsuitable time, inopportune time, poor timing.

V. be ill timed &c *adj.*; mistime, intrude, come amiss, break in upon; have other fish to fry; be busy, be occupied.

lose an opportunity, throw away an opportunity, waste an opportunity, neglect an opportunity &c 460; allow the opportunity to pass, suffer the opportunity to pass, allow the opportunity to slip, suffer the opportunity to slip, allow the opportunity to go by, suffer the opportunity to go by, allow the opportunity to escape, suffer the opportunity to escape, allow the opportunity to lapse, suffer the opportunity to lapse, allow the occasion to pass, allow the occasion to slip by; waste time &c *(be inactive)* 683; let slip through the fingers, lock the barn door after the horse is stolen.

Adj. ill-timed, mistimed; ill-fated, ill-omened, ill-starred; untimely, unseasonable; out of date, out of season; inopportune, timeless, intrusive, untoward, mal a propos *[Fr.]*, unlucky, inauspicious, infelicitous, unbefitting, unpropitious, unfortunate, unfavorable; unsuited &c 24; inexpedient &c 647.

unpunctual &c *(late)* 133; too late for; premature &c *(early)* 132; too soon for; wise after the event, monday morning quarterbacking, twenty-twenty hindsight.

Adv. inopportunely &c *adj.;* as ill luck would have it, in an evil hour, the time having gone by, a day after the fair.

Phr. after death the doctor, after meat mustard.

3. RECURRENT TIME

136. Frequency -- **N.** frequency, oftness[†], oftenness[†], commonness; repetition &c 104; normality &c 80; example *(conformity)* 82; routine, custom *(habit)* 613.

regularity, uniformity, constancy, clock-work precision; punctuality &c *(exactness)* 494; even tenor; system; routine &c *(custom)* 613; formula; rule &c *(form regulation)* 697; keynote, standard, model; precedent &c *(prototype)* 22; conformity &c 82.

V. recur &c 104; do nothing but; keep, keep on.

Adj. frequent, many times, not rare, thickcoming[†], incessant, perpetual, continual, steady, constant, thick; uniform; repeated &c 104; customary &c 613 *(habit)* 613; regular *(normal)* 80; according to rule &c *(conformable)* 82.

common, everyday, usual, ordinary, familiar.

old-hat, boring, well-known, trivial.

Adv. often, oft; ofttimes[†], oftentimes; frequently; repeatedly &c 104; unseldom[†], not unfrequently[†]; in quick succession, in rapid succession; many a time and oft; daily, hourly &c; every day, every hour, every moment &c, perpetually, continually, constantly, incessantly, without ceasing, at all times, daily and hourly, night and day, day and night, day after day, morning noon and night, ever anon, invariably *(habit)* 613.

most often; commonly &c *(habitually)* 613.

sometimes, occasionally, at times, now and then, from time to time, there being times when, toties quoties *[Lat.]*, often enough, when the mood strikes, again and again.

137. Infrequency -- **N.** infrequency, rareness, rarity; fewness &c 103; seldomness†; uncommonness.

V. be rare &c *adj*..

Adj. unfrequent†, infrequent; rare, rare as a blue diamond; few &c 103; scarce; almost unheard of, unprecedented, which has not occurred within the memory of the oldest inhabitant, not within one's previous experience; not since Adam†.

scarce as hen's teeth; one in a million; few and far between.

Adv. seldom, rarely, scarcely, hardly; not often, not much, infrequently, unfrequently†, unoften†; scarcely, scarcely ever, hardly ever; once in a blue moon.

once; once in a blue moon; once in a million years; once for all, once in a way; pro hac vice *[Lat.]*.

Phr. ein mal kein mal *[G.]*.

138. Periodicity *[Regularity of recurrence]* -- **N.** periodicity, intermittence; beat; oscillation &c

314; pulse, pulsation; rhythm; alternation, alternateness, alternativeness, alternity†.

bout, round, revolution, rotation, turn, say.

anniversary, jubilee, centenary.

catamenia†, courses, menses, menstrual flux.

[Regularity of return] rota, cycle, period, stated time, routine; days of the week; Sunday, Monday &c; months of the year; January &c; feast, fast &c; Christmas, Easter, New Year's day &c;Allhallows†, Allhallowmas†, All Saints' Day; All Souls', All Souls' Day; Ash Wednesday, bicentennial, birthday, bissextile†, Candlemas†, Dewali, groundhog day *[U.S.]*, Halloween, Hallowmas†, Lady day, leap year, Midsummer day, Muharram, woodchuck day *[U.S.]*, St.

Swithin's day, natal day; yearbook; yuletide.

punctuality, regularity, steadiness.

V. recur in regular order, recur in regular succession; return, revolve; come again, come in its turn; come round, come round again; beat, pulsate; alternate; intermit.

Adj. periodic, periodical; serial, recurrent, cyclical, rhythmical; recurring &c *v.;* intermittent, remittent; alternate, every other.

hourly; diurnal, daily; quotidian, tertian, weekly; hebdomadal†, hebdomadary†; biweekly, fortnightly; bimonthly; catamenial†; monthly, menstrual; yearly, annual; biennial, triennial, &c;centennial, secular; paschal, lenten, &c regular, steady, punctual, regular as clockwork.

Adv. periodically &c *adj.;* at regular intervals, at stated times; at fixed established, at established periods; punctually &c *adj..* de die in diem *[Lat.]*; from day to day, day by day.

by turns; in turn, in rotation; alternately, every other day, off and on, ride and tie, round and round.

139. Irregularity of recurrence -- **N.** irregularity, uncertainty, unpunctuality; fitfulness &c *adj.;* capriciousness, ecrhythmus†.

Adj. irregular, uncertain, unpunctual, capricious, desultory, fitful, flickering; rambling, rhapsodical; spasmodic; immethodical†, unmethodical, variable.

Adv. irregularly &c *adj.;* by fits and starts &c *(discontinuously)* 70.

SECTION VII.

CHANGE

1. SIMPLE CHANGE

140. *[Difference at different times.]* **Change** --
 N. change, alteration, mutation, permutation, variation, modification, modulation, inflexion, mood, qualification, innovation, metastasis, deviation, turn, evolution, revolution; diversion; break.

transformation, transfiguration; metamorphosis; transmutation; deoxidization *[Chem]*; transubstantiation; *[Genetics],* mutagenesis transanimation†, transmigration, metempsychosis†; avatar; alterative.

conversion &c *(gradual change)* 144; revolution &c *(sudden or radical change)* 146, inversion &c *(reversal)* 218; displacement &c 185; transference &c 270.

changeableness &c 149; tergiversation &c *(change of mind)* 607.

V. change, alter, vary, wax and wane; modulate, diversify, qualify, tamper with; turn, shift, veer, tack, chop, shuffle, swerve, warp, deviate, turn aside, evert, intervert†; pass to, take a turn, turn the corner, resume.

work a change, modify, vamp, superinduce; transform, transfigure, transmute, transmogrify, transume[†]; metamorphose, ring the changes.

innovate, introduce new blood, shuffle the cards; give a turn to, give a color to; influence, turn the scale; shift the scene, turn over a new leaf.

recast &c 146; reverse &c 218; disturb &c 61; convert into &c 144.

Adj. changed &c v.; newfangled; changeable &c 149; transitional; modifiable; alterative.

Adv. mutatis mutandis *[Lat.]*.

Int. quantum mutatus! *[Lat.]*,

Phr. a change came o'er the spirit of my dream [Byron]; nous avons change tout cela [Moliere]; tempora mutantur nos et mutamur in illis *[Lat.]*; non sum qualis eram *[Lat.]* [Horace]; casaque tourner *[Fr.]*; corpora lente augescent cito extinguuntur [Tacitus]; in statu quo ante bellum *[Lat.]*; still ending and beginning still [Cowper]; vox audita perit littera scripta manet*[Lat.]*.

141. *[Absence of change.]* **Permanence --**
N. stability &c 150; quiescence &c 265; obstinacy &c 606.

permanence, persistence, endurance; durability; standing, status quo; maintenance, preservation, conservation; conservation; law of the Medes and Persians; standing dish.

V. let alone, let be, let it be; persist, remain, stay, tarry, rest; stet (copy editing) hold, hold on; last, endure, bide, abide, aby†, dwell, maintain, keep; stand, stand still, stand fast; subsist, live, outlive, survive; hold one's ground, keep one's ground, hold one's footing, keep one's footing; hold good.

Adj. stable &c 150; persisting &c *v.;* permanent; established; unchanged &c *(change)* &c 140; renewed; intact, inviolate; persistent; monotonous, uncheckered†; unfailing.

undestroyed, unrepealed, unsuppressed†; conservative, qualis ab incepto *[Lat.]*; prescriptive &c *(old)* 124; stationary &c 265.

Adv. in statu quo *[Lat.]*; for good, finally; at a stand, at a standstill; uti possidetis *[Lat.]*; without a shadow of turning.

Phr. esto perpetua *[Lat.]*; nolumus leges Angliae mutari *[Lat.]*; j'y suis et j'y ereste *[Fr.]*.

142. *[Change from action to rest.]* **Cessation** --
 N. cessation, discontinuance, desistance, desinence†.

intermission, remission; suspense, suspension; interruption; stop; stopping &c v.; closure, stoppage, halt; arrival &c 292.

pause, rest, lull, respite, truce, drop; interregnum, abeyance; cloture *[U.S.]*.

dead stop, dead stand, dead lock; finis, cerrado *[Sp.]*; blowout, burnout, meltdown, disintegration; comma, colon, semicolon, period, full stop; end &c 67; death &c 360.

V. cease, discontinue, desist, stay, halt; break off, leave off; hold, stop, pull up, stop short; stick, hang fire; halt; pause, rest; burn out, blow out, melt down.

have done with, give over, surcease, shut up shop; give up &c *(relinquish)* 624.

hold one's hand, stay one's hand; rest on one's oars repose on one's laurels.

come to a stand, come to a standstill; come to a deadlock, come to a full stop; arrive &c 292; go out, die away; wear away, wear off; pass away &c *(be past)* 122; be at an end; disintegrate, self-destruct.

intromit, interrupt, suspend, interpel[†]; intermit, remit; put an end to, put a stop to, put a period to; derail; turn off, switch off, power down, deactivate, disconnect; bring to a stand, bring to a standstill; stop, cut short, arrest, stem the tide, stem the torrent; pull the check-string, pull the plug on.

Int. hold!, stop!, enough!, avast!, have done!, a truce to!, soft!, leave off!, tenez! *[Fr.]*,

Phr. I pause for a reply [Julius Caesar].

143. Continuance in action

N. continuance, continuation; run; perpetuation, prolongation; persistence &c *(perseverance)* 604.1; repetition &c 104.

V. continue, persist; go on, jog on, keep on, run on, hold on; abide, keep, pursue, stick to its course, take its course, maintain its course; carry on, keep up.

sustain, uphold, hold up, keep on foot; follow up, perpetuate; maintain; preserve &c 604.1; harp upon &c *(repeat)* 104.

keep going, keep alive, keep the pot boiling, keep up the ball, keep up the good work; die in harness, die with one's boots on; hold on the even tenor of one's way, pursue the even tenor of one's way.

let be; stare super antiquas vias *[Lat.]*; quieta non movere *[Lat.]*; let things take their course; stare decisis (Jurisprudence).

Adj. continuing &c *v.;* uninterrupted, unintermitting†, unvarying, unshifting†; unreversed†, unstopped, unrevoked, unvaried; sustained; undying &c *(perpetual)* 112; inconvertible.

Int. keep it up!, go to it!, right away!, right on!, attaboy!,

Phr. nolumus leges Angliae mutari *[Lat.]*; vestigia nulla retrorsum *[Lat.]* [Horace]; labitur et albetur [Horace].

144. *[Gradual change to something different.]* **Conversion** -- **N.** conversion, reduction, transmutation, resolution, assimilation; evolution, sea change; change of state; assumption; naturalization; transportation; development *[Biol.]*, developing.

[photography] *[conversion of currency]* conversion of currency, exchange of currency; exchange rate; bureau de change.

chemistry, alchemy; progress, growth, lapse, flux.

passage; transit, transition; transmigration, shifting &c *v.;* phase; conjugation; convertibility.

crucible, alembic, caldron, retort.

convert, pervert, renegade, apostate.

V. be converted into; become, get, wax; come to, turn to, turn into, evolve into, develop into; turn out, lapse, shift; run into, fall into, pass into, slide into, glide into, grow into, ripen into, open into, resolve itself into, settle into, merge into, emerge as; melt, grow, come round to, mature, mellow; assume the form of, assume the shape of, assume the state of, assume the nature of, assume the character of; illapse[†]; begin a new phase, assume a new phase, undergo a change.

convert into, resolve into; make, render; mold, form &c 240; remodel, new model, refound[†], reform, reorganize; assimilate to, bring to, reduce to.

Adj. converted into &c *v.;* convertible, resolvable into; transitional; naturalized.

Adv. gradually, &c *(slowly)* 275 in transitu &c *(transference)* 270 [Lat.].

145. Reversion -- **N.** reversion, return; revulsion.

turning point, turn of the tide; status quo ante bellum; calm before a storm.

alternation &c *(periodicity)* 138; inversion &c 219; recoil &c 277; retreat, regression, retrogression &c 283; restoration &c 660; relapse, recidivism &c 661; atavism; vicinism[†];

V. revert, turn back, regress; relapse &c 661; recoil &c 277; retreat &c 283; restore &c 660; undo, unmake; turn the tide, roll back the tide, turn the scale, tip the scale.

Adj. reverting &c *v.;* regressive, revulsive, reactionary; retrorse[†].

Adv. a rebours *[Fr.]*.

146. *[Sudden or violent change.]* **Revolution** -- **N.** revolution, bouleversement, subversion, break up; destruction &c 162; sudden change, radical change, sweeping organic change; change of state, phase change; quantum leap, quantum jump; clean sweep, coup d'etat *[Fr.]*, counter revolution.

jump, leap, plunge, jerk, start, transilience[†]; explosion; spasm, convulsion, throe, revulsion; storm, earthquake, cataclysm.

legerdemain &c *(trick)* 545.

V. revolutionize; new model, remodel, recast; strike out something new, break with the past; change the face of, unsex.

Adj. unrecognizable; revolutionary.

147. *[Change of one thing for another.]* **Substitution** -- **N.** substitution, commutation; supplanting &c *v.;* metaphor, metonymy &c *(figure of speech)* 521.

[Thing substituted] substitute, ersatz, makeshift, temporary expedient, replacement, succedaneum; shift, pis aller *[Fr.]*, stopgap, jury rigging, jury mast, locum tenens, warming pan, dummy, scapegoat; double; changeling; quid pro quo, alternative.

representative &c *(deputy)* 759; palimpsest.

price, purchase money, consideration, equivalent.

V. substitute, put in the place of, change for; make way for, give place to; supply the place of, take the place of; supplant, supersede, replace, cut out, serve as a substitute; step into stand in the shoes of; jury rig, make a shift with, put up with; borrow from Peter to pay Paul, take money out of one pocket and put it in another, cannibalize; commute, redeem, compound for.

Adj. substituted &c*;* ersatz; phony; vicarious, subdititious†.

Adv. instead; in place of, in lieu of, in the stead of, in the room of; faute de mieux *[Fr.]*.

148. *[Double or mutual change.]* **Interchange** --
 N. interchange, exchange; commutation, permutation, intermutation; reciprocation, transposition, rearrangement; shuffling; alternation, reciprocity; castling (at chess); hocus-pocus.

interchangeableness†, interchangeability.

recombination; combination &c 48.

barter &c 794; tit for tat &c *(retaliation)* 718; cross fire, battledore and shuttlecock; quid pro quo.

V. interchange, exchange, counterchange†; bandy, transpose, shuffle, change bands, swap, permute, reciprocate, commute; give and take, return the compliment; play at puss in the corner, play at battledore and shuttlecock; retaliate &c 718; requite.

rearrange, recombine.

Adj. interchanged &c *v.;* reciprocal, mutual, commutative, interchangeable, intercurrent†.

combinatorial *[Math.]*.

recombinant *[Biol.]*.

Adv. in exchange, vice versa, mutatis mutandis *[Lat.]*, backwards and forwards, by turns, turn and turn about; each in his turn, everyone in his turn.

2. COMPLEX CHANGE

149. Changeableness -- **N.** changeableness &c *adj.;* mutability, inconstancy; versatility, mobility; instability, unstable equilibrium; vacillation &c *(irresolution)* 605; fluctuation, vicissitude; alternation &c *(oscillation)* 314.

restlessness &c *adj..* fidgets, disquiet; disquietude, inquietude; unrest; agitation &c 315.

moon, Proteus, chameleon, quicksilver, shifting sands, weathercock, harlequin, Cynthia of the minute, April showers[†]; wheel of Fortune; transientness &c 111 [Obs.].

V. fluctuate, vary, waver, flounder, flicker, flitter, flit, flutter, shift, shuffle, shake, totter, tremble, vacillate, wamble[†], turn and turn about, ring the changes; sway to and fro, shift to and fro; change and change about; waffle, blow with the wind *(irresolute)* 605; oscillate &c 314; vibrate between, two extremes, oscillate between, two extremes; alternate; have as man phases as the moon.

Adj. changeable, changeful; changing &c 140; mutable, variable, checkered, ever changing; protean, proteiform[†]; versatile.

unstaid[†], inconstant; unsteady, unstable, unfixed, unsettled; fluctuating &c *v.;* restless; agitated &c 315; erratic, fickle; irresolute &c 605; capricious &c 608; touch and go; inconsonant, fitful, spasmodic; vibratory; vagrant, wayward; desultory; afloat;

alternating; alterable, plastic, mobile; transient &c 111; wavering.

Adv. seesaw &c *(oscillation)* 314; off and on.

Phr. a rolling stone gathers no moss; pictra mossa non fa muschis *[It]*; honores mutant mores *[Lat.]*; varium et mutabile semper femina *[Lat.]* [Vergil].

150. Stability -- N. stability; immutability &c *adj.;* unchangeability,
&c *adj.;* unchangeableness†; constancy; stable equilibrium, immobility, soundness, vitality, stabiliment†, stiffness, ankylosis†, solidity, aplomb.

establishment, fixture; rock, pillar, tower, foundation, leopard's spots, Ethiopia's skin.

permanence &c 141; obstinacy &c 606.

V. be firm &c *adj.;* stick fast; stand firm, keep firm, remain firm; weather the storm, stay the course, stick to the course, keep the faith, don't give in, don't buckle under.

settle, establish, stablish†, ascertain, fix, set, stabilitate†; retain, keep hold; make good, make sure; fasten &c *(join)* 43; set on its legs, float; perpetuate.

settle down; strike roots, put down roots, take root; take up one's abode &c 184; build one's house on a rock.

Adj. unchangeable, immutable; unaltered, unalterable; not to be changed, constant; permanent &c 141; invariable, undeviating; stable, durable; perennial &c *(diuturnal)* 110 [Obs.].

fixed, steadfast, firm, fast, steady, balanced; confirmed, valid; fiducial[†]; immovable, irremovable, riveted, rooted; settled, established &c *v.;* vested; incontrovertible, stereotyped, indeclinable.

tethered, anchored, moored, at anchor, on a rock, rock solid, firm as a rock; firmly seated, firmly established &c *v.;* deep-rooted, ineradicable; inveterate; obstinate &c 606.

transfixed, stuck fast, aground, high and dry, stranded.

[movable object rendered unmovable] stuck, jammed; unremovable; quiescent &c 265; deterioration &c 659.

indefeasible, irretrievable, intransmutable[†], incommutable[†], irresoluble[†], irrevocable, irreversible, reverseless[†], inextinguishable, irreducible; indissoluble, indissolvable[†]; indestructible, undying, imperishable, incorruptible, indelible, indeciduous[†]; insusceptible, insusceptible of change.

Int. stet.

Phr. littera scripta manet *[Lat.]*.

Present Events

151. Eventuality -- N. eventuality, event, occurrence, incident, affair, matter, thing, episode, happening, proceeding, contingency, juncture, experience, fact; matter of fact; naked fact, bare facts, just the facts; phenomenon; advent.

business, concern, transaction, dealing, proceeding; circumstance, particular, casualty, accident, adventure, passage, crisis, pass, emergency, contingency, consequence;
opportunity *(occasion)* 143.

the world, life, things, doings, affairs in general; things in general, affairs in general; the times, state of affairs, order of the day; course of things, tide of things, stream of things, current of things, run of things, march of things, course of events; ups and downs of life, vicissitudes of life; chapter of accidents &c *(chance)* 156; situation
&c *(circumstances)* 8.

V. happen, occur; take place, take effect; come, become of; come off, comeabout[†], come round, come into existence, come forth, come to pass, come on; pass, present itself; fall; fall out, turn out; run, be on foot, fall in; befall, betide, bechance†; prove, eventuate, draw on; turn up, crop up, spring up, pop up, arise, show up, show its face, appear, come forth, cast up; supervene, survene†; issue, arrive, ensue, arise, start, hold, take its course; pass off &c *(be past)* 122.

meet with; experience, enjoy, encounter, undergo, suffer, pass through, go through, be subjected to, be exposed to; fall to the lot of; be one's chance, be one's fortune, be one's lot; find; endure
&c *(feel)* 821.

Adj. happening &c *v.;* going on, doing, current; in the wind, in the air, afloat; on foot, afoot, on the tapis†; at issue, in question; incidental.

eventful, stirring, bustling, full of incident; memorable, momentous, signal.

Adv. eventually; in the event of, in case, just in case; in the course of things; as things, times go; as the world goes, wags; as the tree falls, cat jumps; as it may turn out, happen.

Phr. that's the way the ball bounces, that's the way the cookie crumbles; you never know what may turn up, you never know what the future will bring; the plot thickens; breasts the blows of circumstance [Tennyson]; so runs round of life from hour to hour

[Keble]; sprinkled along the waste of years [Tennyson].

Future Events

152. Destiny -- **N.** destiny &c *(necessity)* 601; future existence, post existence; hereafter; future state, next world, world to come, after life; futurity &c 121; everlasting life, everlasting death; life beyond the grave, world beyond the grave; prospect &c *(expectation)* 507.

V. impend; hang over, lie over; threaten, loom, await, come on, approach, stare one in the face; foreordain, preordain; predestine, doom, have in store for.

Adj. impending &c *v.;* destined; about to be, happen; coming, in store, to come, going to happen, instant, at hand, near; near, close at hand; over hanging, hanging over one's head, imminent; brewing, preparing, forthcoming; int he wind, on the cards, in reserve; that will, is to be; in prospect &c *(expected)* 507; looming in the distance, horizon, future; unborn, in embryo; int he womb of time, futurity; pregnant &c *(producing)* 161.

Adv. in time, the long run; all in good time; eventually &c 151; whatever may happen &c *(certainly)* 474; as chance would have it &c 156.

SECTION VIII.

CAUSATION

1. CONSTANCY OF SEQUENCE IN EVENTS

153. *[Constant antecedent]*. **Cause** -- N. cause, origin, source, principle, element; occasioner[†], prime mover, primum mobile *[Lat.]*; vera causa *[Lat.]*; author &c *(producer)* 164; mainspring; agent; leaven; groundwork, foundation &c *(support)* 215.

spring, fountain, well, font; fountainhead, spring head, wellhead; fons et origo *[Lat.]*, genesis; descent &c *(paternity)* 166; remote cause; influence.

pivot, hinge, turning point, lever, crux, fulcrum; key; proximate cause, causa causans *[Lat.]*; straw that breaks the camel's back.

ground; reason, reason why; why and wherefore, rationale, occasion, derivation; final cause

&c *(intention)* 620; les dessous des cartes *[Fr.]*; undercurrents.

rudiment.

egg, germ, embryo, bud, root, radix radical, etymon, nucleus, seed, stem, stock, stirps, trunk, tap-root, gemmule†, radicle, semen, sperm.

nest, cradle, nursery, womb, nidus, birthplace, hotbed.

causality, causation; origination; production &c 161.

V. be the cause of &c *n* .; originate; give origin to, give rise, to, give occasion to; cause, occasion, sow the seeds of, kindle, suscitate†; bring on, bring to bring pass, bring about; produce; create &c 161; set up, set afloat, set on foot; found, broach, institute, lay the foundation of; lie at the root of.

procure, induce, draw down, open the door to, superinduce, evoke, entail, operate; elicit, provoke.

conduce to &c *(tend to)* 176; contribute; have a hand in the pie, have a finger in the pie; determine, decide, turn the scale; have a common origin; derive its origin &c *(effect)* 154.

Adj. caused &c *v.;* causal, original; primary, primitive, primordial; aboriginal; protogenal†; radical; embryonic, embryotic†; in embryo, in ovo *[Lat.]*; seminal, germinal; at the bottom of; connate, having a common origin.

Adv. because &c 155; behind the scenes.

Phr. causa latet vis est notissima *[Lat.]* [Ovid]; felix qui potuit rerum cognoscere causas *[Lat.]* [Vergil].

154. *[Constant sequent.]* **Effect** -- N. effect, consequence; aftergrowth†, aftercome†; derivative, derivation; result; resultant, resultance†; upshot, issue, denouement; end &c 67; development, outgrowth, fruit, crop, harvest, product, bud.

production, produce, work, handiwork, fabric, performance; creature, creation; offspring, offshoot; firstfruits†, firstlings; heredity, telegony†; premices premises†.

V. be the effect of &c *n.;* be due to, be owing to; originate in, originate from; rise from, arise, take its rise spring from, proceed from, emanate from, come from, grow from, bud from, sprout from, germinate from, issue from, flow from, result from, follow from, derive its origin from, accrue from; come to, come of, come out of; depend upon, hang upon, hinge upon, turn upon.

take the consequences, sow the wind and reap the whirlwind.

Adj. owing to; resulting from &c v.; derivable from; due to; caused by &c 153; dependent upon; derived from, evolved from; derivative; hereditary; telegonous†.

Adv. of course, it follows that, naturally, consequently; as a consequence, in consequence; through, all along of, necessarily, eventually.

Phr. cela va sans dire *[Fr.]*, thereby hangs a tale [Taming of the Shrew].

155. *[Assignment of cause]* **Attribution** --
 N. attribution, theory, etiology, ascription, reference to, rationale; accounting for &c v.; palaetiology1, imputation, derivation from.

filiation†, affiliation; pedigree &c *(paternity)* 166.

explanation &c *(interpretation)* 522; reason why &c *(cause)* 153.

V. attribute to, ascribe to, impute to, refer to, lay to, point to, trace to, bring home to; put down to, set down to, blame; charge on, ground on; invest with, assign as cause, lay at, the door of, father upon; account for, derive from, point out the reason &c 153; theorize; tell how it comes; put the saddle on the right horse.

Adj. attributed &c v.; attributable &c v.; referable to, referrible to†, due to, derivable from; owing to &c *(effect)* 154; putative; ecbatic†.

Adv. hence, thence, therefore, for, since, on account of, because, owing to; on that account; from this cause, from that cause; thanks to, forasmuch as; whence, propter hoc *[Lat.]*.

why? wherefore? whence? how comes it, how is it, how happens it? how does it happen? in some way, in some such way; somehow, somehow or other.

Phr. that is why; hinc illae lachrymae *[Lat.]* [Horace].

156. *[Absence of assignable cause.]* **Chance** --
 N. chance, indetermination, accident, fortune, hazard, hap, haphazard, chance medley, random, luck, raccroc†, casualty, contingence, adventure, hit; fate &c *(necessity)* 601; equal chance; lottery; tombola†; toss up &c 621; turn of the table, turn of the cards; hazard of the die, chapter of accidents, fickle finger of fate; cast of the dice, throw of the dice; heads or tails, flip of a coin, wheel of Fortune; sortes†, sortes Virgilianae†.

probability, possibility, odds; long odds, run of luck; accidentalness; main chance, odds on, favorable odds.

contingency, dependence *(uncertainty)* 475; situation *(circumstance)* 8.

statistics, theory of Probabilities, theory of Chances; bookmaking; assurance; speculation, gaming &c 621.

V. chance, hap, turn up; fall to one's lot; be one's fate &c 601; stumble on light upon; take one's chance &c 621.

Adj. casual, fortuitous, accidental, adventitious, causeless, incidental, contingent, uncaused, undetermined, indeterminate; random, statistical; possible &c 470; unintentional &c 621.

Adv. by chance, accidentally, by accident; casually; perchance &c *(possibly)* 470; for aught one knows; as good would have it, as bad would have it, as luck would have it, as ill-luck would have it, as chance would have it; as it may be, as it may chance, as it may turn up, as it may happen; as the case may be.

Phr. grasps the skirts of happy chance [Tennyson]; the accident of an accident [Lord Thurlow].

There but for the grace of God go I

2. CONNECTION BETWEEN CAUSE AND EFFECT

157. Power -- N. power; potency, potentiality; jiva†; puissance, might, force, energy &c 171; dint; right hand, right arm; ascendency†, sway, control; prepotency, prepollence†; almightiness, omnipotence; authority &c 737; strength &c 159.

ability; ableness &c *adj.*†; competency; efficacy; efficiency, productivity, expertise *(skill)* 698; validity, cogency; enablement†; vantage ground; influence &c 175.

pressure; conductivity; elasticity; gravity, electricity, magnetism, galvanism, voltaic electricity, voltaism, electromagnetism; atomic power, nuclear power, thermonuclear power; fuel cell; hydraulic power, water power, hydroelectric power; solar power, solar energy, solar panels; tidal power; wind power; attraction; vis inertiae *[Lat.]*, vis mortua *[Lat.]*, vis viva *[Lat.]*; potential energy, dynamic energy; dynamic friction, dynamic suction; live circuit, live rail, live wire.

capability, capacity; quid valeant humeri quid ferre recusent *[Lat.]*; faculty, quality, attribute, endowment, virtue, gift, property, qualification, susceptibility.

V. be powerful &c *adj.*; gain power &c *n.*. belong to, pertain to; lie in one's power, be in one's power; can, be able.

give power, confer power, exercise power &c *n.;* empower, enable, invest; indue†, endue; endow, arm; strengthen &c 159; compel &c 744.

Adj. powerful, puissant; potential; capable, able; equal to, up to; cogent, valid; efficient, productive; effective, effectual, efficacious, adequate, competent; multipotent†, plenipotent†, omnipotent; almighty.

forcible &c *adj.. (energetic)* 171; influential &c 175; productive &c 168.

Adv. powerfully &c *adj.;* by virtue of, by dint of.

Phr. a toute force *[Fr.]*; dos moi pou sto kai kino ten gen *[Gr.]*; eripuit coelo fulmen sceptrumque tyrannis *[Lat.]*; fortis cadere cedere non potest *[Lat.]*.

158. Impotence -- N. impotence; inability, disability; disablement, impuissance, imbecility; incapacity, incapability; inaptitude, ineptitude, incompetence, unproductivity†; indocility†; invalidity, disqualification; inefficiency, wastefulness.

telum imbelle *[Lat.]*, brutum fulmen *[Lat.]*, blank, blank cartridge, flash in the pan, vox et proeterea nihil *[Lat.]*, dead letter, bit of waste paper, dummy; paper tiger; Quaker gun.

inefficacy &c *(inutility)* 645 [Obs.]; failure &c 732.

helplessness &c *adj.;* prostration, paralysis, palsy, apoplexy, syncope, sideration†, deliquium *[Lat.]*, collapse, exhaustion, softening of the brain, inanition; emasculation, orchiotomy *[Med.]*, orchotomy *[Med.]*.

cripple, old woman, muff, powder puff, creampuff, pussycat, wimp, mollycoddle; eunuch.

V. be impotent &c *adj.;* not have a leg to stand on.

vouloir rompre l'anguille au genou *[Fr.]*, vouloir prendre la lune avec les dents *[Fr.]*.

collapse, faint, swoon, fall into a swoon, drop; go by the board, go by the wayside; go up in smoke, end in smoke &c *(fail)* 732.

render powerless &c *adj.;* deprive of power; disable, disenable†; disarm, incapacitate, disqualify, unfit, invalidate, deaden, cramp, tie the hands; double up, prostrate, paralyze, muzzle, cripple, becripple†, maim, lame, hamstring, draw the teeth of; throttle, strangle, garrotte, garrote; ratten†, silence, sprain, clip the wings of, put hors de combat *[Fr.]*, spike the guns; take the wind out of one's sails, scotch the snake, put a spoke in one's wheel; break the neck, break the back; unhinge, unfit; put out of gear.

unman, unnerve, enervate; emasculate, castrate, geld, alter, neuter, sterilize, fix.

shatter, exhaust, weaken &c 160.

Adj. powerless, impotent, unable, incapable, incompetent; inefficient, ineffective; inept; unfit, unfitted; unqualified, disqualified; unendowed; inapt, unapt; crippled, disabled &c *v.;* armless[†].

harmless, unarmed, weaponless, defenseless, sine ictu *[Lat.]*, unfortified, indefensible, vincible, pregnable, untenable.

paralytic, paralyzed; palsied, imbecile; nerveless, sinewless[†], marrowless[†], pithless[†], lustless[†]; emasculate, disjointed; out of joint, out of gear; unnerved, unhinged; water-logged, on one's beam ends, rudderless; laid on one's back; done up, dead beat, exhausted, shattered, demoralized; graveled &c *(in difficulty)* 704; helpless, unfriended[†], fatherless; without a leg to stand on, hors de combat *[Fr.]*, laid on the shelf.

null and void, nugatory, inoperative, good for nothing; ineffectual &c *(failing)* 732; inadequate &c 640; inefficacious &c *(useless)* 645.

Phr. der kranke Mann *[G.]*; desirous still but impotent to rise [Shenstone]; the spirit is willing but the flesh is weak.

159. *[Degree of power.]* **Strength** -- **N.** strength; power &c 157; energy &c 171; vigor, force; main force, physical force, brute force; spring, elasticity, tone, tension, tonicity.

stoutness &c *adj.;* lustihood[†], stamina, nerve, muscle, sinew, thews and sinews, physique; pith, pithiness; virtility, vitality.

athletics, athleticism[†]; gymnastics, feats of strength.

adamant, steel, iron, oak, heart of oak; iron grip; grit, bone.

athlete, gymnast, acrobat; superman, Atlas, Hercules, Antaeus[†], Samson, Cyclops, Goliath; tower of strength; giant refreshed.

strengthening &c *v.;* invigoration, refreshment, refocillation[†].

[Science of forces] dynamics, statics.

V. be strong &c *adj.,* be stronger; overmatch.

render strong &c *adj.;* give strength &c *n.;* strengthen, invigorate, brace, nerve, fortify, sustain, harden, case harden, steel, gird; screw up, wind up, set up; gird up one's loins, brace up one's loins; recruit, set on one's legs; vivify; refresh &c 689; refect[†]; reinforce, reenforce &c *(restore)* 660.

Adj. strong, mighty, vigorous, forcible, hard, adamantine, stout, robust, sturdy, hardy, powerful, potent, puissant, valid.

resistless, irresistible, invincible, proof against, impregnable, unconquerable, indomitable, dominating, inextinguishable, unquenchable; incontestable; more than a match for; overpowering, overwhelming; all powerful, all sufficient; sovereign.

able-bodied; athletic; Herculean, Cyclopean, Atlantean†; muscular, brawny, wiry, well-knit, broad-shouldered, sinewy, strapping, stalwart, gigantic.

manly, man-like, manful; masculine, male, virile.

unweakened†, unallayed, unwithered†, unshaken, unworn, unexhausted†; in full force, in full swing; in the plenitude of power.

stubborn, thick-ribbed, made of iron, deep-rooted; strong as a lion, strong as a horse, strong as an ox, strong as brandy; sound as a roach; in fine feather, in high feather; built like a brick shithouse; like a giant refreshed.

Adv. strongly &c *adj.;* by force &c *n.;* by main force &c *(by compulsion)* 744.

Phr. our withers are unwrung [Hamlet].

Blut und Eisen *[G.]*; coelitus mihi vires *[Lat.]*; du fort au diable *[Fr.]*; en habiles gens *[Lat.]*; ex vi termini; flecti non frangi *[Lat.]*; he that wrestles with us strengthens our nerves and sharpens our skill

[Burke]; inflexible in faith invincible in arms [Beattie].

160. Weakness -- **N.** weakness &c *adj.;* debility, atony†, relaxation, languor, enervation; impotence &c 158; infirmity; effeminacy, feminality†; fragility, flaccidity; inactivity &c 683.

anaemia, bloodlessness, deficiency of blood, poverty of blood.

declension of strength, loss of strength, failure of strength; delicacy, invalidation, decrepitude, asthenia†, adynamy†, cachexy†, cachexia *[Med.]*, sprain, strain.

reed, thread, rope of sand, house of cards.

softling†, weakling; infant &c 129; youth &c 127.

V. be weak &c *adj.;* drop, crumble, give way, totter, tremble, shake, halt, limp, fade, languish, decline, flag, fail, have one leg in the grave.

render weak &c *adj.;* weaken, enfeeble, debilitate, shake, deprive of strength, relax, enervate, eviscerate; unbrace, unnerve; cripple, unman &c *(render powerless)* 158; cramp, reduce, sprain, strain, blunt the edge of; dilute, impoverish; decimate; extenuate; reduce in strength, reduce the strength of; mettre de l'eau dans son vin *[Fr.]*.

Adj. weak, feeble, debile†; impotent &c 158; relaxed, unnerved, &c *v.;* sapless, strengthless†, powerless; weakly, unstrung, flaccid, adynamic†, asthenic†; nervous.

soft, effeminate, feminate†, womanly.

frail, fragile, shattery†; flimsy, unsubstantial, insubstantial, gimcrack, gingerbread; rickety, creaky, creaking, cranky; craichy†; drooping, tottering &c *v..* broken, lame, withered, shattered, shaken, crazy, shaky; palsied &c 158; decrepit.

languid, poor, infirm; faint, faintish†; sickly &c *(disease)* 655; dull, slack, evanid†, spent, short-winded, effete; weather-beaten; decayed, rotten, worn, seedy, languishing, wasted, washy, laid low, pulled down, the worse for wear.

unstrengthened &c 159 [Obs.], unsupported, unaided, unassisted; aidless†, defenseless &c 158; cantilevered *(support)* 215.

on its last legs; weak as a child, weak as a baby, weak as a chicken, weak as a cat, weak as a rat; weak as water, weak as water gruel, weak as gingerbread, weak as milk and water; colorless &c 429.

Phr. non sum qualis eram *[Lat.]*.

3. POWER IN OPERATION

161. Production -- N. {ant.

162,, 158} production, creation, construction, formation, fabrication, manufacture; building, architecture, erection, edification; coinage; diaster†; organization; nisus formativus *[Lat.]*; putting together &c *v.;* establishment; workmanship, performance; achievement &c *(completion)* 729.

flowering, fructification; inflorescence.

bringing forth &c *v.;* parturition, birth, birth-throe, childbirth, delivery, confinement, accouchement, travail, labor, midwifery, obstetrics; geniture†; gestation &c *(maturation)* 673; assimilation; evolution, development, growth; entelechy *[Phil.]*; fertilization, gemination, germination, heterogamy *[Biol.]*, genesis, generation, epigenesis†, procreation, progeneration†, propagation; fecundation, impregnation; albumen &c 357.

spontaneous generation; archegenesis†, archebiosis†; biogenesis, abiogenesis†, digenesis†, dysmerogenesis†, eumerogenesis†, heterogenesis†, oogenesis, merogenesis†, metogenesis†, monogenesis†, parthenogenesis, homogenesis†, xenogenesis1†; authorship, publication; works, opus, oeuvre.

biogeny†, dissogeny†, xenogeny†; tocogony†, vacuolization.

edifice, building, structure, fabric, erection, pile, tower, flower, fruit.

V. produce, perform, operate, do, make, gar, form, construct, fabricate, frame, contrive, manufacture; weave, forge, coin, carve, chisel; build, raise, edify, rear, erect, put together, set up, run up; establish, constitute, compose, organize, institute; achieve, accomplish &c *(complete)* 729.

flower, bear fruit, fructify, teem, ean†, yean†, farrow, drop, pup, kitten, kindle; bear, lay, whelp, bring forth, give birth to, lie in, be brought to bed of, evolve, pullulate, usher into the world.

make productive &c 168; create; beget, get, generate, fecundate, impregnate; procreate, progenerate†, propagate; engender; bring into being, call into being, bring into existence; breed, hatch, develop, bring up.

induce, superinduce; suscitate†; cause &c 153; acquire &c 775.

Adj. produced, producing &c *v.;* productive of; prolific &c 168; creative; formative, genetic, genial, genital; pregnant; enceinte, big with, fraught with; in the family way, teeming, parturient, in the straw, brought to bed of; puerperal, puerperous†.

digenetic†, heterogenetic†, oogenetic, xenogenetic†; ectogenous†, gamic†, haematobious†, sporogenous *[Biol.]*, sporophorous *[Biol.]*.

architectonic.

Phr. ex nihilo nihil *[Lat.]*; fiat lux *[Lat.]*; materiam superabat opus *[Lat.]* [Ovid]; nemo dat quod non habet *[Lat.]*.

162. *[Nonproduction.]* **Destruction** -- N. {ant. 161} destruction; waste, dissolution, breaking up; diruption†, disruption; consumption; disorganization.

fall, downfall, devastation, ruin, perdition, crash; eboulement *[Fr.]*, smash, havoc, delabrement *[Fr.]*, debacle; break down, break up, fall apart; prostration; desolation, bouleversement*[Fr.]*, wreck, wrack, shipwreck, cataclysm; washout.

extinction, annihilation; destruction of life &c 361; knock-down blow; doom, crack of doom.

destroying &c *v.;* demolition, demolishment; overthrow, subversion, suppression; abolition &c *(abrogation)* 756; biblioclasm†; sacrifice; ravage, razzia†; inactivation; incendiarism; revolution &c 146; extirpation &c *(extraction)* 301; beginning of the end, commencement de la fin *[Fr.]*, road to ruin; dilapidation &c *(deterioration)* 659; sabotage.

V. be destroyed &c; perish; fall to the ground; tumble, topple; go to pieces, fall to pieces; break up; crumble to dust; go to the dogs, go to the wall, go to smash, go to shivers, go to wreck, go to pot, go to wrack and ruin; go by the board, go all to smash; be all over, be all up, be all with; totter to its fall.

destroy; do away with, make away with; nullify; annual &c 756; sacrifice, demolish; tear up; overturn, overthrow, overwhelm; upset, subvert, put an end to; seal the doom of, do in, do for, dish *[Slang]*, undo; break up, cut up; break down, cut down, pull down, mow down, blow down, beat down; suppress, quash, put down, do a job on; cut short, take off, blot out; dispel, dissipate, dissolve; consume.

smash, crash, quell, squash, squelch, crumple up, shatter, shiver; batter to pieces, tear to pieces, crush to pieces, cut to pieces, shake to pieces, pull to pieces, pick to pieces; laniate†; nip; tear to rags, tear to tatters; crush to atoms, knock to atoms; ruin; strike out; throw over, knock down over; fell, sink, swamp, scuttle, wreck, shipwreck, engulf, ingulf†, submerge; lay in ashes, lay in ruins; sweep away, erase, wipe out, expunge, raze; level with the dust, level with the ground; waste; atomize, vaporize.

deal destruction, desolate, devastate, lay waste, ravage gut; disorganize; dismantle &c *(render useless)* 645; devour, swallow up, sap, mine, blast, bomb, blow to smithereens, drop the big one, confound; exterminate, extinguish, quench, annihilate; snuff out, put out, stamp out, trample out; lay in the dust, trample in the dust; prostrate; tread under foot; crush under foot, trample under foot; lay the ax to the root of; make short work of, make clean sweep of, make mincemeat of; cut up root and branch, chop into pieces, cut into ribbons; fling to the winds, scatter to the winds; throw overboard; strike at the root of, sap the foundations of, spring a mine, blow up, ravage with fire and sword; cast to the dogs; eradicate &c 301.

Adj. destroyed &c *v.;* perishing &c *v.;* trembling to its fall, nodding to its fall, tottering to its fall; in course of destruction &c *n.;* extinct.

all-destroying, all-devouring, all-engulfing.

destructive, subversive, ruinous, devastating; incendiary, deletory†; destroying &c *n..* suicidal; deadly &c *(killing)* 361.

Adv. with crushing effect, with a sledge hammer.

Phr. delenda est Carthago *[Lat.]*; dum Roma deliberat Saguntum perit *[Lat.]*; ecrasez l'infame [Voltaire].

163. Reproduction -- **N.** reproduction, renovation; restoration &c 660; renewal; new edition, reprint, revival, regeneration, palingenesis†, revivification;

apotheosis; resuscitation, reanimation, resurrection, reappearance; regrowth; Phoenix.

generation &c *(production)* 161; multiplication.

V. reproduce; restore &c 660; revive, renovate, renew, regenerate, revivify, resuscitate, reanimate; remake, refashion, stir the embers, put into the crucible; multiply, repeat; resurge†.

crop up, spring up like mushrooms.

Adj. reproduced &c *v.;* renascent, reappearing; reproductive; suigenetic†.

164. Producer -- **N.** producer, originator, inventor, author, founder, generator, mover, architect, creator, prime mover; maker &c *(agent)* 690; prime mover.

165. Destroyer -- **N.** destroyer &c *(destroy)* &c 162; cankerworm &c *(bane)* 663; assassin &c *(killer)* 361; executioner &c *(punish)* 975; biblioclast†, eidoloclast†, iconoclast, idoloclast†; nihilist.

166. Paternity -- **N.** paternity; parentage; consanguinity &c 11.

parent; father, sire, dad, papa, paterfamilias, abba†; genitor, progenitor, procreator; ancestor; grandsire†, grandfather; great-grandfather; fathership†, fatherhood; mabap†.

house, stem, trunk, tree, stock, stirps, pedigree, lineage, line, family, tribe, sept, race, clan; genealogy, descent, extraction, birth, ancestry; forefathers, forbears, patriarchs.

motherhood, maternity; mother, dam, mamma, materfamilias *[Lat.]*, grandmother.

Adj. paternal, parental; maternal; family, ancestral, linear, patriarchal.

Phr. avi numerantur avorum *[Lat.]*; happy he with such a mother [Tennyson]; hombre bueno no le busquen abolengo *[Sp.]*; philosophia stemma non inspicit *[Lat.]* [Seneca].

167. Posterity -- N. posterity, progeny, breed, issue, offspring, brood, litter, seed, farrow, spawn, spat; family, grandchildren, heirs; great-grandchild.

child, son, daughter; butcha†; bantling, scion; acrospire†, plumule†, shoot, sprout, olive-branch, sprit†, branch; off-shoot, off-set; ramification; descendant; heir, heiress; heir-apparent, heir-presumptive; chip off the old block; heredity; rising generation.

straight descent, sonship†, line, lineage, filiation†, primogeniture.

Adj. filial; diphyletic†.

Phr. the child is father of the man [Wordsworth]; the fruit doesn't fall far from the tree, like father, like son.

168. Productiveness -- **N.** productiveness &c *adj.;* fecundity, fertility, luxuriance, uberty†.

pregnancy, pullulation, fructification, multiplication, propagation, procreation; superfetation.

milch cow, rabbit, hydra, warren, seed plot, land flowing with milk and honey; second crop, aftermath; aftercrop, aftergrowth†; arrish†, eddish†, rowen†; protoplasm; fertilization.

V. make productive &c *adj.;* fructify; procreate, generate, fertilize, spermative†, impregnate; fecundate, fecundify†; teem, multiply; produce &c 161; conceive.

Adj. productive, prolific; teeming, teemful†; fertile, fruitful, frugiferous†, fruit-bearing; fecund, luxuriant; pregnant, uberous†.

procreant†, procreative; generative, life-giving, spermatic; multiparous; omnific†, propagable.

parturient &c *(producing)* 161; profitable &c *(useful)* 644.

169. Unproductiveness -- **N.** unproductiveness &c *adj.;* infertility, sterility, infecundity†; masturbation; impotence &c 158; unprofitableness &c *(inutility)* 645.

waste, desert, Sahara, wild, wilderness, howling wilderness.

V. be unproductive &c *adj.;* hang fire, flash in the pan, come to nothing.

[make unproductive] sterilize, addle; disable, inactivate.

Adj. unproductive, acarpous†, inoperative, barren, addled, infertile, unfertile, unprolific†, arid, sterile, unfruitful, infecund†; sine prole; fallow; teemless†, issueless†, fruitless; unprofitable &c *(useless)* 645; null and void, of no effect.

170. Agency -- **N.** agency, operation, force, working, strain, function, office, maintenance, exercise, work, swing, play; interworking†, interaction; procurement.

causation &c 153; instrumentality &c 631; influence &c 175; action &c *(voluntary)* 680; modus operandi &c 627.

quickening power, maintaining power, sustaining power; home stroke.

V. be in action &c *adj.;* operate, work; act, act upon; perform, play, support, sustain, strain, maintain, take effect, quicken, strike.

come play, come bring into operation; have play, have free play; bring to bear upon.

Adj. operative, efficient, efficacious, practical, effectual.

at work, on foot; acting &c *(doing)* 680; in operation, in force, in action, in play, in exercise; acted upon, wrought upon.

Adv. by the agency of, &c *n.;* through &c *(instrumentality)* 631; by means of &c 632.

Phr. I myself must mix with action lest I wither by despair [Tennyson].

171. Physical Energy -- **N.** energy, physical energy, force, power &c 157; keenness &c *adj.;* intensity, vigor, strength, elasticity; go; high pressure; fire; rush.

acrimony, acritude†; causiticity†, virulence; poignancy; harshness &c *adj.;* severity, edge, point; pungency &c 392.

cantharides; seasoning &c *(condiment)* 393.

activity, agitation, effervescence; ferment, fermentation; ebullition, splutter, perturbation, stir, bustle; voluntary energy &c 682; quicksilver.

resolution &c *(mental energy)* 604; exertion &c *(effort)* 686; excitation &c *(mental)* 824.

V. give energy &c *n.;* energize, stimulate, kindle, excite, exert; sharpen, intensify; inflame &c *(render violent)* 173; wind up &c *(strengthen)* 159.

strike home, into home, hard home; make an impression.

Adj. strong, energetic, forcible, active; intense, deep-dyed, severe, keen, vivid, sharp, acute, incisive, trenchant, brisk.

rousing, irritation; poignant; virulent, caustic, corrosive, mordant, harsh, stringent; double-edged, double-shotted†, double-distilled; drastic, escharotic†; racy &c *(pungent)* 392.

potent &c *(powerful)* 157; radioactive.

Adv. strongly &c *adj.;* fortiter in re *[Lat.]*; with telling effect.

Phr. the steam is up; vires acquirit eundo *[Lat.]*; the race by vigor not by vaunts is won [Pope].

172. Physical Inertness

N. inertness, dullness &c *adj.;* inertia, vis inertiae *[Lat.]*, inertion†, inactivity, torpor, languor; quiescence &c 265; latency, inaction; passivity.

mental inertness; sloth &c *(inactivity)* 683; inexcitability &c 826 [Obs.]; irresolution &c 605; obstinacy &c 606; permanence &c 141.

rare gas, paraffin, noble metal, unreactivity.

V. be inert &c *adj.;* hang fire, smolder.

Adj. inert, inactive, passive; torpid &c 683; sluggish, dull, heavy, flat, slack, tame, slow, blunt; unreactive; lifeless, dead, uninfluential†.

latent, dormant, smoldering, unexerted†.

Adv. inactively &c *adj.;* in suspense, in abeyance.

173. Violence

N. violence, inclemency, vehemence, might, impetuosity; boisterousness &c *adj.;* effervescence, ebullition; turbulence, bluster; uproar, callithump *[U.S.]*, riot, row, rumpus, le diable a quatre *[Fr.]*, devil to pay, all the fat in the fire.

severity &c 739; ferocity, rage, fury; exacerbation, exasperation, malignity; fit, paroxysm; orgasm, climax, aphrodisia†; force, brute force; outrage; coup de main; strain, shock, shog†; spasm, convulsion, throe; hysterics, passion &c *(state of excitability)* 825.

outbreak, outburst; debacle; burst, bounce, dissilience†, discharge, volley, explosion, blow up, blast, detonation, rush, eruption, displosion†, torrent.

turmoil &c *(disorder)* 59; ferment &c *(agitation)* 315; storm, tempest, rough weather; squall &c *(wind)* 349; earthquake, volcano, thunderstorm.

berserk, berserker; fury, dragon, demon, tiger, beldame, Tisiphone†, Megaera, Alecto†, madcap, wild beast; fire eater &c *(blusterer)* 887.

V. be violent &c *adj.;* run high; ferment, effervesce; romp, rampage, go on a rampage; run wild, run amuck, run riot; break the peace; rush, tear; rush headlong, rush foremost; raise a storm, make a riot; rough house *[Slang]*; riot, storm; wreak, bear down, ride roughshod, out Herod, Herod; spread like wildfire (person).

[shout or act in anger at something], explode, make a row, kick up a row; boil, boil over; fume, foam,

come on like a lion, bluster, rage, roar, fly off the handle, go bananas, go ape, blow one's top, blow one's cool, flip one's lid, hit the ceiling, hit the roof; fly into a rage *(anger)* 900.

break out, fly out, burst out; bounce, explode, go off, displode[†], fly, detonate, thunder, blow up, crump[†], flash, flare, burst; shock, strain; break open, force open, prize open.

render violent &c *adj.;* sharpen, stir up, quicken, excite, incite, annoy, urge, lash, stimulate, turn on; irritate, inflame, kindle, suscitate[†], foment; accelerate, aggravate, exasperate, exacerbate, convulse, infuriate, madden, lash into fury; fan the flame; add fuel to the flame, pour oil on the fire, oleum addere camino *[Lat.]*.

explode; let fly, fly off; discharge, detonate, set off, detonize[†], fulminate.

Adj. violent, vehement; warm; acute, sharp; rough, rude, ungentle, bluff, boisterous, wild; brusque, abrupt, waspish; impetuous; rampant.

turbulent; disorderly; blustering, raging &c *v.;* troublous[†], riotous; tumultuary[†], tumultuous; obstreperous, uproarious; extravagant; unmitigated; ravening, inextinguishable, tameless; frenzied &c *(insane)* 503.

desperate &c *(rash)* 863; infuriate, furious, outrageous, frantic, hysteric, in hysterics.

fiery, flaming, scorching, hot, red-hot, ebullient.

savage, fierce, ferocious, fierce as a tiger.

excited &c v.; unquelled[†], unquenched, unextinguished[†], unrepressed, unbridled, unruly; headstrong, ungovernable, unappeasable, immitigable, unmitigable[†]; uncontrollable, incontrollable[†]; insuppressible, irrepressible; orgastic, orgasmatic, orgasmic.

spasmodic, convulsive, explosive; detonating &c v.; volcanic, meteoric; stormy &c *(wind)* 349.

Adv. violently &c *adj.;* amain[†]; by storm, by force, by main force; with might and main; tooth and nail, vi et armis *[Lat.]*, at the point of the sword, at the point of the bayonet; at one fell swoop; with a high hand, through thick and thin; in desperation, with a vengeance; a outrance[†], a toute outrance *[Fr.]*; headlong, head foremost.

Phr. furor arma ministrat *[Lat.]*; blown with restless violence round about the pendent world [Measure for Measure].

174. Moderation -- **N.** moderation, lenity &c 740; temperateness, gentleness &c *adj.;* sobriety; quiet; mental calmness &c *(inexcitability)* 826 [Obs.].

moderating &c v.; anaphrodisia†; relaxation, remission, mitigation, tranquilization†, assuagement, contemporation†, pacification.

measure, juste milieu *[Fr.]*, golden mean, ariston metron *[Gr.]*.

moderator; lullaby, sedative, lenitive, demulcent, antispasmodic, carminative, laudanum; rose water, balm, poppy, opiate, anodyne, milk, opium, poppy or mandragora; wet blanket; palliative.

V. be moderate &c *adj.;* keep within bounds, keep within compass; sober down, settle down; keep the peace, remit, relent, take in sail.

moderate, soften, mitigate, temper, accoy†; attemper†, contemper†; mollify, lenify†, dulcify†, dull, take off the edge, blunt, obtund†, sheathe, subdue, chasten; sober down, tone down, smooth down; weaken &c 160; lessen &c *(decrease)* 36; check palliate.

tranquilize, pacify, assuage, appease, swag, lull, soothe, compose, still, calm, calm down, cool, quiet, hush, quell, sober, pacify, tame, damp, lay, allay, rebate, slacken, smooth, alleviate, rock to sleep, deaden, smooth, throw cold water on, throw a wet blanket over, turn off; slake; curb &c *(restrain)* 751; tame &c *(subjugate)* 749; smooth over; pour oil on the waves, pour oil on the troubled waters; pour balm into, mattre de l'eau dans son vin *[Fr.]*.

go out like a lamb, roar you as gently as any sucking dove [Midsummer-Night's Dream].

Adj. moderate; lenient &c 740; gentle, mild, mellow; cool, sober, temperate, reasonable, measured; tempered &c *v.;* calm, unruffled, quiet, tranquil, still; slow, smooth, untroubled; tame; peaceful, peaceable; pacific, halcyon.

unexciting, unirritating†; soft, bland, oily, demulcent, lenitive, anodyne; hypnotic &c 683; sedative; antiorgastic†, anaphrodisiac†.

mild as mother's milk; milk and water.

Adv. moderately &c *adj.;* gingerly; piano; under easy sail, at half speed; within bounds, within compass; in reason.

Phr. est modue in rebus†; pour oil on troubled waters.

4. INDIRECT POWER

175. Influence -- **N.** influence; importance &c 642; weight, pressure, preponderance, prevalence, sway; predominance, predominancy†; ascendency†; dominance, reign; control, domination, pull *[Slang]*;

authority &c 737; capability &c *(power)* 157; effect &c 154; interest.

synergy *(cooperation)* 709.

footing; purchase &c *(support)* 215; play, leverage, vantage ground.

tower of strength, host in himself; protection, patronage, auspices.

V. have influence &c *n.;* be influential &c *adj.;* carry weight, weigh, tell; have a hold upon, magnetize, bear upon, gain a footing, work upon; take root, take hold; strike root in.

run through, pervade; prevail, dominate, predominate; out weigh, over weigh; over-ride, over-bear; gain head; rage; be rife &c *adj.;* spread like wildfire; have the upper hand, get the upper hand, gain the upper hand, have full play, get full play, gain full play.

be recognized, be listened to; make one's voice heard, gain a hearing; play a part, play a leading part, play a leading part in; take the lead, pull the strings; turn the scale, throw one's weight into the scale; set the fashion, lead the dance.

Adj. influential, effective; important &c 642; weighty; prevailing &c *v.;* prevalent, rife, rampant, dominant, regnant, predominant, in the ascendant, hegemonical[†].

Adv. with telling effect.

Phr. tel maure tel valet *[Fr.]*.

175a. Absence of Influence -- **N.** impotence &c 158; powerlessness; inertness &c 172; irrelevancy &c 10.

V. have no influence &c 175.

Adj. uninfluential†, ineffective; inconsequential, nugatory; unconducing, unconducive, unconducting to†; powerless &c 158; irrelevant &c 10.

176. Tendency -- **N.** tendency; aptness, aptitude; proneness, proclivity, bent, turn, tone, bias, set, leaning to, predisposition, inclination, propensity, susceptibility; conatus *[Lat.]*, nisus *[Lat.]*; liability &c 177; quality, nature, temperament; idiocrasy†, idiosyncrasy; cast, vein, grain; humor, mood; drift &c *(direction)* 278; conduciveness, conducement†; applicability &c *(utility)* 644; subservience &c *(instrumentality)* 631.

V. tend, contribute, conduce, lead, dispose, incline, verge, bend to, trend, affect, carry, redound to, bid fair to, gravitate towards; promote &c *(aid)* 707.

Adj. tending &c *v.;* conducive, working towards, in a fair way to, calculated to; liable &c 177; subservient &c *(instrumental)* 631; useful &c 644; subsidiary &c *(helping)* 707.

Adv. for, whither.

177. Liability -- **N.** liability, liableness[†]; possibility, contingency; susceptivity[†], susceptibility, exposure.

V. be liable &c *adj.;* incur, lay oneself open to; run the chance, stand a chance; lie under, expose oneself to, open a door to.

Adj. liable, subject; in danger &c 665; open to, exposed to, obnoxious to; answerable; unexempt from[†]; apt to; dependent on; incident to.

contingent, incidental, possible, on the cards, within range of, at the mercy of.

5. COMBINATIONS OF CAUSES

178. Concurrence -- **N.** concurrence, cooperation, coagency[†]; union; agreement &c 23; consilience[†]; consent, coincidence &c *(assent)* 488; alliance;

concert, additivity, synergy &c 709; partnership &c 712.

common cause.

V. concur, conduce, conspire, contribute; agree, unite; hang together, pull together, join forces, make common cause.

&c *(cooperate)* 709; help to &c *(aid)* 707.

keep pace with, run parallel; go with, go along with, go hand in hand with, coincide.

Adj. concurring &c *v.;* concurrent, in alliance with, banded together, of one mind, at one with, coinciding.

Adv. with one consent.

179. Counteraction -- **N.** counteraction, opposition; contrariety &c 14; antagonism, polarity; clashing &c *v.;* collision, interference, inhibition, resistance, renitency, friction; reaction; retroaction &c *(recoil)* 277; counterblast[†]; neutralization &c *(compensation)* 30; vis inertiae *[Lat.]*; check &c *(hindrance)* 706.

voluntary opposition &c 708, voluntary resistance &c 719; repression &c *(restraint)* 751.

opposites, action and reaction, yang and yin, yang-yin *(contrariety)* 14.

V. counteract; run counter, clash, cross; interfere with, conflict with; contravene; jostle; go against, run against, beat against, militate against; stultify; antagonize, block, oppose &c 708; traverse; withstand &c *(resist)* 719; hinder &c 706; repress &c *(restrain)* 751; react &c *(recoil)* 277.

undo, neutralize; counterpoise &c *(compensate)* 30; overpoise[†].

Adj. counteracting &c *v.;* antagonistic, conflicting, retroactive, renitent, reactionary; contrary &c 14.

Adv. although &c 30; in spite of &c 708; against.

Phr. for every action there is a reaction, equal in force and opposite in direction [Newton].

CLASS II

WORDS RELATING TO SPACE

SECTION I.

SPACE IN GENERAL

1. ABSTRACT SPACE

180. *[Indefinite space.]* **Space** -- **N.** space, extension, extent, superficial extent, expanse, stretch, hyperspace; room, scope, range, field, way, expansion, compass, sweep, swing, spread.

dimension, length &c 200; distance &c 196; size &c 192; volume; hypervolume.

latitude, play, leeway, purchase, tolerance, room for maneuver.

spare room, elbow room, house room; stowage, roomage[†], margin; opening, sphere, arena.

open space, free space; void &c *(absence)* 187; waste; wildness, wilderness; moor, moorland; campagna[†].

abyss &c *(interval)* 198; unlimited space; infinity &c 105; world; ubiquity &c *(presence)* 186; length and breadth of the land.

proportions, acreage; acres, acres and

perches, roods and perches, hectares, square miles; square inches, square yards, square centimeters, square meters, yards *(clothing)* &c; ares, arpents†.

Adj. spacious, roomy, extensive, expansive, capacious, ample; widespread, vast, world-wide, uncircumscribed; boundless &c *(infinite)* 105; shoreless†, trackless, pathless; extended.

Adv. extensively &c *adj.;* wherever; everywhere; far and near, far and wide; right and left, all over, all the world over; throughout the world, throughout the length and breadth of the land; under the sun, in every quarter; in all quarters, in all lands; here there and everywhere; from pole to pole, from China to Peru [Johnson], from Indus to the pole [Pope], from Dan to Beersheba, from end to end; on the face of the earth, in the wide world, from all points of the compass; to the four winds, to the uttermost parts of the earth.

180a. Inextension -- **N.** inextension†, nonextension†, point; dot; atom &c *(smallness)* 32.

181. *[Definite space.]* **Region** -- **N.** region, sphere, ground, soil, area, field, realm, hemisphere, quarter, district, beat, orb, circuit, circle; reservation, pale &c *(limit)* 233; compartment, department; clearing.

[political divisions: see] (property) &c 780 *(Government)* &c 737.1 arena, precincts, enceinte, walk, march; patch, plot, parcel, inclosure, close, field, court; enclave, reserve, preserve; street &c *(abode)* 189.

clime, climate, zone, meridian, latitude.

biosphere; lithosphere.

Adj. territorial, local, parochial, provincial, regional.

182. *[Limited space.]* **Place** -- **N.** place, lieu, spot, point, dot; niche, nook &c *(corner)* 244; hole; pigeonhole &c *(receptacle)* 191; compartment; premises, precinct, station; area, courtyard, square; abode &c 189; locality &c *(situation)* 183.

ins and outs; every hole and corner.

Adv. somewhere, in some place, wherever it may be, here and there, in various places, passim.

2. RELATIVE SPACE

183. Situation -- **N.** situation, position, locality, locale, status, latitude and longitude; footing, standing, standpoint, post; stage; aspect, attitude, posture, pose.

environment, surroundings *(location)* 184; circumjacence &c 227 [Obs.].

place, site, station, seat, venue, whereabouts; ground; bearings &c *(direction)* 278; spot &c *(limited space)* 182.

topography, geography, chorography[†]; map &c 554.

V. be situated, be situate; lie, have its seat in.

Adj. situate, situated; local, topical, topographical &c *n..*

Adv. in situ, in loco; here and there, passim; hereabouts, thereabouts, whereabouts; in place, here, there.

in such and such surroundings, in such and such environs, in such and such entourage, amidst such and such surroundings, amidst such and such environs, amidst such and such entourage.

184. Location -- **N.** location, localization; lodgment; deposition, reposition; stowage, package; collocation; packing, lading; establishment, settlement, installation; fixation; insertion &c 300.

habitat, environment, surroundings *(situation)* 183; circumjacence &c 227 [Obs.].

anchorage, mooring, encampment.

plantation, colony, settlement, cantonment; colonization, domestication, situation; habitation &c *(abode)* 189; cohabitation; a local habitation and a name [Midsummer Night's Dream]; endenization†, naturalization.

V. place, situate, locate, localize, make a place for, put, lay, set, seat, station, lodge, quarter, post, install; house, stow; establish, fix, pin, root; graft; plant &c *(insert)* 300; shelve, pitch, camp, lay down, deposit, reposit†; cradle; moor, tether, picket; pack, tuck in; embed, imbed; vest, invest in.

billet on, quarter upon, saddle with; load, lade, freight; pocket, put up, bag.

inhabit &c *(be present)* 186; domesticate, colonize; take root, strike root; anchor; cast anchor, come to an anchor; sit down, settle down; settle; take up one's abode, take up one's quarters; plant oneself, establish oneself, locate oneself; squat, perch, hive, se nicher *[Fr.]*, bivouac, burrow, get a footing; encamp, pitch one's tent; put up at, put up one's horses at; keep house.

endenizen†, naturalize, adopt.

put back, replace &c *(restore)* 660.

Adj. placed &c *v.;* situate, posited, ensconced, imbedded, embosomed†, rooted; domesticated; vested in, unremoved†.

moored &c *v.;* at anchor.

185. Displacement -- N. displacement, elocation†, transposition.

ejectment &c 297 [Obs.]; exile &c *(banishment)* 893; removal &c *(transference)* 270.

misplacement, dislocation &c 61; fish out of water.

V. displace, misplace, displant†, dislodge, disestablish; exile &c *(seclude)* 893; ablegate†, set aside, remove; take away, cart away; take off, draft off; lade &c 184.

unload, empty &c *(eject)* 297; transfer &c 270; dispel.

vacate; depart &c 293.

Adj. displaced &c *v.;* unplaced, unhoused†, unharbored†, unestablished†, unsettled; houseless†, homeless; out of place, out of a situation; in the wrong place.

misplaced, out of its element.

3. EXISTENCE IN SPACE

186. Presence -- **N.** presence; occupancy, occupation; attendance; whereness†.

permeation, pervasion; diffusion &c *(dispersion)* 73.

ubiety†, ubiquity, ubiquitariness†; omnipresence.

bystander &c *(spectator)* 444.

V. exist in space, be present &c *adj.;* assister†; make one of, make one at; look on, attend, remain; find oneself, present oneself; show one's face; fall in the way of, occur in a place; lie, stand; occupy; be there.

people; inhabit, dwell, reside, stay, sojourn, live, abide, lodge, nestle, roost, perch; take up one's abode &c *(be located)* 184; tenant.

resort to, frequent, haunt; revisit.

fill, pervade, permeate; be diffused, be disseminated, be through; over spread, overrun; run through; meet one at every turn.

Adj. present; occupying, inhabiting &c *v.;* moored &c 184; resiant†, resident, residentiary†; domiciled.

ubiquitous, ubiquitary†; omnipresent; universally present.

peopled, populous, full of people, inhabited.

Adv. here, there, where, everywhere, aboard, on board, at home, afield; here there and everywhere &c *(space)* 180; in presence of, before; under the eyes of, under the nose of; in the face of; in propria persona *[Lat.]*.

on the spot; in person, in the flesh.

Phr. nusquam est qui ubique est *[Lat.]* [Seneca].

187. *[Nullibiety.1]* **Absence** -- **N.** absence; inexistence &c 2 [Obs.]; nonresidence, absenteeism; nonattendance, alibi.

emptiness &c *adj.;* void, vacuum; vacuity, vacancy; tabula rasa *[Lat.]*; exemption; hiatus &c *(interval)* 198; lipotype†.

truant, absentee.

nobody; nobody present, nobody on earth; not a soul; ame qui vive *[Fr.]*.

V. be absent &c *adj.;* keep away, keep out of the way; play truant, absent oneself, stay away; keep aloof, hold aloof.

withdraw, make oneself scarce, vacate; go away &c 293.

Adj. absent, not present, away, nonresident, gone, from home; missing; lost; wanting; omitted; nowhere to be found; inexistence &c 2 [Obs.].

empty, void; vacant, vacuous; untenanted, unoccupied, uninhabited; tenantless; barren, sterile; desert, deserted; devoid; uninhabitable.

Adv. without, minus, nowhere; elsewhere; neither here nor there; in default of; sans; behind one's back.

Phr. the bird has flown, non est inventus *[Lat.]*.

absence makes the heart grow fonder [Bayley]; absent in body but present in spirit [1 Corinthians verse 3]; absento nemo ne nocuisse velit *[Lat.]* [Propertius]; Achilles absent was Achilles still [Homer]; aux absents les os; briller par son absence *[Fr.]*; conspicuous by his absence [Russell]; in the hope to meet shortly again and make our absence sweet [B.

Jonson].

188. Inhabitant -- **N.** inhabitant; resident, residentiary†; dweller, indweller†; addressee; occupier, occupant; householder, lodger, inmate, tenant, incumbent, sojourner, locum tenens, commorant†; settler, squatter, backwoodsman, colonist; islander; denizen, citizen; burgher, oppidan†, cockney, cit, townsman, burgess; villager; cottager, cottier†, cotter; compatriot; backsettler†, boarder; hotel keeper, innkeeper; habitant; paying guest; planter.

native, indigene, aborigines, autochthones†; Englishman, John Bull; newcomer &c *(stranger)* 57.

aboriginal, American†, Caledonian, Cambrian, Canadian, Canuck *[Slang]*, downeaster *[U.S.]*, Scot, Scotchman, Hibernian, Irishman, Welshman, Uncle Sam, Yankee, Brother Jonathan.

garrison, crew; population; people &c *(mankind)* 372; colony, settlement; household; mir†.

V. inhabit &c *(be present)* 186; endenizen &c *(locate oneself)* 184 [Obs.].

Adj. indigenous; native, natal; autochthonal†, autochthonous; British; English; American†; Canadian, Irish, Scotch, Scottish, Welsh; domestic; domiciliated†, domiciled; naturalized, vernacular, domesticated; domiciliary.

in the occupation of; garrisoned by, occupied by.

189. *[Place of habitation, or resort.]* **Abode --**
N. abode, dwelling, lodging, domicile, residence, apartment, place, digs, pad, address, habitation, where one's lot is cast, local habitation, berth, diggings, seat, lap, sojourn, housing, quarters, headquarters, resiance†, tabernacle, throne, ark.

home, fatherland; country; homestead, homestall†; fireside; hearth, hearth stone; chimney corner, inglenook, ingle side; harem, seraglio, zenana†; household gods, lares et penates *[Lat.]*, roof, household, housing, dulce domum *[Lat.]*, paternal domicile; native soil, native land.

habitat, range, stamping ground; haunt, hangout; biosphere; environment, ecological niche.

nest, nidus, snuggery†; arbor, bower, &c 191; lair, den, cave, hole, hiding place, cell, sanctum sanctorum *[Lat.]*, aerie, eyrie, eyry†, rookery, hive; covert, resort, retreat, perch, roost; nidification; kala jagah†.

bivouac, camp, encampment, cantonment, castrametation†; barrack, casemate†, casern†.

tent &c *(covering)* 223; building
&c *(construction)* 161; chamber
&c *(receptacle)* 191; xenodochium†.

tenement, messuage, farm, farmhouse, grange, hacienda, toft†.

cot, cabin, hut, chalet, croft, shed, booth, stall, hovel, bothy†, shanty, dugout *[U.S.]*, wigwam; pen &c *(inclosure)* 232; barn, bawn†; kennel, sty, doghold†, cote, coop, hutch, byre; cow house, cow shed; stable, dovecote, columbary†, columbarium; shippen†; igloo, iglu†, jacal†; lacustrine dwelling†, lacuslake dwelling†, lacuspile dwelling†; log cabin, log house; shack, shebang *[Slang]*, tepee, topek†.

house, mansion, place, villa, cottage, box, lodge, hermitage, rus in urbe *[Lat.]*, folly, rotunda, tower, chateau, castle, pavilion, hotel, court, manor-house, capital messuage, hall, palace; kiosk, bungalow; casa *[Sp.]*, country seat, apartment house, flat house, frame house, shingle house, tenement house; temple &c 1000.

hamlet, village, thorp†, dorp†, ham, kraal; borough, burgh, town, city, capital, metropolis; suburb; province, country; county town, county seat; courthouse *[U.S.]*; ghetto.

street, place, terrace, parade, esplanade, alameda†, board walk, embankment, road, row, lane, alley, court, quadrangle, quad, wynd *[Scot.]*, close *[Scot.]*, yard, passage, rents, buildings, mews.

square, polygon, circus, crescent, mall, piazza, arcade, colonnade, peristyle, cloister; gardens, grove, residences; block of buildings, market place, place, plaza.

anchorage, roadstead, roads; dock, basin, wharf, quay, port, harbor.

quarter, parish &c *(region)* 181.

assembly room, meetinghouse, pump room, spa, watering place; inn; hostel, hostelry; hotel, tavern, caravansary, dak bungalow†, khan, hospice; public house, pub, pot house, mug house; gin mill, gin palace; bar, bar room; barrel house *[U.S.]*, cabaret, chophouse; club, clubhouse; cookshop†, dive *[U.S.]*, exchange *[Euph.]*; grill room, saloon *[U.S.]*, shebeen†; coffee house, eating house; canteen, restaurant, buffet, cafe, estaminet†, posada†; almshouse†, poorhouse, townhouse *[U.S.]*.

garden, park, pleasure ground, plaisance†, demesne.

[quarters for animals] cage, terrarium, doghouse; pen, aviary; barn, stall; zoo.

V. take up one's abode &c *(locate oneself)* 184; inhabit &c *(be present)* 186.

Adj. urban, metropolitan; suburban; provincial, rural, rustic; domestic; cosmopolitan; palatial.

Phr. eigner Hert ist goldes Werth *[G.]*; even cities have their graves [Longfellow]; ubi libertas ibi patria *[Lat.]*; home sweet home.

190. *[Things contained.]* **Contents** -- **N.** contents; cargo, lading, freight, shipment, load, bale, burden, jag; cartload†, shipload; cup of, basket of, &c *(receptacle)* 191 of; inside &c 221; stuffing, ullage.

191. Receptacle -- **N.** receptacle; inclosure &c 232; recipient, receiver, reservatory.

compartment; cell, cellule; follicle; hole, corner, niche, recess, nook; crypt, stall, pigeonhole, cove, oriel; cave &c *(concavity)* 252.

capsule, vesicle, cyst, pod, calyx, cancelli, utricle, bladder; pericarp, udder.

stomach, paunch, venter, ventricle, crop, craw, maw, gizzard, breadbasket; mouth.

pocket, pouch, fob, sheath, scabbard, socket, bag, sac, sack, saccule, wallet, cardcase, scrip, poke, knit, knapsack, haversack, sachel, satchel, reticule, budget, net; ditty bag, ditty box; housewife, hussif; saddlebags; portfolio; quiver &c *(magazine)* 636.

chest, box, coffer, caddy, case, casket, pyx, pix, caisson, desk, bureau, reliquary; trunk, portmanteau, band-box, valise; grip, grip sack *[U.S.]*; skippet, vasculum; boot, imperial; vache; cage, manger, rack.

vessel, vase, bushel, barrel; canister, jar; pottle, basket, pannier, buck-basket, hopper, maund†, creel, cran, crate, cradle, bassinet, wisket, whisket, jardiniere, corbeille, hamper, dosser, dorser, tray, hod, scuttle, utensil; brazier; cuspidor, spittoon.

[For liquids] cistern &c *(store)* 636; vat, caldron, barrel, cask, drum, puncheon, keg, rundlet, tun, butt, cag, firkin, kilderkin, carboy, amphora, bottle, jar, decanter, ewer, cruse, caraffe, crock, kit, canteen, flagon; demijohn; flask, flasket; stoup, noggin, vial, phial, cruet, caster; urn, epergne, salver, patella, tazza, patera; pig gin, big gin; tyg, nipperkin, pocket pistol; tub, bucket, pail, skeel, pot, tankard, jug, pitcher, mug, pipkin; galipot, gallipot; matrass, receiver, retort, alembic, bolthead, capsule, can, kettle; bowl, basin, jorum, punch bowl, cup, goblet, chalice, tumbler, glass, rummer, horn, saucepan, skillet, posnet†, tureen.

[laboratory vessels for liquids] beaker, flask, Erlenmeyer flask, Florence flask, round-bottom flask, graduated cylinder, test tube, culture tube, pipette, Pasteur pipette, disposable pipette, syringe, vial, carboy, vacuum flask, Petri dish, microtiter tray, centrifuge tube.

bail, beaker, billy, canakin; catch basin, catch drain; chatti, lota, mussuk, schooner *[U.S.]*, spider, terrine, toby, urceus.

plate, platter, dish, trencher, calabash, porringer, potager, saucer, pan, crucible; glassware, tableware; vitrics.

compote, gravy boat, creamer, sugar bowl, butter dish, mug, pitcher, punch bowl, chafing dish.

shovel, trowel, spoon, spatula, ladle, dipper, tablespoon, watch glass, thimble.

closet, commode, cupboard, cellaret, chiffonniere, locker, bin, bunker, buffet, press, clothespress, safe, sideboard, drawer, chest of drawers, chest on chest, highboy, lowboy, till, scrutoire[†], secretary, secretaire, davenport, bookcase, cabinet, canterbury; escritoire, etagere, vargueno, vitrine.

chamber, apartment, room, cabin; office, court, hall, atrium; suite of rooms, apartment *[U.S.]*, flat, story; saloon, salon, parlor; by-room, cubicle; presence chamber; sitting room, best room, keeping room, drawing room, reception room, state room; gallery, cabinet, closet; pew, box; boudoir; adytum, sanctum; bedroom, dormitory; refectory, dining room, salle-a-manger; nursery, schoolroom; library, study; studio; billiard room, smoking room; den; stateroom, tablinum, tenement.

[room for defecation and urination] bath room, bathroom, toilet, lavatory, powder room; john, jakes, necessary, loo; *[in public places]* men's room, ladies' room, rest room; *[fixtures](uncleanness)*. 653 attic,

loft, garret, cockloft, clerestory; cellar, vault, hold, cockpit; cubbyhole; cook house; entre-sol; mezzanine floor; ground floor, rez-de-chaussee; basement, kitchen, pantry, bawarchi-khana, scullery, offices; storeroom &c *(depository)* 636; lumber room; dairy, laundry.

coach house; garage; hangar; outhouse; penthouse; lean-to.

portico, porch, stoop, stope, veranda, patio, lanai, terrace, deck; lobby, court, courtyard, hall, vestibule, corridor, passage, breezeway; ante room, ante chamber; lounge; piazza, veranda.

conservatory, greenhouse, bower, arbor, summerhouse, alcove, grotto, hermitage.

lodging &c *(abode)* 189; bed &c *(support)* 215; carriage &c *(vehicle)* 272.

Adj. capsular; saccular, sacculated; recipient; ventricular, cystic, vascular, vesicular, cellular, camerated, locular, multilocular, polygastric; marsupial; siliquose, siliquous.

SECTION II.

DIMENSIONS

1. GENERAL DIMENSIONS

192. Size -- **N.** size, magnitude, dimension, bulk, volume; largeness &c *adj.;* greatness &c *(of quantity)* 31; expanse &c *(space)* 180; amplitude, mass; proportions.

capacity, tonnage, tunnage; cordage; caliber, scantling.

turgidity &c *(expansion)* 194; corpulence, obesity; plumpness &c *adj.;* embonpoint, corporation, flesh and blood, lustihood.

hugeness &c *adj.;* enormity, immensity, monstrosity.

giant, Brobdingnagian, Antaeus, Goliath, Gog and Magog, Gargantua, monster, mammoth, Cyclops; cachalot, whale, porpoise, behemoth, leviathan, elephant, hippopotamus; colossus; tun, cord, lump, bulk, block, loaf, mass, swad, clod, nugget, bushel, thumper, whooper, spanker, strapper; Triton among the minnows [Coriolanus].

mountain, mound; heap &c *(assemblage)* 72.

largest portion &c 50; full size, life size.

V. be large &c *adj.;* become large &c *(expand)* 194.

Adj. large, big; great &c *(in quantity)* 31; considerable, bulky, voluminous, ample, massive, massy; capacious, comprehensive; spacious &c 180; mighty, towering, fine, magnificent.

corpulent, stout, fat, obese, plump, squab, full, lusty, strapping, bouncing; portly, burly, well-fed, full-grown; corn fed, gram fed; stalwart, brawny, fleshy; goodly; in good case, in good condition; in condition; chopping, jolly; chub faced, chubby faced.

lubberly, hulky, unwieldy, lumpish, gaunt, spanking, whacking, whopping, walloping, thumping, thundering, hulking; overgrown; puffy &c *(swollen)* 194.

huge, immense, enormous, mighty; vast, vasty; amplitudinous, stupendous; monster, monstrous, humongous, monumental; elephantine, jumbo, mammoth; gigantic, gigantean, giant, giant like, titanic; prodigious, colossal, Cyclopean, Brobdingnagian, Bunyanesque, Herculean, Gargantuan; infinite &c 105.

large as life; plump as a dumpling, plump as a partridge; fat as a pig, fat as a quail, fat as butter, fat as brawn, fat as bacon.

immeasurable, unfathomable, unplumbed; inconceivable, unimaginable, unheard-of.

of cosmic proportions; of epic proportions, the mother of all, teh granddaddy of all.

193. Littleness -- N. littleness &c *adj.;* smallness &c *(of quantity)* 32; exiguity, inextension†; parvitude†, parvity†; duodecimo†; Elzevir edition, epitome, microcosm; rudiment; vanishing point; thinness &c 203.

dwarf, pygmy, pigmy†, Liliputian, chit, pigwidgeon†, urchin, elf; atomy†, dandiprat†; doll, puppet; Tom Thumb, Hop-o'-my-thumb†; manikin, mannikin; homunculus, dapperling†, cock-sparrow.

animalcule, monad, mite, insect, emmet†, fly, midge, gnat, shrimp, minnow, worm, maggot, entozoon†; bacteria; infusoria†; microzoa *[Micro.]*; phytozoaria†; microbe; grub; tit, tomtit, runt, mouse, small fry; millet seed, mustard seed; barleycorn; pebble, grain of sand; molehill, button, bubble.

point; atom &c *(small quantity)* 32; fragment &c *(small part)* 51; powder &c 330; point of a pin, mathematical point; minutiae &c *(unimportance)* 643.

micrometer; vernier; scale.

microphotography, photomicrography, micrography†; photomicrograph, microphotograph; microscopy; microscope *(optical instruments)* 445.

V. be little &c *adj.;* lie in a nutshell; become small &c *(decrease)* 36, *(contract)* 195.

Adj. little; small &c *(in quantity)* 32; minute, diminutive, microscopic; microzoal; inconsiderable &c *(unimportant)* 643; exiguous, puny, tiny, wee, petty, minikin[†], miniature, pygmy, pigmy[†], elfin; undersized; dwarf, dwarfed, dwarfish; spare, stunted, limited; cramp, cramped; pollard, Liliputian, dapper, pocket; portative[†], portable; duodecimo[†]; dumpy, squat; short &c 201.

impalpable, intangible, evanescent, imperceptible, invisible, inappreciable, insignificant, inconsiderable, trivial; infinitesimal, homoeopathic[†]; atomic, subatomic, corpuscular, molecular; rudimentary, rudimental; embryonic, vestigial.

weazen[†], scant, scraggy, scrubby; thin &c *(narrow)* 203; granular &c *(powdery)* 330; shrunk &c 195; brevipennate[†].

Adv. in a small compass, in a nutshell; on a small scale; minutely, microscopically.

194. Expansion -- **N.** expansion; increase of size &c 35; enlargement, extension, augmentation; amplification, ampliation[†]; aggrandizement, spread, increment, growth, development, pullulation, swell, dilation, rarefaction; turgescence[†], turgidness, turgidity; dispansion[†]; obesity &c *(size)* 192;

hydrocephalus, hydrophthalmus *[Med.]*; dropsy, tumefaction, intumescence, swelling, tumor, diastole, distension; puffing, puffiness; inflation; pandiculation†.

dilatability, expansibility.

germination, growth, upgrowth†; accretion &c 35; budding, gemmation†.

overgrowth, overdistension†; hypertrophy, tympany†.

bulb &c *(convexity)* 250; plumper; superiority of size.

[expansion of the universe] big bang; Hubble constant.

V. become larger &c *(large)* &c 192; expand, widen, enlarge, extend, grow, increase, incrassate†, swell, gather; fill out; deploy, take open order, dilate, stretch, distend, spread; mantle, wax; grow up, spring up; bud, bourgeon *[Fr.]*, shoot, sprout, germinate, put forth, vegetate, pullulate, open, burst forth; gain flesh, gather flesh; outgrow; spread like wildfire, overrun.

be larger than; surpass &c *(be superior)* 33.

render larger &c *(large)* &c 192; expand, spread, extend, aggrandize, distend, develop, amplify, spread out, widen, magnify, rarefy, inflate, puff, blow up, stuff, pad, cram; exaggerate; fatten.

Adj. expanded, &c v.; larger, &c *(large)* &c 192; swollen; expansive; wide open, wide spread; flabelliform†; overgrown, exaggerated, bloated, fat, turgid, tumid, hypertrophied, dropsical; pot bellied, swag bellied†; edematous, oedematous†, obese, puffy, pursy†, blowzy, bigswoln†, distended; patulous; bulbous &c *(convex)* 250; full blown, full grown, full formed; big &c 192; abdominous†, enchymatous†, rhipidate†; tumefacient†, tumefying†.

195. Contraction -- **N.** contraction, reduction, diminution; decrease of size &c 36; defalcation, decrement; lessening, shrinking &c *v.*; compaction; tabes†, collapse, emaciation, attenuation, tabefaction†, consumption, marasmus†, atrophy; systole, neck, hourglass.

condensation, compression, compactness; compendium &c 596; squeezing
&c *v.*; strangulation; corrugation; astringency; astringents, sclerotics; contractility, compressibility; coarctation†.

inferiority in size.

V. become small, become smaller; lessen, decrease &c 36; grow less, dwindle, shrink, contract, narrow, shrivel, collapse, wither, lose flesh, wizen, fall away, waste, wane, ebb; decay &c *(deteriorate)* 659.

be smaller than, fall short of; not come up to &c *(be inferior)* 34.

render smaller, lessen, diminish, contract, draw in, narrow, coarctate†; boil down; constrict, constringe†; condense, compress, squeeze, corrugate, crimp, crunch, crush, crumple up, warp, purse up, pack, squeeze, stow; pinch, tighten, strangle; cramp; dwarf, bedwarf†; shorten &c 201; circumscribe &c 229; restrain &c 751.

*[reduce in size by abrasion or paring.
] (subtraction)* 38 abrade, pare, reduce, attenuate, rub down, scrape, file, file down, grind, grind down, chip, shave, shear, wear down.

Adj. contracting &c *v.;* astringent; shrunk, contracted &c *v.;* strangulated, tabid†, wizened, stunted; waning &c *v.;* neap, compact.

unexpanded &c *(expand)* &c 194 [Obs.]; contractile; compressible; smaller &c *(small)* &c 193.

196. Distance -- **N.** distance; space &c 180; remoteness, farness†, far-cry to; longinquity†, elongation; offing, background; remote region; removedness†; parallax; reach, span, stride.

outpost, outskirt; horizon; aphelion; foreign parts, ultima Thule *[Lat.]*, ne plus ultra *[Lat.]*, antipodes; long range, giant's stride.

dispersion &c 73.

[units of distance] length &c 200.

cosmic distance, light-years.

V. be distant &c *adj.;* extend to, stretch to, reach to, spread to, go to, get to, stretch away to; range.

remain at a distance; keep away, keep off, keep aloof, keep clear of, stand away, stand off, stand aloof, stand clear of, stay away, keep one's distance.

distance; distance oneself from.

Adj. distant; far off, far away; remote, telescopic, distal, wide of; stretching to &c *v.;* yon, yonder; ulterior; transmarine†, transpontine†, transatlantic, transalpine; tramontane; ultramontane, ultramundane†; hyperborean, antipodean; inaccessible, out of the way; unapproached†, unapproachable; incontiguous†.

Adv. far off, far away; afar, afar off; off; away; a long way off, a great way off, a good way off; wide away, aloof; wide of, clear of; out of the way, out of reach; abroad, yonder, farther, further, beyond; outre mer *[Fr.]*, over the border, far and wide, over the hills and far away [Gay]; from pole to pole &c *(over great space)* 180; to the uttermost parts, to the ends of the earth; out of hearing, nobody knows where, a perte de vue *[Fr.]*, out of the sphere of, wide of the mark; a far cry to.

apart, asunder; wide apart, wide asunder; longo intervallo *[It]*; at arm's length.

Phr. distance lends enchantment [Campbell]; it's a long long way to Tipperary; out of sight, out of mind.

197. Nearness -- **N.** nearness &c *adj.;* proximity, propinquity; vicinity, vicinage; neighborhood, adjacency; contiguity &c 199.

short distance, short step, short cut; earshot, close quarters, stone's throw; bow shot, gun shot, pistol shot; hair's breadth, span.

purlieus, neighborhood, vicinage, environs, alentours *[Fr.]*, suburbs, confines, banlieue†, borderland; whereabouts.

bystander; neighbor, borderer†.

approach &c 286; convergence &c 290; perihelion.

V. be near &c *adj.;* adjoin, hang about, trench on; border upon, verge upon; stand by, approximate, tread on the heels of, cling to, clasp, hug; huddle; hang upon the skirts of, hover over; burn.

touch &c 199; bring near, draw near &c 286; converge &c 290; crowd &c 72; place side by side &c *adv.*.

Adj. near, nigh; close at hand, near at hand; close, neighboring; bordering upon, contiguous, adjacent, adjoining; proximate, proximal; at hand, handy; near the mark, near run; home, intimate.

Adv. near, nigh; hard by, fast by; close to, close upon; hard upon; at the point of; next door to; within reach, within call, within hearing, within earshot; within an ace of; but a step, not far from, at no great distance; on the verge of, on the brink of, on the skirts of; in the environs &c *n.;* at one's door, at one's feet, at one's elbow, at one's finger's end, at one's side; on the tip of one's tongue; under one's nose; within a stone's throw &c *n.;* in sight of, in presence of; at close quarters; cheek by jole[†], cheek by jowl; beside, alongside, side by side, tete-a-tete; in juxtaposition &c *(touching)* 199; yardarm to yardarm, at the heels of; on the confines of, at the threshold, bordering upon, verging to; in the way.

about; hereabouts, thereabouts; roughly, in round numbers; approximately, approximatively[†]; as good as, well-nigh.

198. Interval -- **N.** interval, interspace[†]; separation &c 44; break, gap, opening; hole &c 260; chasm, hiatus, caesura; interruption, interregnum; interstice, lacuna, cleft, mesh, crevice, chink, rime, creek, cranny, crack, chap, slit, fissure, scissure[†], rift, flaw, breach, rent, gash, cut, leak, dike, ha-ha.

gorge, defile, ravine, canon, crevasse, abyss, abysm; gulf; inlet, frith†, strait, gully; pass; furrow &c 259; abra†; barranca†, barranco†; clove *[U.S.]*, gulch *[U.S.]*, notch *[U.S.]*; yawning gulf; hiatus maxime *[Lat.]*, hiatus valde deflendus *[Lat.]*; parenthesis &c *(interjacence)* 228 [Obs.]; void &c *(absence)* 187; incompleteness &c 53.

[interval of time] period &c 108; interim *(time)* 106.

V. gape &c *(open)* 260.

Adj. with an interval, far between; breachy†, rimose†, rimulose†.

Adv. at intervals &c *(discontinuously)* 70; longo intervallo *[It]*.

199. Contiguity -- **N.** contiguity, contact, proximity, apposition, abuttal†, juxtaposition; abutment, osculation; meeting, appulse†, rencontre†, rencounter†, syzygy *[Astr.]*, coincidence, coexistence; adhesion &c 46; touching &c v.. *(touch)* 379.

borderland; frontier &c *(limit)* 233; tangent; abutter.

V. be contiguous &c *adj.;* join, adjoin, abut on, march with; graze, touch, meet, osculate, come in contact, coincide; coexist; adhere &c 46.

[cause to be contiguous] juxtapose; contact; join *(unite)* 43; link *(vinculum)* 45.

Adj. contiguous; touching &c *v.;* in contact &c *n.;* conterminous, end to end, osculatory; pertingent†; tangential.

hand to hand; close to &c *(near)* 197; with no interval &c 198.

2. LINEAR DIMENSIONS

200. Length -- N. length, longitude, span; mileage; distance &c 196.

line, bar, rule, stripe, streak, spoke, radius.

lengthening &c *v.;* prolongation, production, protraction; tension, tensure†; extension.

[Measures of length] line, nail, inch, hand, palm, foot, cubit, yard, ell, fathom, rood, pole, furlong, mile, league; chain, link; arpent†, handbreadth†, jornada *[U.S.]*, kos†, vara†.

[astronomical units of distance] astronomical unit, AU, light-year, parsec.

[metric units of length] nanometer, nm, micron, micrometer, millimicron, millimeter, mm, centimeter, cm, meter, kilometer, km.

pedometer, perambulator; scale &c *(measurement)* 466.

V. be long &c *adj.;* stretch out, sprawl; extend to, reach to, stretch to; make a long arm, drag its slow length along.

render long &c *adj.;* lengthen, extend, elongate; stretch; prolong, produce, protract; let out, draw out, spin out[†]; drawl.

enfilade, look along, view in perspective.

distend *(expand)* 194.

Adj. long, longsome[†]; lengthy, wiredrawn[†], outstretched; lengthened &c *v.;* sesquipedalian &c *(words)* 577; interminable, no end of; macrocolous[†].

linear, lineal; longitudinal, oblong.

as long as my arm, as long as today and tomorrow; unshortened &c *(shorten)* &c 201 [Obs.].

Adv. lengthwise, at length, longitudinally, endlong[†], along; tandem; in a line &c *(continuously)* 69; in perspective.

from end to end, from stem to stern, from head to foot, from the crown of the head to the sole of the foot, from top to toe; fore and aft.

201. Shortness -- **N.** shortness &c *adj.;* brevity; littleness &c 193; a span.

shortening &c *v.;* abbreviation, abbreviature[†]; abridgment, concision, retrenchment, curtailment, decurtation[†]; reduction &c *(contraction)* 195; epitome &c *(compendium)* 596.

elision, ellipsis; conciseness &c *(in style)* 572.

abridger, epitomist[†], epitomizer[†].

V. be short &c *adj.;* render short &c *adj.;* shorten, curtail, abridge, abbreviate, take in, reduce; compress &c *(contract)* 195; epitomize &c 596.

retrench, cut short, obtruncate[†]; scrimp, cut, chop up, hack, hew; cut down, pare down; clip, dock, lop, prune, shear, shave, mow, reap, crop; snub; truncate, pollard, stunt, nip, check the growth of; foreshorten (in drawing).

Adj. short, brief, curt; compendious, compact; stubby, scrimp; shorn, stubbed; stumpy, thickset, pug; chunky *[U.S.]*, decurtate[†]; retroussé[†]; stocky; squab, squabby[†]; squat, dumpy; little &c 193;

curtailed of its fair proportions; short by; oblate; concise &c 572; summary.

Adv. shortly &c *adj.;* in short &c *(concisely)* 572.

202. Breadth, Thickness, -- **N.** breadth, width, latitude, amplitude; diameter, bore, caliber, radius; superficial extent &c *(space)* 180.

thickness, crassitude†; corpulence &c *(size)* 192; dilation &c *(expansion)* 194.

V. be broad &c *adj.;* become broad, render broad &c *adj.;* expand &c 194; thicken, widen, calibrate.

Adj. broad, wide, ample, extended; discous†; fanlike; outspread, outstretched; wide as a church-door [Romeo and Juliet]; latifoliate†, latifolous†.

thick, dumpy, squab, squat, thickset; thick as a rope.

203. Narrowness. Thinness -- **N.** narrowness &c *adj.;* closeness, exility†; exiguity &c *(little)* 193.

line; hair's breadth, finger's breadth; strip, streak, vein.

monolayer; epitaxial deposition *[Eng.]*.

thinness &c *adj.;* tenuity; emaciation, macilency†, marcor†.

shaving, slip &c *(filament)* 205; thread paper, skeleton, shadow, anatomy, spindleshanks†, lantern jaws, mere skin and bone.

middle constriction, stricture, neck, waist, isthmus, wasp, hourglass; ridge, ghaut†, ghat†, pass; ravine &c 198.

narrowing, coarctation†, angustation†, tapering; contraction &c 195.

V. be narrow &c *adj.;* narrow, taper, contract &c 195; render narrow &c *adj.;* waste away.

Adj. narrow, close; slender, thin, fine; thread-like &c *(filament)* 205; finespun†, gossamer; paper-thin; taper, slim, slight-made; scant, scanty; spare, delicate, incapacious†; contracted &c 195; unexpanded &c *(expand)* &c 194 [Obs.]; slender as a thread.

[in reference to people or animals] emaciated, lean, meager, gaunt, macilent†; lank, lanky; weedy, skinny; scrawny slinky *[U.S.]*; starved, starveling; herring gutted; worn to a shadow, lean as a rake [Chaucer]; thin as a lath, thin as a whipping post, thin as a wafer; hatchet-faced; lantern-jawed.

attenuated, shriveled, extenuated, tabid†, marcid†, barebone, rawboned.

monomolecular.

204. Layer -- **N.** layer, stratum, strata, course, bed, zone, substratum, substrata, floor, flag, stage, story, tier, slab, escarpment; table, tablet; dess[†]; flagstone; board, plank; trencher, platter.

plate; lamina, lamella; sheet, foil; wafer; scale, flake, peel; coat, pellicle; membrane, film; leaf; slice, shive[†], cut, rasher, shaving, integument &c *(covering)* 223; eschar[†].

stratification, scaliness, nest of boxes, coats of an onion.

monolayer; bilayer; trilayer *[Bioch.]*.

V. slice, shave, pare, peel; delaminate; plate, coat, veneer; cover &c 223.

Adj. lamellar, lamellated[†], lamelliform[†], layered; laminated, laminiferous[†]; micaceous[†]; schistose, schistous[†]; scaly, filmy, membranous, pellicular, flaky, squamous *[Anat.]*; foliated, foliaceous[†]; stratified, stratiform; tabular, discoid; spathic[†], spathose[†].

trilamellar[†].

graphitic[†].

205. Filament -- N. filament, line; fiber, fibril; funicle[†], vein; hair, capillament[†], cilium, cilia, pilus, pili; tendril, gossamer; hair stroke; veinlet[†], venula[†], venule[†].

wire, string, thread, packthread, cotton, sewing silk, twine, twist, whipcord, tape, ribbon, cord, rope, yarn, hemp, oakum, jute.

strip, shred, slip, spill, list, band, fillet, fascia, ribbon, riband, roll, lath, splinter, shiver, shaving.

beard &c *(roughness)* 256; ramification; strand.

Adj. filamentous, filamentiferous[†], filaceous[†], filiform[†]; fibrous, fibrillous[†]; thread-like, wiry, stringy, ropy; capillary, capilliform[†]; funicular, wire-drawn; anguilliform[†]; flagelliform[†]; hairy &c *(rough)* 256; taeniate[†], taeniform[†], taenioid[†]; venose[†], venous.

206. Height -- N. height, altitude, elevation; eminence, pitch; loftiness &c *adj.;* sublimity.

tallness &c *adj.;* stature, procerity[†]; prominence &c 250.

colossus &c *(size)* 192; giant, grenadier, giraffe, camelopard.

mount, mountain; hill alto, butte *[U.S.]*, monticle†, fell, knap†; cape; headland, foreland†; promontory; ridge, hog's back, dune; rising ground, vantage ground; down; moor, moorland; Alp; uplands, highlands; heights &c *(summit)* 210; knob, loma†, pena *[U.S.]*, picacho†, tump†; knoll, hummock, hillock, barrow, mound, mole; steeps, bluff, cliff, craig†, tor†, peak, pike, clough†; escarpment, edge, ledge, brae; dizzy height.

tower, pillar, column, obelisk, monument, steeple, spire, minaret, campanile, turret, dome, cupola; skyscraper.

pole, pikestaff, maypole, flagstaff; top mast, topgallant mast.

ceiling &c *(covering)* 223.

high water; high tide, flood tide, spring tide.

altimetry &c *(angel)* 244 [Obs.]; batophobia†.

satellite, spy-in-the-sky.

V. be high &c *adj.;* tower, soar, command; hover, hover over, fly over; orbit, be in orbit; cap, culminate; overhang, hang over, impend, beetle, bestride, ride, mount; perch, surmount; cover &c 223; overtop &c *(be superior)* 33; stand on tiptoe.

become high &c *adj.;* grow higher, grow taller; upgrow†; rise &c *(ascend)* 305; send into orbit.

render high &c *adj.;* heighten &c *(elevate)* 307.

Adj. high, elevated, eminent, exalted, lofty, tall; gigantic &c *(big)* 192; Patagonian; towering, beetling, soaring, hanging (gardens); elevated &c 307; upper; highest &c *(topmost)* 210; high reaching, insessorial†, perching.

upland, moorland; hilly, knobby *[U.S.]*; mountainous, alpine, subalpine, heaven kissing; cloudtopt†, cloudcapt†, cloudtouching†; aerial.

overhanging &c *v.;* incumbent, overlying, superincumbent†, supernatant, superimposed; prominent &c *v.* 250.

tall as a maypole, tall as a poplar, tall as a steeple, lanky &c *(thin)* 203.

Adv. on high, high up, aloft, up, above, aloof, overhead; airwind†; upstairs, abovestairs†; in the clouds; on tiptoe, on stilts, on the shoulders of; over head and ears; breast high.

over, upwards; from top to bottom &c *(completely)* 52.

Phr. e meglio cader dalle finistre che dal tetto *[It]*.

207. Lowness -- **N.** lowness &c *adj.;* debasement, depression, prostration &c *(horizontal)* 213; depression &c *(concave)* 252.

molehill; lowlands; basement floor, ground floor; rez de chaussee *[Fr.]*; cellar; hold, bilge; feet, heels.

low water; low tide, ebb tide, neap tide, spring tide.

V. be low &c *adj.;* lie low, lie flat; underlie; crouch, slouch, wallow, grovel; lower &c *(depress)* 308.

Adj. low, neap, debased; nether, nether most; flat, level with the ground; lying low &c *v.;* crouched, subjacent, squat, prostrate &c *(horizontal)* 213.

Adv. under; beneath, underneath; below; downwards; adown[†], at the foot of; under foot, under ground; down stairs, below stairs; at a low ebb; below par.

208. Depth -- **N.** depth; deepness &c *adj.;* profundity, depression &c *(concavity)* 252.

hollow, pit, shaft, well, crater; gulf &c 198; bowels of the earth, botttomless pit[†], hell.

soundings, depth of water, water, draught, submersion; plummet, sound, probe; sounding rod, sounding line; lead.

bathymetry.

[instrument to measure depth] sonar, side-looking sonar; bathometer†.

V. be deep &c *adj.;* render deep &c *adj.;* deepen.

plunge &c 310; sound, fathom, plumb, cast the lead, heave the lead, take soundings, make soundings; dig &c *(excavate)* 252.

Adj. deep, deep seated; profound, sunk, buried; submerged &c 310; subaqueous, submarine, subterranean, subterraneous, subterrene†; underground.

bottomless, soundless, fathomless; unfathomed, unfathomable; abysmal; deep as a well; bathycolpian†; benthal†, benthopelagic†; downreaching†, yawning.

knee deep, ankle deep.

Adv. beyond one's depth, out of one's depth; over head and ears; mark twine, mark twain.

209. Shallowness -- **N.** shallowness &c *adj.;* shoals; mere scratch.

Adj. shallow, slight, superficial; skin deep, ankle deep, knee deep; just enough to wet one's feet; shoal, shoaly†.

210. Summit -- **N.** summit, summity†; top, peak, vertex, apex, zenith, pinnacle, acme, culmination, meridian, utmost height, ne plus utra, height, pitch, maximum, climax, culminating point, crowning point, turning point; turn of the tide, fountain head; water shed, water parting; sky, pole.

tip, tip top; crest, crow's nest, cap, truck, nib; end &c 67; crown, brow; head, nob†, noddle†, pate; capsheaf†.

high places, heights.

topgallant mast, sky scraper; quarter deck, hurricane deck.

architrave, frieze, cornice, coping stone, zoophorus†, capital, epistyle†, sconce, pediment, entablature†; tympanum; ceiling &c *(covering)* 223.

attic, loft, garret, house top, upper story.

[metaphorical use] summit conference, summit; peak of achievement, peak of performance; peaks and troughs, peaks and valleys (in graphs).

V. culminate, crown, top; overtop &c *(be superior to)* 33.

Adj. highest &c *(high)* &c 206; top; top most, upper most; tiptop; culminating &c *v.;* meridian, meridional†; capital, head, polar, supreme, supernal, topgallant.

Adv. atop, at the top of the tree.

Phr. en flute; fleur deau *[Fr.]*.

211. Base -- **N.** base, basement; plinth, dado, wainscot; baseboard, mopboard†; bedrock, hardpan *[U.S.]*; foundation &c *(support)* 215; substructure, substratum, ground, earth, pavement, floor, paving, flag, carped, ground floor, deck; footing, ground work, basis; hold, bilge.

bottom, nadir, foot, sole, toe, hoof, keel, root; centerboard.

Adj. bottom, undermost, nethermost; fundamental; founded on, based on, grounded on, built on.

212. Verticality -- **N.** verticality; erectness &c *adj.;* perpendicularity &c 216.1; right angle, normal; azimuth circle.

wall, precipice, cliff.

elevation, erection; square, plumb line, plummet.

V. be vertical &c *adj.*; stand up, stand on end, stand erect, stand upright; stick up, cock up.

render vertical &c *adj.*; set up, stick up, raise up, cock up; erect, rear, raise on its legs.

Adj. vertical, upright, erect, perpendicular, plumb, normal, straight, bolt, upright; rampant; standing up &c *v.*; rectangular, orthogonal &c 216.1.

Adv. vertically &c *adj.*; up, on end; up on end, right on end; a plomb *[Fr.]*, endwise; one one's legs; at right angles.

213. Horizontality -- N. horizontality†; flatness; level, plane; stratum &c 204; dead level, dead flat; level plane.

recumbency, lying down &c *v.*; reclination†, decumbence†; decumbency†, discumbency†; proneness &c *adj.*; accubation†, supination†, resupination†, prostration; azimuth.

plain, floor, platform, bowling green; cricket ground; croquet ground, croquet lawn; billiard table; terrace, estrade†, esplanade, parterre.

[flat land area] table land, plateau, ledge; butte; mesa *(plain)* 344.

[instrument to measure horizontality] level, spirit level.

V. be horizontal &c *adj.;* lie, recline, couch; lie down, lie flat, lie prostrate; sprawl, loll, sit down.

render horizontal &c *adj.;* lay down, lay out; level, flatten; prostrate, knock down, floor, fell.

Adj. horizontal, level, even, plane; flat &c 251; flat as a billiard table, flat as a bowling green; alluvial; calm, calm as a mill pond; smooth, smooth as glass.

recumbent, decumbent, procumbent, accumbent[†]; lying &c *v.;* prone, supine, couchant, jacent[†], prostrate, recubant[†].

Adv. horizontally &c *adj.;* on one's back, on all fours, on its beam ends.

214. Pendency -- **N.** pendency[†], dependency; suspension, hanging &c *v.;* pedicel, pedicle, peduncle; tail, train, flap, skirt, pigtail, pony tail, pendulum; hangnail peg, knob, button, hook, nail, stud, ring, staple, tenterhook; fastening &c 45; spar, horse.

V. be pendent &c *adj.;* hang, depend, swing, dangle; swag; daggle†, flap, trail, flow; beetle.

suspend, hang, sling, hook up, hitch, fasten to, append.

Adj. pendent, pendulous; pensile; hanging &c *v.;* beetling, jutting over, overhanging, projecting; dependent; suspended &c *v.;* loose, flowing.

having a peduncle &c *n.;* pedunculate†, tailed, caudate.

215. Support -- **N.** support, ground, foundation, base, basis; terra firma; bearing, fulcrum, bait *[U.S.]*, caudex crib†; point d'appui *[Fr.]*, pou sto *[Gr.]*, purchase footing, hold, locus standi*[Lat.]*; landing place, landing stage; stage, platform; block; rest, resting place; groundwork, substratum, riprap, sustentation, subvention; floor &c *(basement)* 211.

supporter; aid &c 707; prop, stand, anvil, fulciment†; cue rest, jigger; monkey; stay, shore, skid, rib, truss, bandage; sleeper; stirrup, stilts, shoe, sole, heel, splint, lap, bar, rod, boom, sprit†, outrigger; ratlings†.

staff, stick, crutch, alpenstock, baton, staddle†; bourdon†, cowlstaff†, lathi†, mahlstick†.

post, pillar, shaft, thill†, column, pilaster; pediment, pedicle; pedestal; plinth, shank, leg, socle†, zocle†; buttress, jamb, mullion, abutment; baluster, banister, stanchion; balustrade; headstone; upright; door post, jamb, door jamb.

frame, framework; scaffold, skeleton, beam, rafter, girder, lintel, joist, travis†, trave†, corner stone, summer, transom; rung, round, step, sill; angle rafter, hip rafter; cantilever, modillion†; crown post, king post; vertebra.

columella†, backbone; keystone; axle, axletree; axis; arch, mainstay.

trunnion, pivot, rowlock†; peg &c *(pendency)* 214 [Obs.]; tiebeam &c *(fastening)* 45; thole pin†.

board, ledge, shelf, hob, bracket, trevet†, trivet, arbor, rack; mantel, mantle piece *[Fr.]*, mantleshelf†; slab, console; counter, dresser; flange, corbel; table, trestle; shoulder; perch; horse; easel, desk; clotheshorse, hatrack; retable; teapoy†.

seat, throne, dais; divan, musnud†; chair, bench, form, stool, sofa, settee, stall; arm chair, easy chair, elbow chair, rocking chair; couch, fauteuil *[Fr.]*, woolsack†, ottoman, settle, squab, bench; aparejo†, faldstool†, horn; long chair, long sleeve chair, morris chair; lamba chauki†, lamba kursi†; saddle, pannel†, pillion; side saddle, pack saddle; pommel.

bed, berth, pallet, tester, crib, cot, hammock, shakedown, trucklebed†, cradle, litter, stretcher, bedstead; four poster, French bed, bunk, kip, palang†; bedding, bichhona, mattress, paillasse†; pillow, bolster; mat, rug, cushion.

footstool, hassock; tabouret†; tripod, monopod.

Atlas, Persides, Atlantes†, Caryatides, Hercules.

V. be supported &c; lie on, sit on, recline on, lean on, loll on, rest on, stand on, step on, repose on, abut on, bear on, be based on &c; have at one's back; bestride, bestraddle†.

support, bear, carry, hold, sustain, shoulder; hold up, back up, bolster up, shore up; uphold, upbear†; prop; under prop, under pin, under set; riprap; bandage &c 43.

give support, furnish support, afford support, supply support, lend support, give foundations, furnish foundations, afford foundations, supply foundations, lend foundations; bottom, found, base, ground, imbed, embed.

maintain, keep on foot; aid &c 707.

Adj. supporting, supported &c v.; fundamental; dorsigerous†.

Adv. astride on, straddle.

216. Parallelism -- N. {ant.

216a} parallelism; coextension†; equidistance†; similarity &c 17.

Adj. parallel; coextensive; equidistant.

Adv. alongside &c *(laterally)* 236.

216a. Perpendicularity -- N. {ant.

216} perpendicularity, orthogonality; verticality, &c 212.

V. be perpendicular, be orthogonal; intersect at right angles, be rectangular, be at right angles to, intersect at 90 degrees; have no correlation.

Adj. orthogonal, perpendicular; rectangular; uncorrelated.

217. Obliquity -- N. obliquity, inclination, slope, slant, crookedness &c *adj.;* slopeness†; leaning &c *v.;* bevel, tilt; bias, list, twist, swag, cant, lurch; distortion &c 243; bend &c *(curve)* 245; tower of Pisa.

acclivity, rise, ascent, gradient, khudd†, rising ground, hill, bank, declivity, downhill, dip, fall, devexity†; gentle slope, rapid slope, easy ascent, easy descent; shelving beach; talus; monagne Russe *[Fr.]*; facilis descensus averni *[Lat.]*.

V. intersect; lack parallelism.

218. Inversion -- **N.** inversion, eversion, subversion, reversion, retroversion, introversion; contraposition &c 237 [Obs.]; contrariety &c 14; reversal; turn of the tide.

overturn; somersault, somerset; summerset†; culbute†; revulsion; pirouette.

transposition, transposal†, anastrophy†, metastasis, hyperbaton†, anastrophe†, hysteron proteron *[Gr.]*, hypallage†, synchysis†, tmesis†, parenthesis; metathesis; palindrome.

pronation and supination *[Anat.]*.

V. be inverted &c; turn round, turn about, turn to the right about, go round, go about, go to the right about, wheel round, wheel about, wheel to the right about; turn over, go over, tilt over, topple over; capsize, turn turtle.

invert, subvert, retrovert†, introvert; reverse; up turn, over turn, up set, over set; turn topsy turvy

&c *adj.;* culbuter†; transpose, put the cart before the horse, turn the tables.

Adj. inverted &c *v.;* wrong side out, wrong side up; inside out, upside down; bottom upwards, keel upwards; supine, on one's head, topsy-turvy, sens dessus dessous *[Fr.].*

inverse; reverse &c *(contrary)* 14; opposite &c 237.

top heavy.

Adv. inversely &c *adj.;* hirdy-girdy†; heels over head, head over heels.

219. Crossing --
N. crossing &c *v.;* intersection, interdigitation; decussation†, transversion†; convolution &c 248; level crossing.

reticulation, network; inosculation†, anastomosis, intertexture†, mortise.

net, plexus, web, mesh, twill, skein, sleeve, felt, lace; wicker; mat, matting; plait, trellis, wattle, lattice, grating, grille, gridiron, tracery, fretwork, filigree, reticle; tissue, netting, mokes†; rivulation†.

cross, chain, wreath, braid, cat's cradle, knot; entangle &c *(disorder)* 59.

[woven fabrics] cloth, linen, muslin, cambric &c

V. cross, decussate†; intersect, interlace, intertwine, intertwist†, interweave, interdigitate, interlink.

twine, entwine, weave, inweave†, twist, wreathe; anastomose *[Med.]*, inosculate†, dovetail, splice, link; lace, tat.

mat, plait, plat, braid, felt, twill; tangle, entangle, ravel; net, knot; dishevel, raddle†.

Adj. crossing &c *v.;* crossed, matted &c, *v..* transverse.

cross, cruciform, crucial; retiform†, reticular, reticulated; areolar†, cancellated†, grated, barred, streaked; textile; crossbarred†, cruciate†, palmiped†, secant; web-footed.

Adv. cross, thwart, athwart, transversely; at grade *[U.S.]*; crosswise.

3. CENTRICAL DIMENSIONS
1. General.

220. Exteriority -- **N.** exteriority†; outside, exterior; surface, superficies; skin &c *(covering)* 223; superstratum†; disk, disc; face, facet; extrados†.

excentricity†; eccentricity; circumjacence &c 227 [Obs.].

V. be exterior &c *adj.;* lie around &c 227.

place exteriorly, place outwardly, place outside; put out, turn out.

Adj. exterior, external; outer most; outward, outlying, outside, outdoor; round about &c 227; extramural; extralimitary†, extramundane.

superficial, skin-deep; frontal, discoid.

extraregarding†; excentric†, eccentric; outstanding; extrinsic &c 6; ecdemic *[Med.]*, exomorphic†.

Adv. externally &c *adj.;* out, with out, over, outwards, ab extra, out of doors; extra muros *[Lat.]*.

in the open air; sub Jove, sub dio *[Lat.]*; a la belle etoile *[Fr.]*, al fresco.

221. Interiority -- **N.** interiority; inside, interior; interspace†, subsoil, substratum; intrados.

contents &c 190; substance, pith, marrow; backbone &c *(center)* 222; heart, bosom, breast; abdomen; vitals, viscera, entrails, bowels, belly, intestines, guts, chitterings†, womb, lap; penetralia *[Lat.]*, recesses, innermost recesses; cave &c *(concavity)* 252.

V. be inside &c *adj.;* within &c *adv..* place within, keep within; inclose &c *(circumscribe)* 229; intern; imbed &c *(insert)* 300.

Adj. interior, internal; inner, inside, inward, intraregarding†; inmost, innermost; deep seated, gut; intestine, intestinal; inland; subcutaneous; abdominal, coeliac, endomorphic *[Physio.]*; interstitial &c *(interjacent)* 228 [Obs.]; inwrought &c *(intrinsic)* 5; inclosed &c *v..* home, domestic, indoor, intramural, vernacular; endemic.

Adv. internally &c *adj.;* inwards, within, in, inly†; here in, there in, where in; ab intra, withinside†; in doors, within doors; at home, in the bosom of one's family.

222. Centrality -- **N.** centrality, centricalness†, center; middle &c 68; focus &c 74.

core, kernel; nucleus, nucleolus; heart, pole axis, bull's eye; nave, navel; umbilicus, backbone, marrow, pith; vertebra, vertebral column; hotbed;

concentration &c *(convergence)* 290; centralization; symmetry.

center of gravity, center of pressure, center of percussion, center of oscillation, center of buoyancy &c; metacenter[†].

V. be central &c *adj.*; converge &c 290.

render central, centralize, concentrate; bring to a focus.

Adj. central, centrical[†]; middle &c 68; azygous, axial, focal, umbilical, concentric; middlemost; rachidian[†]; spinal, vertebral.

Adv. middle; midst; centrally &c *adj.*.

223. Covering -- **N.** covering, cover; baldachin, baldachino[†], baldaquin[†]; canopy, tilt, awning, tent, marquee, tente d'abri *[Fr.]*, umbrella, parasol, sunshade; veil *(shade)* 424; shield &c *(defense)* 717.

roof, ceiling, thatch, tile; pantile, pentile[†]; tiling, slates, slating, leads; barrack *[U.S.]*, plafond, planchment *[U.S.]*, tiling, shed &c *(abode)* 189.

top, lid, covercle[†], door, operculum; bulkhead *[U.S.]*.

bandage, plaster, lint, wrapping, dossil[†], finger stall.

coverlet, counterpane, sheet, quilt, tarpaulin, blanket, rug, drugget†; housing; antimacassar, eiderdown, numdah†, pillowcase, pillowslip†; linoleum; saddle cloth, blanket cloth; tidy; tilpah*[U.S.]*, apishamore *[U.S.]*.

integument, tegument; skin, pellicle, fleece, fell, fur, leather, shagreen†, hide; pelt, peltry†; cordwain†; derm†; robe, buffalo robe *[U.S.]*; cuticle, scarfskin, epidermis.

clothing &c 225; mask &c *(concealment)* 530.

peel, crust, bark, rind, cortex, husk, shell, coat; eggshell, glume†.

capsule; sheath, sheathing; pod, cod; casing, case, theca†; elytron†; elytrum†; involucrum *[Lat.]*; wrapping, wrapper; envelope, vesicle; corn husk, corn shuck *[U.S.]*; dermatology, conchology; testaceology†.

inunction†; incrustation, superimposition, superposition, obduction†; scale &c *(layer)* 204.

[specific coverings] veneer, facing; overlay; plate, silver plate, gold plate, copper plate; engobe†; ormolu; Sheffield plate; pavement; coating, paint; varnish &c *(resin)* 216.1; plating, barrel plating, anointing &c *v.;* enamel; epitaxial deposition *[Eng.]*, vapor deposition; ground, whitewash, plaster, spackel, stucco, compo; cerement; ointment &c *(grease)* 356.

V. cover; superpose, superimpose; overlay, overspread; wrap &c 225; encase, incase†; face, case, veneer, pave, paper; tip, cap, bind; bulkhead, bulkhead in; clapboard *[U.S.]*.

coat, paint, varnish, pay, incrust, stucco, dab, plaster, tar; wash; besmear, bedaub; anoint, do over; gild, plate, japan, lacquer, lacker†, enamel, whitewash; parget†; lay it on thick.

overlie, overarch†; endome†; conceal &c 528.

[of aluminum] anodize.

[of steel] galvanize.

Adj. covering &c *v.;* superimposed, overlaid, plated &c *v.;* cutaneous, dermal, cortical, cuticular, tegumentary†, skinny, scaly, squamous *[Anat.]*; covered &c *v.;* imbricated, loricated†, armor plated, ironclad; under cover; cowled, cucullate†, dermatoid†, encuirassed†, hooded, squamiferous†, tectiform†; vaginate†.

224. Lining -- **N.** lining, inner coating; coating &c *(covering)* 223; stalactite, stalagmite.

filling, stuffing, wadding, padding.

wainscot, parietes *[Lat.]*, wall.

V. line, stuff, incrust, wad, pad, fill.

Adj. lined &c *v..*

225. Clothing -- N. clothing, investment; covering &c 223; dress, raiment, drapery, costume, attire, guise, toilet, toilette, trim; habiliment; vesture, vestment; garment, garb, palliament†, apparel, wardrobe, wearing apparel, clothes, things; underclothes.

array; tailoring, millinery; finery &c *(ornament)* 847; full dress &c *(show)* 882; garniture; theatrical properties.

outfit, equipment, trousseau; uniform, regimentals; continentals *[U.S.]*; canonicals &c 999; livery, gear, harness, turn-out, accouterment, caparison, suit, rigging, trappings, traps, slops, togs, toggery†; day wear, night wear, zoot suit; designer clothes; masquerade.

dishabille, morning dress, undress.

kimono; lungi†; shooting-coat; mufti; rags, tatters, old clothes; mourning, weeds; duds; slippers.

robe, tunic, paletot†, habit, gown, coat, frock, blouse, toga, smock frock, claw coat, hammer coat, Prince Albert coat†, sack coat, tuxedo coat, frock coat, dress coat, tail coat.

cloak, pall, mantle, mantlet mantua†, shawl, pelisse, wrapper; veil; cape, tippet, kirtle†, plaid, muffler, comforter, haik†, huke†, chlamys†, mantilla, tabard, housing, horse cloth, burnoose, burnous, roquelaure†; houppelande *[Fr.]*; surcoat, overcoat, great coat; surtout *[Fr.]*, spencer†; mackintosh, waterproof, raincoat; ulster, P-coat, dreadnought, wraprascal†, poncho, cardinal, pelerine†; barbe†, chudder†, jubbah†, oilskins, pajamas, pilot jacket, talma jacket†, vest, jerkin, waistcoat, doublet, camisole, gabardine; farthingale, kilt, jupe†, crinoline, bustle, panier, skirt, apron, pinafore; bloomer, bloomers; chaqueta†, songtag *[G.]*, tablier†.

pants, trousers, trowsers†; breeches, pantaloons, inexpressibles†, overalls, smalls, small clothes; shintiyan†; shorts, jockey shorts, boxer shorts; tights, drawers, panties, unmentionables; knickers, knickerbockers; philibeg†, fillibeg†; pants suit; culottes; jeans, blue jeans, dungarees, denims.

[brand names for jeans] Levis, Calvin Klein, Calvins, Bonjour, Gloria Vanderbilt.

headdress, headgear; chapeau *[Fr.]*, crush hat, opera hat; kaffiyeh; sombrero, jam, tam-o-shanter, tarboosh†, topi, sola topi *[Lat.]*, pagri†, puggaree†; cap, hat, beaver hat, coonskin cap; castor, bonnet, tile, wideawake, billycock†, wimple; nightcap, mobcap†, skullcap; hood, coif; capote†, calash; kerchief, snood, babushka; head, coiffure; crown &c *(circle)* 247; chignon, pelt, wig, front, peruke, periwig, caftan, turban, fez, shako, csako†, busby; kepi†, forage cap, bearskin; baseball cap; fishing hat; helmet &c 717; mask, domino.

body clothes; linen; hickory shirt *[U.S.]*; shirt, sark†, smock, shift, chemise; night gown, negligee, dressing gown, night shirt; bedgown†, sac de nuit *[Fr.]*.

underclothes *[underclothing]*, underpants, undershirt; slip *[for women]*, brassiere, corset, stays, corsage, corset, corselet, bodice, girdle &c *(circle)* 247; stomacher; petticoat, panties; under waistcoat; jock *[for men]*, athletic supporter, jockstrap.

sweater, jersey; cardigan; turtleneck, pullover; sweater vest.

neckerchief, neckcloth†; tie, ruff, collar, cravat, stock, handkerchief, scarf; bib, tucker; boa; cummerbund, rumal†, rabat†.

shoe, pump, boot, slipper, sandal, galoche†, galoshes, patten, clog; sneakers, running shoes, hiking boots; high-low; Blucher boot, wellington boot, Hessian boot, jack boot, top boot; Balmoral†; arctics, bootee, bootikin†, brogan, chaparajos†; chavar†, chivarras†, chivarros†; gums *[U.S.]*, larrigan *[U.S.]*, rubbers, showshoe, stogy†, veldtschoen *[G.]*, legging, buskin, greave†, galligaskin†, gamache†, gamashes†, moccasin, gambado, gaiter, spatterdash†, brogue, antigropelos†; stocking, hose, gaskins†, trunk hose, sock; hosiery.

glove, gauntlet, mitten, cuff, wristband, sleeve.

swaddling cloth, baby linen, layette; ice wool; taffeta.

pocket handkerchief, hanky†, hankie.

clothier, tailor, milliner, costumier, sempstress†, snip; dressmaker, habitmaker†, breechesmaker†, shoemaker; Crispin; friseur *[Fr.]*; cordwainer†, cobbler, hosier†, hatter; draper, linen draper, haberdasher, mercer.

[underpants for babies] diaper, nappy *[Brit.]*; disposable diaper, cloth diaper; *[brand names for diapers],* Luvs Huggies.

V. invest; cover &c 223; envelope, lap, involve; inwrap†, enwrap; wrap; fold up, wrap up, lap up, muffle up; overlap; sheath, swathe, swaddle, roll up in, circumvest.

vest, clothe, array, dress, dight†, drape, robe, enrobe, attire, apparel, accounter†, rig, fit out; deck &c *(ornament)* 847; perk, equip, harness, caparison.

wear; don; put on, huddle on, slip on; mantle.

Adj. invested &c *v.;* habited; dighted†; barbed, barded; clad, costume, shod, chausse *[Fr.]*; en grande tenue &c *(show)* 882 [Fr.].

sartorial.

Phr. the soul of this man is his clothes [All's Well].

226. Divestment -- **N.** divestment; taking off &c *v..* nudity; bareness &c *adj.;* undress; dishabille &c 225; the altogether; nudation†, denudation; decortication, depilation, excoriation, desquamation; molting; exfoliation; trichosis *[Med.]*.

V. divest; uncover &c *(cover)* &c 223; denude, bare, strip; disfurnish†; undress, disrobe &c *(dress, enrobe)* &c 225; uncoif†; dismantle; put off, take off, cast off; doff; peel, pare, decorticate, excoriate, skin, scalp, flay; expose, lay open; exfoliate, molt, mew; cast the skin.

Adj. divested &c *v.;* bare, naked, nude; undressed, undraped; denuded; exposed; in dishabille; bald, threadbare, ragged, callow, roofless.

in a state of nature, in nature's garb, in the buff, in native buff, in birthday suit; in puris naturalibus *[Lat.]*; with nothing on, stark naked, stark raving naked *[Joc.]*; bald as a coot, bare as the back of one's hand; out at elbows; barefoot; bareback, barebacked; leafless, napless†, hairless.

227. Circumjacence -- **N.** circumjacence†, circumambience†; environment, encompassment; atmosphere, medium, surroundings.

outpost; border &c *(edge)* 231; girdle &c *(circumference)* 230; outskirts, boulebards, suburbs, purlieus, precincts, faubourgs†, environs, entourage, banlieue†; neighborhood, vicinage, vicinity.

V. lie around &c *adv.;* surround, beset, compass, encompass, environ, inclose, enclose, encircle, embrace, circumvent, lap, gird; belt; begird, engird†; skirt, twine round; hem in &c *(circumscribe)* 229.

Adj. circumjacent, circumambient†, circumfluent†; ambient; surrounding &c *v.;* circumferential, suburban.

Adv. around, about; without; on every side; on all sides; right and left, all round, round about.

228. Interposition -- **N.** interposition, interjacence†, intercurrence†, intervenience†, interlocation†, interdigitation, interjection, interpolation, interlineation, interspersion, intercalation.

[interposition at a fine-grained level] interpenetration; permeation; infiltration.

[interposition by one person in another's affairs, at the intervenor's initiative] intervention, interference; intrusion, obtrusion; insinuation.

insertion &c 300; dovetailing; embolism.

intermediary, intermedium†; go between, bodkin†, intruder, interloper; parenthesis, episode, flyleaf.

partition, septum, diaphragm; midriff; dissepiment†; party wall, panel, room divider.

halfway house.

V. lie between, come between, get between; intervene, slide in, interpenetrate, permeate.

put between, introduce, import, throw in, wedge in, edge in, jam in, worm in, foist in, run in, plow in, work in; interpose, interject, intercalate, interpolate, interline, interleave, intersperse, interweave, interlard, interdigitate, sandwich in, fit in, squeeze in; let in, dovetail, splice, mortise; insinuate, smuggle; infiltrate, ingrain.

interfere, put in an oar, thrust one's nose in; intrude, obtrude; have a finger in the pie; introduce the thin end of the wedge; thrust in &c *(insert)* 300.

Adj. interjacent†, intercurrent†, intervenient†, intervening &c *v.*, intermediate, intermediary, intercalary, interstitial; embolismal†.

parenthetical, episodic; mediterranean; intrusive; embosomed†; merged.

Adv. between, betwixt; twixt; among, amongst; amid, amidst; mid, midst; in the thick of; betwixt and between; sandwich-wise; parenthetically, obiter dictum.

229. Circumscription -- N. circumscription, limitation, inclosure; confinement &c *(restraint)* 751; circumvallation†; encincture; envelope &c 232.

container *(receptacle)* 191.

V. circumscribe, limit, bound, confine, inclose; surround &c 227; compass about; imprison &c *(restrain)* 751; hedge in, wall in, rail in; fence round, fence in, hedge round; picket; corral.

enfold, bury, encase, incase†, pack up, enshrine, inclasp†; wrap up &c *(invest)* 225; embay†, embosom†.

containment *(inclusion)* 76.

Adj. circumscribed &c *v.;* begirt†, lapt†; buried in, immersed in; embosomed†, in the bosom of, imbedded, encysted, mewed up; imprisoned &c 751; landlocked, in a ring fence.

230. Outline -- **N.** outline, circumference; perimeter, periphery, ambit, circuit, lines tournure†, contour, profile, silhouette; bounds; coast line.

zone, belt, girth, band, baldric, zodiac, girdle, tyre *[Brit.]*, cingle†, clasp, girt; cordon &c *(inclosure)* 232; circlet, &c 247.

231. Edge -- **N.** edge, verge, brink, brow, brim, margin, border, confine, skirt, rim, flange, side, mouth; jaws, chops, chaps, fauces; lip, muzzle.

threshold, door, porch; portal &c *(opening)* 260; coast, shore.

frame, fringe, flounce, frill, list, trimming, edging, skirting, hem, selvedge, welt, furbelow, valance, gimp.

Adj. border, marginal, skirting; labial, labiated†, marginated†.

232. Inclosure -- **N.** inclosure, envelope; case &c *(receptacle)* 191; wrapper; girdle &c 230.

pen, fold; pen fold, in fold, sheep fold; paddock, pound; corral; yard; net, seine net.

wall, hedge, hedge row; espalier; fence &c *(defense)* 717; pale, paling, balustrade, rail, railing, quickset hedge, park paling, circumvallation†, enceinte, ring fence.

barrier, barricade; gate, gateway; bent, dingle *[U.S.]*; door, hatch, cordon; prison &c 752.

dike, dyke, ditch, fosse†, moat.

V. inclose, circumscribe &c 229.

233. Limit -- **N.** limit, boundary, bounds, confine, enclave, term, bourn, verge, curbstone†, but, pale, reservation; termination, terminus; stint, frontier, precinct, marches; backwoods.

boundary line, landmark; line of demarcation, line of circumvallation†; pillars of Hercules; Rubicon, turning point; ne plus ultra *[Lat.]*; sluice, floodgate.

Adj. definite; conterminate†, conterminable†; terminal, frontier; bordering.

Adv. thus far, thus far and no further.

Phr. stick to the reservation; go beyond the pale.

2. Special

234. Front -- N. front; fore, forepart; foreground; face, disk, disc, frontage; facade, proscenium, facia *[Lat.]*, frontispiece; anteriority[†]; obverse (of a medal or coin).

fore rank, front rank; van, vanguard; advanced guard; outpost; first line; scout.

brow, forehead, visage, physiognomy, phiz[†], countenance, mut *[Slang]*; rostrum, beak, bow, stem, prow, prore[†], jib.

pioneer &c *(precursor)* 64; metoposcopy[†].

V. be in front, stand in front &c *adj.;* front, face, confront; bend forwards; come to the front, come to the fore.

Adj. fore, anterior, front, frontal.

Adv. before; in front, in the van, in advance; ahead, right ahead; forehead, foremost; in the foreground, in the lee of; before one's face, before one's eyes; face to face, vis-a-vis; front a front.

Phr. formosa muta commendatio est *[Lat.]* [Syrus]; frons est animi janua *[Lat.]* [Cicero]; Human face divine [Milton]; imago animi vultus est indices oculi *[Lat.]* [Cicero]; sea of upturned faces [Scott].

235. Rear -- N. rear, back, posteriority; rear rank, rear guard; background, hinterland.

occiput *[Anat.]*, nape, chine; heels; tail, rump, croup, buttock, posteriors, backside scut[†], breech, dorsum, loin; dorsal region, lumbar region; hind quarters; aitchbone[†]; natch, natch bone.

stern, poop, afterpart[†], heelpiece[†], crupper.

wake; train &c *(sequence)* 281.

reverse; other side of the shield.

V. be behind &c *adv.;* fall astern; bend backwards; bring up the rear.

Adj. back, rear; hind, hinder, hindmost, hindermost[†]; postern, posterior; dorsal, after; caudal, lumbar; mizzen, tergal[†].

Adv. behind; in the rear, in the background; behind one's back; at the heels of, at the tail of, at the back of; back to back.

after, aft, abaft, astern, sternmost[†], aback, rearward.

Phr. ogni medaglia ha il suo rovescio *[It]*; the other side of the coin.

236. Laterality -- **N.** laterality†; side, flank, quarter, lee; hand; cheek, jowl, jole†, wing; profile; temple, parietes *[Lat.]*, loin, haunch, hip; beam.

gable, gable end; broadside; lee side.

points of the compass; East, Orient, Levant; West; orientation.

V. be on one side &c *adv.;* flank, outflank; sidle; skirt; orientate.

Adj. lateral, sidelong; collateral; parietal, flanking, skirting; flanked; sideling.

many sided; multilateral, bilateral, trilateral, quadrilateral.

Eastern; orient, oriental; Levantine; Western, occidental, Hesperian.

Adv. sideways, sidelong; broadside on; on one side, abreast, alongside, beside, aside; by the side of; side by side; cheek by jowl &c *(near)* 197; to windward, to leeward; laterally &c *adj.;* right and left; on her beam ends.

Phr. his cheek the may of days outworn [Shakespeare].

237. Contraposition -- **N.** contraposition†, opposition; polarity; inversion &c 218; opposite side; reverse, inverse; counterpart; antipodes; opposite poles, North and South.

antonym, opposite *(contrariety)* 14.

V. be opposite &c *adj.;* subtend.

Adj. opposite; reverse, inverse; converse, antipodal, subcontrary†; fronting, facing, diametrically opposite.

Northern, septentrional, Boreal, arctic; Southern, Austral, antarctic.

Adv. over, over the way, over against; against; face to face, vis-a-vis; as poles asunder.

238. Dextrality -- **N.** dextrality†; right, right hand; dexter, offside, starboard.

Adj. dextral, right-handed; dexter, dextrorsal†, dextrorse†; ambidextral†, ambidextrous; dextro-.

Adv. dextrad†, dextrally†.

239. Sinistrality -- **N.** sinistrality†; left, left hand, a gauche; sinister, nearside†, larboard, port.

Adj. left-handed; sinister; sinistral, sinistrorsal†, sinistrorse†, sinistrous†; laevo- *[Pref.]*.

Adv. sinistrally, sinistrously†.

SECTION III.

FORM

1. GENERAL FORM

240. Form -- **N.** form, figure, shape; conformation, configuration; make, formation, frame, construction, cut, set, build, trim, cut of one's jib; stamp, type, cast, mold; fashion; contour &c *(outline)* 230; structure &c 329; plasmature†.

feature, lineament, turn; phase &c *(aspect)* 448; posture, attitude, pose.

[Science of form] morphism.

[Similarity of form] isomorphism.

forming &c *v.;* formation, figuration, efformation†; sculpture; plasmation†.

V. form, shape, figure, fashion, efform[†], carve, cut, chisel, hew, cast; rough hew, rough cast; sketch; block out, hammer out; trim; lick into shape, put into shape; model, knead, work up into, set, mold, sculpture; cast, stamp; build &c *(construct)* 161.

Adj. formed &c *v..* *[Receiving form]* plastic, fictile[†]; formative; fluid.

[Giving form] plasmic[†].

[Similar in form] isomorphous.

[taking several forms] pleomorphic; protean; changeable, &c 149.

241. *[Absence of form.]* **Amorphism** --
N. amorphism[†], informity[†]; unlicked cub[†]; rudis indigestaque moles *[Lat.]*; disorder &c 59; deformity &c 243.

disfigurement, defacement; mutilation; deforming.

chaos, randomness *(disorder)* 59.

[taking form from surroundings] fluid &c 333.

V. deface *[Destroy form]*, disfigure, deform, mutilate, truncate; derange &c 61; blemish, mar.

Adj. shapeless, amorphous, formless; unformed, unhewn†, unfashioned†, unshaped, unshapen; rough, rude, Gothic, barbarous, rugged.

242. *[Regularity of form.]* **Symmetry** --
 N. symmetry, shapeliness, finish; beauty &c 845; proportion, eurythmy†, uniformity, parallelism; bilateral symmetry, trilateral symmetry, multilateral symmetry; centrality &c 222.

arborescence†, branching, ramification; arbor vitae.

Adj. symmetrical, shapely, well set, finished; beautiful &c 845; classic, chaste, severe.

regular, uniform, balanced; equal &c 27; parallel, coextensive.

arborescent†, arboriform†; dendriform†, dendroid†; branching; ramous†, ramose; filiciform†, filicoid†; subarborescent†; papilionaceous†.

fuji-shaped, fujigata *[Jap.]*.

243. *[Irregularity of form.]* **Distortion** --
 N. distortion, detortion†, contortion; twist, crookedness &c *(obliquity)* 217; grimace; deformity; malformation, malconformation†; harelip;

monstrosity, misproportion†, want of symmetry, anamorphosis†; ugliness &c 846; talipes†; teratology.

asymmetry; irregularity.

V. distort, contort, twist, warp, wrest, writhe, make faces, deform, misshape.

Adj. distorted &c *v.;* out of shape, irregular, asymmetric, unsymmetric†, awry, wry, askew, crooked; not true, not straight; on one side, crump†, deformed; harelipped; misshapen, misbegotten; misproportioned†, ill proportioned; ill-made; grotesque, monstrous, crooked as a ram's horn; camel backed, hump backed, hunch backed, bunch backed, crook backed; bandy; bandy legged, bow legged; bow kneed, knock kneed; splay footed, club footed; round shouldered; snub nosed; curtailed of one's fair proportions; stumpy &c *(short)* 201; gaunt &c *(thin)* 203; bloated &c 194; scalene; simous†; taliped†, talipedic†.

Adv. all manner of ways.

Phr. crooked as a Virginia fence *[U.S.]*.

2. SPECIAL FORM

244. Angularity -- N. angularity, angularness†; aduncity†; angle, cusp, bend; fold &c 258; notch &c 257; fork, bifurcation.

elbow, knee, knuckle, ankle, groin, crotch, crutch, crane, fluke, scythe, sickle, zigzag, kimbo†, akimbo.

corner, nook, recess, niche, oriel *[Arch.]*, coign†.

right angle &c *(perpendicular)* 216.1, 212; obliquity &c 217; angle of 45 degrees, miter; acute angle, obtuse angle, salient angle, reentering angle, spherical angle.

angular measurement, angular elevation, angular distance, angular velocity; trigonometry, goniometry; altimetry†; clinometer, graphometer†, goniometer; theodolite; sextant, quadrant; dichotomy.

triangle, trigon†, wedge; rectangle, square, lozenge, diamond; rhomb, rhombus; quadrangle, quadrilateral; parallelogram; quadrature; polygon, pentagon, hexagon, heptagon, octagon, oxygon†, decagon.

pyramid, cone.

Platonic bodies; cube, rhomboid; tetrahedron, pentahedron, hexahedron, octahedron, dodecahedron, icosahedron, eicosahedron; prism, pyramid; parallelopiped; curb roof, gambrel roof, mansard roof.

V. bend, fork, bifurcate, crinkle.

Adj. angular, bent, crooked, aduncous†, uncinated†, aquiline, jagged, serrated; falciform†, falcated†; furcated†, forked, bifurcate, zigzag; furcular†; hooked; dovetailed; knock kneed, crinkled, akimbo, kimbo†, geniculated†; oblique &c 217.

fusiform *[Micro.]*, wedge-shaped, cuneiform; cuneate†, multangular†, oxygonal†; triangular, trigonal†, trilateral; quadrangular, quadrilateral; foursquare; rectangular, square, multilateral; polygonal &c *n.;* cubical, rhomboid, rhomboidal, pyramidal.

245. Curvature -- N. curvature, curvity†, curvation†; incurvature†, incurvity†; incurvation†; bend; flexure, flexion, flection†; conflexure†; crook, hook, bought, bending; deflection, deflexion†; inflection, inflexion†; concameration†; arcuation†, devexity†, turn, deviation, detour, sweep; curl, curling; bough; recurvity†, recurvation†; sinuosity &c 248.

kink.

carve, arc, arch, arcade, vault, bow, crescent, half-moon, lunule†, horseshoe, loop, crane neck; parabola, hyperbola; helix, spiral; catenary†, festoon; conchoid†, cardioid; caustic; tracery; arched ceiling, arched roof; bay window, bow window.

sine curve; spline, spline curve, spline function; obliquity &c 217.

V. be curved, &c *adj.;* curve, sweep, sway, swag, sag; deviate &c 279; curl, turn; reenter.

render curved &c *adj.;* flex, bend, curve, incurvate†; inflect; deflect, scatter *[Phys.]*; refract *(light)* 420; crook; turn, round, arch, arcuate, arch over, concamerate†; bow, curl, recurve, frizzle.

rotundity &c 249; convexity &c 250.

Adj. curved &c *v.;* curviform†, curvilineal†, curvilinear; devex†, devious; recurved, recurvous†; crump†; bowed &c *v.;* vaulted, hooked; falciform†, falcated†; semicircular, crescentic; sinusoid *[Geom.]*, parabolic, paraboloid; luniform†, lunular†; semilunar, conchoidal†; helical, double helical, spiral; kinky; cordiform†, cordated†; cardioid; heart shaped, bell shaped, boat shaped, crescent shaped, lens shaped, moon shaped, oar shaped, shield shaped, sickle shaped, tongue shaped, pear shaped, fig shaped; kidney-shaped, reniform; lentiform†, lenticular; bow-legged &c *(distorted)* 243; oblique &c 217; circular &c 247.

aduncated†, arclike†, arcuate, arched, beaked; bicorn†, bicornuous†, bicornute†; clypeate†, clypeiform†; cymbiform†, embowed†, galeiform†; hamate†, hamiform†, hamous†; hooked; linguiform†, lingulate†; lobiform†, lunate, navicular†, peltate†, remiform†, rhamphoid†; rostrate†, rostriferous†, rostroid†; scutate†, scaphoid†, uncate†; unguiculate†, unguiform†.

246. Straightness -- **N.** straightness, rectilinearity†, directness; inflexibility &c *(stiffness)* 323; straight line, right line, direct line; short cut.

V. be straight &c *adj.;* have no turning; not incline to either side, not bend to either side, not turn to either side, not deviate to either side; go straight; steer for &c *(directions)* 278.

render straight, straighten, rectify; set straight, put straight; unbend, unfold, uncurl &c 248, unravel &c 219, unwrap.

Adj. straight; rectilinear, rectilineal†; direct, even, right, true, in a line; unbent, virgate† &c *v.;* undeviating, unturned, undistorted, unswerving; straight as an arrow &c *(direct)* 278; inflexible &c 323.

laser-straight; ramrod-straight.

247. *[Simple circularity.]* **Circularity** -- **N.** circularity, roundness; rotundity &c 249.

circle, circlet, ring, areola, hoop, roundlet†, annulus, annulet†, bracelet, armlet; ringlet; eye, loop, wheel; cycle, orb, orbit, rundle, zone, belt, cordon, band; contrate wheel†, crown wheel; hub; nave; sash, girdle, cestus†, cincture, baldric, fillet, fascia, wreath, garland; crown, corona, coronet, chaplet, snood, necklace, collar; noose, lasso, lassoo†.

ellipse, oval, ovule; ellipsoid, cycloid; epicycloid *[Geom.]*, epicycle; semicircle; quadrant, sextant, sector.

sphere &c 249.

V. make round &c *adj.;* round.

go round; encircle &c 227; describe a circle &c 311.

Adj. round, rounded, circular, annular, orbicular; oval, ovate; elliptic, elliptical; egg-shaped; pear-shaped &c 245; cycloidal &c *n.*†; spherical &c 249.

Phr. I watched the little circles die [Tennyson].

248. *[Complex curvature.]* **Convolution** --
 N. winding &c *v.;* convolution, involution, circumvolution; wave, undulation, tortuosity, anfractuosity†; sinuosity, sinuation†; meandering, circuit, circumbendibus†, twist, twirl, windings and turnings, ambages†; torsion; inosculation†;

reticulation &c *(crossing)* 219; rivulation†; roughness &c 256.

coil, roll, curl; buckle, spiral, helix, corkscrew, worm, volute, rundle; tendril; scollop†, scallop, escalop†; kink; ammonite, snakestone†.

serpent, eel, maze, labyrinth.

knot.

V. be convoluted &c *adj.;* wind, twine, turn and twist, twirl; wave, undulate, meander; inosculate†; entwine, intwine†; twist, coil, roll; wrinkle, curl, crisp, twill; frizzle; crimp, crape, indent, scollop†, scallop, wring, intort†; contort; wreathe &c *(cross)* 219.

Adj. convoluted; winding, twisted &c *v.;* tortile†, tortive†; wavy; undated, undulatory; circling, snaky, snake-like, serpentine; serpent, anguill†, vermiform; vermicular; mazy, tortuous, sinuous, flexuous, anfractuous†, reclivate†, rivulose†, scolecoid†; sigmoid, sigmoidal *[Geom.]*; spiriferous†, spiroid†; involved, intricate, complicated, perplexed; labyrinth, labyrinthic†, labyrinthian†, labyrinthine; peristaltic; daedalian†; kinky, knotted.

wreathy†, frizzly, crepe, buckled; raveled &c *(in disorder)* 59.

spiral, coiled, helical; cochleate, cochleous; screw-shaped; turbinated, turbiniform†.

Adv. in and out, round and round; a can of worms; Gordian knot.

249. Rotundity -- N. rotundity; roundness &c *adj.;* cylindricity†; sphericity, spheroidity†; globosity†.

cylinder, cylindroid†, cylindrical; barrel, drum; roll, roller; rouleau†, column, rolling-pin, rundle.

cone, conoid†; pear shape, egg shape, bell shape.

sphere, globe, ball, boulder, bowlder†; spheroid, ellipsoid; oblong spheroid; oblate spheroid, prolate spheroid; drop, spherule, globule, vesicle, bulb, bullet, pellet, pelote†, clew, pill, marble, pea, knob, pommel, horn; knot *(convolution)* 248.

curved surface, hypersphere; hyperdimensional surface.

V. render spherical &c *adj.;* form into a sphere, sphere, roll into a ball; give rotundity &c *n.;* round.

Adj. rotund; round &c *(circular)* 247; cylindric, cylindrical, cylindroid†; columnar, lumbriciform†; conic, conical; spherical, spheroidal; globular, globated†, globous†, globose; egg shaped, bell shaped, pear shaped; ovoid, oviform; gibbous; rixiform†; campaniform†, campanulate†, campaniliform†; fungiform†, bead-like, moniliform†, pyriform†, bulbous; tres atque rotundus *[Lat.]*; round as an orange, round as an apple, round as a ball, round as a billiard ball, round as a cannon ball.

3. SUPERFICIAL FORM

250. Convexity -- N. convexity, prominence, projection, swelling, gibbosity†, bilge, bulge, protuberance, protrusion; camber, cahot *[U.S.]*.

thank-ye-ma'am *[U.S.]*.

swell.

intumescence; tumour *[Brit.]*, tumor; tubercle, tuberosity *[Anat.]*; excrescence; hump, hunch, bunch.

boss, embossment, hub, hubble; *[convex body parts]* tooth *[U.S.]*, knob, elbow, process, apophysis†, condyle, bulb, node, nodule, nodosity†, tongue, dorsum, bump, clump; sugar loaf &c *(sharpness)* 253; bow; mamelon†; molar; belly, corporation†, pot belly, gut *[Coll.]*; withers, back, shoulder, lip, flange.

[convexities on skin] pimple, zit *[Slang]*; wen, wheel, papula *[Med.]*, pustule, pock, proud flesh, growth, sarcoma, caruncle†, corn, wart, pappiloma,

furuncle, polypus†, fungus, fungosity†, exostosis†, bleb, blister, blain†; boil &c *(disease)* 655; airbubble†, blob, papule, verruca.

[convex body parts on chest] papilla, nipple, teat, tit *[Vulg.]*, titty *[Vulg.]*, boob *[Vulg.]*, knocker *[Vulg.]*, pap, breast, dug, mammilla†.

[prominent convexity on the face] proboscis, nose, neb, beak, snout, nozzle, schnoz *[Coll.]*.

peg, button, stud, ridge, rib, jutty, trunnion, snag.

cupola, dome, arch, balcony, eaves; pilaster.

relief, relievo *[It]*, cameo; bassorilievo†, mezzorilevo†, altorivievo; low relief, bas relief *[Fr.]*, high relief.

hill &c *(height)* 206; cape, promontory, mull; forehead, foreland†; point of land, mole, jetty, hummock, ledge, spur; naze†, ness.

V. be prominent &c *adj.;* project, bulge, protrude, pout, bouge *[Fr.]*, bunch; jut out, stand out, stick out, poke out; stick up, bristle up, start up, cock up, shoot up; swell over, hang over, bend over; beetle.

render prominent &c *adj.;* raise 307; emboss, chase.

[become convex] belly out.

Adj. convex, prominent, protuberant, projecting &c *v.;* bossed, embossed, bossy, nodular, bunchy; clavate, clavated†, claviform; hummocky†, moutonne†, mammiliform†; papulous†, papilose†; hemispheric, bulbous; bowed, arched; bold; bellied; tuberous, tuberculous; tumous†; cornute†, odontoid†; lentiform†, lenticular; gibbous; club shaped, hubby *[U.S.]*, hubbly *[U.S.]*, knobby, papillose, saddle-shaped, selliform†, subclavate†, torose†, ventricose†, verrucose†.

salient, in relief, raised, repousse; bloated &c, *(expanded)* 194.

251. Flatness -- **N.** flatness &c *adj.;* smoothness &c 255.

plane; level &c 213; plate, platter, table, tablet, slab.

V. render flat, flatten; level &c 213.

Adj. flat, plane, even, flush, scutiform†, discoid; level &c *(horizontal)* 213; flat as a pancake, flat as a fluke, flat as a flounder, flat as a board, flat as my hand.

252. Concavity -- **N.** concavity, depression, dip; hollow, hollowness; indentation, intaglio, cavity, dent, dint, dimple, follicle, pit, sinus, alveolus†,

lacuna; excavation, strip mine; trough &c *(furrow)* 259; honeycomb.

cup, basin, crater, punch bowl; cell &c *(receptacle)* 191; socket.

valley, vale, dale, dell, dingle, combe†, bottom, slade†, strath†, glade, grove, glen, cave, cavern, cove; grot†, grotto; alcove, cul-de-sac; gully &c 198; arch &c *(curve)* 245; bay &c *(of the sea)* 343.

excavator, sapper, miner.

honeycomb *(sponge)* 252.1.

V. be concave &c *adj.;* retire, cave in.

render concave &c *adj.;* depress, hollow; scoop, scoop out; gouge, gouge out, dig, delve, excavate, dent, dint, mine, sap, undermine, burrow, tunnel, stave in.

Adj. depressed &c *v.;* alveolate†, calathiform†, cup-shaped, dishing; favaginous†, faveolate†, favose†; scyphiform†, scyphose†; concave, hollow, stove in; retiring; retreating; cavernous; porous &c *(with holes)* 260; infundibul†, infundibular†, infundibuliform†; funnel shaped, bell shaped; campaniform†, capsular; vaulted, arched.

252a Sponge -- **N.** sponge, honeycomb, network; frit *[Chem]*, filter.

sieve, net, screen *(opening)* 260.

Adj. cellular, spongy, spongious†; honeycombed, alveolar; sintered; porous *(opening)* 260.

253. Sharpness -- **N.** sharpness &c *adj.;* acuity, acumination†; spinosity†.

point, spike, spine, spicule *[Biol.]*, spiculum†; needle, hypodermic needle, tack, nail, pin; prick, prickle; spur, rowel, barb; spit, cusp; horn, antler; snag; tag thorn, bristle; Adam's needle†, bear grass *[U.S.]*, tine, yucca.

nib, tooth, tusk; spoke, cog, ratchet.

crag, crest, arete *[Fr.]*, cone peak, sugar loaf, pike, aiguille†; spire, pyramid, steeple.

beard, chevaux de frise *[Fr.]*, porcupine, hedgehog, brier, bramble, thistle; comb; awn, beggar's lice, bur, burr, catchweed†, cleavers, clivers†, goose, grass, hairif†, hariff, flax comb, hackle, hatchel†, heckle.

wedge; knife edge, cutting edge; blade, edge tool, cutlery, knife, penknife, whittle, razor, razor blade, safety razor, straight razor, electric razor; scalpel; bistoury†, lancet; plowshare, coulter, colter†; hatchet, ax, pickax, mattock, pick, adze, gill; billhook, cleaver, cutter; scythe, sickle; scissors, shears, pruning shears, cutters, wire cutters, nail clipper, paper cutter; sword &c *(arms)* 727; bodkin &c *(perforator)* 262; belduque†, bowie knife†, paring knife; bushwhacker *[U.S.]*; drawing knife, drawing shave; microtome *[Micro.]*; chisel, screwdriver blade; flint blade; guillotine.

sharpener, hone, strop; grindstone, whetstone; novaculite†; steel, emery.

V. be sharp &c *adj.;* taper to a point; bristle with.

render sharp &c *adj.;* sharpen, point, aculeate, whet, barb, spiculate†, set, strop, grind; chip (flint).

cut &c *(sunder)* 44.

Adj. sharp, keen; acute; acicular, aciform†; aculeated†, acuminated†; pointed; tapering; conical, pyramidal; mucronate†, mucronated†; spindle shaped, needle shaped; spiked, spiky, ensiform†, peaked, salient; cusped, cuspidate, cuspidated†; cornute†, cornuted†, cornicultate†; prickly; spiny, spinous†, spicular; thorny, bristling, muricated†, pectinated†, studded, thistly, briary†; craggy &c *(rough)* 256; snaggy, digitated†, two-edged, fusiform *[Micro.]*; dentiform†, denticulated; toothed; odontoid†; starlike; stellated†, stelliform†; sagittate†, sagittiform†; arrowheaded†; arrowy†, barbed, spurred.

acinaciform; apiculate†, apiculated†; aristate†, awned, awny†, bearded, calamiform†, cone-shaped, coniform†, crestate†, echinate†, gladiate†; lanceolate†, lanciform; awl, awl-shaped, lance-shaped, awl-shaped, scimitar-shaped, sword-shaped; setarious†, spinuliferous†, subulate†, tetrahedral, xiphoid†.

cutting; sharp edged, knife edged; sharp as a razor, keen as a razor; sharp as a needle, sharp as a tack; sharpened &c v.; set

254. Bluntness -- N. bluntness &c *adj..*

V. be blunt, render blunt &c *adj.;* obtund†, dull; take off the point, take off the edge; turn.

Adj. blunt, obtuse, dull, bluff; edentate, toothless.

255. Smoothness -- N. smoothness &c *adj.;* polish, gloss; lubricity, lubrication.

[smooth materials] down, velvet, velure, silk, satin; velveteen, velour, velours, velumen†; glass, ice.

slide; bowling green &c *(level)* 213; asphalt, wood pavement, flagstone, flags.

[objects used to smooth other objects] roller, steam roller, lawn roller, rolling pin, rolling mill; sand

paper, emery paper, emery cloth, sander; flat iron, sad iron; burnisher, turpentine and beeswax; polish, shoe polish.

[art of cutting and polishing gemstones] lapidary.

[person who polishes gemstones] lapidary, lapidarian.

V. smooth, smoothen†; plane; file; mow, shave; level, roll; macadamize; polish, burnish, calender†, glaze; iron, hot-press, mangle; lubricate &c *(oil)* 332.

Adj. smooth; polished &c *v.;* leiodermatous†, slick, velutinous†; even; level &c 213; plane &c *(flat)* 251; sleek, glossy; silken, silky; lanate†, downy, velvety; glabrous, slippery, glassy, lubricous, oily, soft, unwrinkled†; smooth as glass, smooth as ice, smooth as monumental alabaster, smooth as velvet, smooth as oil; slippery as an eel; woolly &c *(feathery)* 256.

Phr. smooth as silk; slippery as coonshit on a pump handle; slippery as a greased pig.

256. Roughness -- **N.** roughness &c *adj.;* tooth, grain, texture, ripple; asperity, rugosity†, salebrosity†, corrugation, nodosity†; arborescence† &c 242; pilosity†.

brush, hair, beard, shag, mane, whisker, moustache, imperial, tress, lock, curl, ringlet; fimbriae, pili, cilia, villi; lovelock; beaucatcher†; curl paper; goatee; papillote, scalp lock.

plumage, plumosity†; plume, panache, crest; feather, tuft, fringe, toupee.

wool, velvet, plush, nap, pile, floss, fur, down; byssus†, moss, bur; fluff.

knot *(convolution)* 248.

V. be rough &c *adj.;* go against the grain.

render-rough &c *adj.;* roughen, ruffle, crisp, crumple, corrugate, set on edge, stroke the wrong way, rumple.

Adj. rough, uneven, scabrous, scaly, knotted; rugged, rugose†, rugous†; knurly†; asperous†, crisp, salebrous†, gnarled, unpolished, unsmooth†, roughhewn†; craggy, cragged; crankling†, scraggy; prickly &c *(sharp)* 253; arborescent &c 242 [Obs.]; leafy, well-wooded; feathery; plumose, plumigerous†; laciniate†, laciniform†, laciniose†; pappose†; pileous†, pilose†; trichogenous†, trichoid *[Med.]*; tufted, fimbriated, hairy, ciliated, filamentous, hirsute; crinose†, crinite†; bushy, hispid, villous, pappous†, bearded, pilous†, shaggy, shagged; fringed, befringed†; setous†, setose†, setaceous; like quills upon the fretful porcupine [Hamlet]; rough as a nutmeg grater, rough as a bear.

downy, velvety, flocculent, woolly; lanate†, lanated†; lanuginous†, lanuginose†; tomentose†; fluffy.

Adv. against the grain.

Phr. cabello luengo y corto el seso *[Sp.]*.

257. Notch -- **N.** notch, dent, nick, cut; indent, indentation; dimple.

embrasure, battlement, machicolation†; saw, tooth, crenelle†, scallop, scollop†, vandyke; depression; jag.

V. notch, nick, cut, dent, indent, jag, scarify, scotch, crimp, scallop, scollop†, crenulate†, vandyke.

Adj. notched &c *v.;* crenate†, crenated†; dentate, dentated; denticulate, denticulated; toothed, palmated†, serrated.

258. Fold -- **N.** fold, plicature†, plait, pleat, ply, crease; tuck, gather; flexion, flexure, joint, elbow, double, doubling, duplicature†, gather, wrinkle, rimple†, crinkle, crankle†, crumple, rumple, rivel†, ruck†, ruffle, dog's ear, corrugation, frounce†, flounce, lapel; pucker, crow's feet; plication†.

V. fold, double, plicate†, plait, crease, wrinkle, crinkle, crankle†, curl, cockle up, cocker, rimple†, rumple, flute, frizzle, frounce†, rivel†, twill, corrugate, ruffle, crimple†, crumple, pucker; turn down, double down, down under; tuck, ruck†, hem, gather.

Adj. folded, fluted, pleated &c *v.*.

259. Furrow -- N. furrow, groove, rut, sulcus *[Anat.]*, scratch, streak, striae, crack, score, incision, slit; chamfer, fluting; corduroy road, cradle hole.

channel, gutter, trench, ditch, dike, dyke; moat, fosse†, trough, kennel; ravine &c *(interval)* 198; tajo *[U.S.]*, thank-ye-ma'am *[U.S.]*.

V. furrow &c *n.;* flute, plow; incise, engrave, etch, bite in.

Adj. furrowed &c *v.;* ribbed, striated, sulcated *[Anat.]*, fluted, canaliculated†; bisulcous†, bisulcate†, bisulcated†; canaliferous†; trisulcate†; corduroy; unisulcate†; costate†, rimiform†.

260. Opening -- N. hole, foramen; puncture, perforation; fontanel†; transforation†; pinhole, keyhole, loophole, porthole, peephole, mousehole, pigeonhole; eye of a needle; eyelet; slot.

opening; aperture, apertness†; hiation†, yawning, oscitancy†, dehiscence, patefaction†, pandiculation†; chasm &c *(interval)* 198.

embrasure, window, casement; abatjour†; light; sky light, fan light; lattice; bay window, bow window; oriel *[Arch.]*; dormer, lantern.

outlet, inlet; vent, vomitory; embouchure; orifice, mouth, sucker, muzzle, throat, gullet, weasand†, wizen, nozzle; placket.

portal, porch, gate, ostiary†, postern, wicket, trapdoor, hatch, door; arcade; cellarway†, driveway, gateway, doorway, hatchway, gangway; lich gate†.

way, path &c 627; thoroughfare; channel; passage, passageway; tube, pipe; water pipe &c 350; air pipe &c 351; vessel, tubule, canal, gut, fistula; adjutage†, ajutage†; ostium†; smokestack; chimney, flue, tap, funnel, gully, tunnel, main; mine, pit, adit†, shaft; gallery.

alley, aisle, glade, vista.

bore, caliber; pore; blind orifice; fulgurite†, thundertube†.

porousness, porosity.

sieve, cullender†, colander; cribble†, riddle, screen; honeycomb.

apertion†, perforation; piercing &c v.; terebration†, empalement†, pertusion†, puncture, acupuncture, penetration.

key &c 631, opener, master key, password, combination, passe-partout.

V. open, ope†, gape, yawn, bilge; fly open.

perforate, pierce, empierce†, tap, bore, drill; mine &c *(scoop out)* 252; tunnel; transpierce†, transfix; enfilade, impale, spike, spear, gore, spit, stab, pink, puncture, lance, stick, prick, riddle, punch; stave in.

cut a passage through; make way for, make room for.

uncover, unclose, unrip†; lay open, cut open, rip open, throw open, pop open, blow open, pry open, tear open, pull open.

Adj. open; perforated &c v.; perforate; wide open, ajar, unclosed, unstopped; oscitant†, gaping, yawning; patent.

tubular, cannular†, fistulous; pervious, permeable; foraminous†; vesicular, vasicular†; porous, follicular, cribriform†, honeycombed, infundibular†, riddled; tubulous†, tubulated†; piped, tubate†.

opening &c v.; aperient†.

Int. open sesame!,

261. Closure -- **N.** closure, occlusion, blockade; shutting up &c *v.;* obstruction &c *(hindrance)* 706; embolus; contraction &c 195; infarction; constipation, obstipation†; blind alley, blind corner; keddah†; cul-de-sac, caecum; imperforation†, imperviousness &c *adj.;* impermeability; stopper &c 263.

V. close, occlude, plug; block up, stop up, fill up, bung up, cork up, button up, stuff up, shut up, dam up; blockade, obstruct &c *(hinder)* 706; bar, bolt, stop, seal, plumb; choke, throttle; ram down, dam, cram; trap, clinch; put to the door, shut the door.

Adj. closed &c *v.;* shut, operculated†; unopened.

unpierced†, imporous†, caecal *[Med.]*; closable; imperforate, impervious, impermeable; impenetrable; impassable, unpassable†; invious†; pathless, wayless†; untrodden, untrod.

unventilated; air tight, water tight; hermetically sealed; tight, snug.

262. Perforator -- **N.** perforator, piercer, borer, auger, chisel, gimlet, stylet†, drill, wimble†, awl, bradawl, scoop, terrier, corkscrew, dibble, trocar *[Med.]*, trepan, probe, bodkin, needle, stiletto, rimer, warder, lancet; punch, puncheon; spikebit†, gouge; spear &c *(weapon)* 727; puncher; punching machine, punching press; punch pliers.

263. Stopper -- **N.** stopper, stopple; plug, cork, bung, spike, spill, stopcock, tap; rammer†; ram, ramrod; piston; stop-gap; wadding, stuffing, padding, stopping, dossil†, pledget†, tompion†, tourniquet.

cover &c 223; valve, vent peg, spigot, slide valve.

janitor, doorkeeper, porter, warder, beadle, cerberus, ostiary†.

SECTION IV.

MOTION

1. MOTION IN GENERAL

264. *[Successive change of place.]* **Motion** -- **N.** motion, movement, move; going &c *v.;* unrest.

stream, flow, flux, run, course, stir; evolution; kinematics; telekinesis.

step, rate, pace, tread, stride, gait, port, footfall, cadence, carriage, velocity, angular velocity; clip, progress, locomotion; journey &c 266; voyage &c 267; transit &c 270.

restlessness &c *(changeableness)* 149; mobility; movableness, motive power; laws of motion; mobilization.

V. be in motion &c *adj.;* move, go, hie, gang, budge, stir, pass, flit; hover about, hover round, hover about; shift, slide, glide; roll, roll on; flow, stream, run, drift, sweep along; wander &c*(deviate)* 279; walk &c 266; change one's place, shift one's place, change one's quarters, shift one's quarters; dodge; keep going, keep moving; put in motion, set in motion; move; impel &c 276; propel &c 284; render movable, mobilize.

Adj. moving &c *v.;* in motion; transitional; motory†, motive; shifting, movable, mobile, mercurial, unquiet; restless &c *(changeable)* 149; nomadic &c 266; erratic &c 279.

Adv. under way; on the move, on the wing, on the tramp, on the march.

Phr. eppur si muove [Galileo]; es bildet ein Talent sich in der Stille *[G.]*, sich ein Charakter in dem Strom der Welt *[G.]*.

265. Quiescence -- N. rest; stillness
&c *adj.;* quiescence; stagnation, stagnancy; fixity, immobility, catalepsy; indisturbance†; quietism.

quiet, tranquility, calm; repose &c 687; peace; dead calm, anticyclone†; statue-like repose; silence &c 203; not a breath of air, not a mouse stirring; sleep &c *(inactivity)* 683.

pause, lull &c *(cessation)* 142; stand still; standing still &c *v.;* lock; dead lock, dead stop, dead stand; full stop; fix; embargo.

resting place; gite *[Fr.]*; bivouac; home &c *(abode)* 189; pillow &c *(support)* 215; haven &c *(refuge)* 666; goal &c *(arrival)* 292.

V. be quiescent &c *adj.;* stand still, lie still; keep quiet, repose, hold the breath.

remain, stay; stand, lie to, ride at anchor, remain in situ, tarry, mark time; bring to, heave to, lay to; pull up, draw up; hold, halt; stop, stop short; rest, pause, anchor; cast to an anchor, come to an anchor; rest on one's oars; repose on one's laurels, take breath; stop &c *(discontinue)* 142.

stagnate; quieta non movere *[Lat.]*; let alone; abide, rest and be thankful; keep within doors, stay at home, go to bed.

dwell &c *(be present)* 186; settle &c *(be located)* 184; alight &c *(arrive)* 292; stick, stick fast;

stand like a post; not stir a peg, not stir a step; be at a stand &c *n.*. quell, becalm, hush, stay, lull to sleep, lay an embargo on.

Adj. quiescent, still; motionless, moveless; fixed; stationary; immotile; at rest at a stand, at a standstill, at anchor; stock, still; standing still &c *v.;* sedentary, untraveled, stay-at-home; becalmed, stagnant, quiet; unmoved, undisturbed, unruffled; calm, restful; cataleptic; immovable &c *(stable)* 150; sleeping &c *(inactive)* 683; silent &c 403; still as a statue, still as a post, still as a mouse, still as death; vegetative, vegetating.

Adv. at a stand &c *adj.;* tout court; at the halt.

Int. stop!, stay!, avast!, halt!, hold hard!, whoa!, hold!, sabr karo![†].

Phr. requiescat in pace *[Lat.]*; Deus nobis haec otia fecit *[Lat.]* [Vergil]; the noonday quiet holds the hill [Tennyson].

266. *[Locomotion by land.]* **Journey** -- **N.** travel; traveling &c *v.*. wayfaring, campaigning.

journey, excursion, expedition, tour, trip, grand tour, circuit, peregrination, discursion[†], ramble, pilgrimage, hajj, trek, course, ambulation[†], march, walk, promenade, constitutional, stroll, saunter, tramp, jog trot, turn, stalk, perambulation;

noctambulation†, noctambulism; somnambulism; outing, ride, drive, airing, jaunt.

equitation, horsemanship, riding, manege *[Fr.]*, ride and tie; basophobia†.

roving, vagrancy, pererration†; marching and countermarching; nomadism; vagabondism, vagabondage; hoboism *[U.S.]*; gadding; flit, flitting, migration; emigration, immigration, demigration†, intermigration†; wanderlust.

plan, itinerary, guide; handbook, guidebook, road book; Baedeker†, Bradshaw, Murray; map, road map, transportation guide, subway map.

procession, cavalcade, caravan, file, cortege, column.

[Organs and instruments of locomotion] vehicle &c 272; automobile, train, bus, airplane, plane, autobus, omnibus, subway, motorbike, dirt bike, off-road vehicle, van, minivan, motor scooter, trolley, locomotive; legs, feet, pegs, pins, trotters.

traveler &c 268.

depot *[U.S.]*, railway station, station.

V. travel, journey, course; take a journey, go a journey; take a walk, go out for walk &c *n.;* have a run; take the air.

flit, take wing; migrate, emigrate; trek; rove, prowl, roam, range, patrol, pace up and down, traverse; scour the country, traverse the country; peragrate†; circumambulate, perambulate; nomadize†, wander, ramble, stroll, saunter, hover, go one's rounds, straggle; gad, gad about; expatiate.

walk, march, step, tread, pace, plod, wend, go by shank's mare; promenade; trudge, tramp; stalk, stride, straddle, strut, foot it, hoof it, stump, bundle, bowl along, toddle; paddle; tread a path.

take horse, ride, drive, trot, amble, canter, prance, fisk†, frisk, caracoler†, caracole; gallop &c *(move quickly)* 274.

[start riding] embark, board, set out, hit the road, get going, get underway.

peg on, jog on, wag on, shuffle on; stir one's stumps; bend one's steps, bend one's course; make one's way, find one's way, wend one's way, pick one's way, pick one's way, thread one's way, plow one's way; slide, glide, coast, skim, skate; march in procession, file on, defile.

go to, repair to, resort to, hie to, betake oneself to.

Adj. traveling &c *v.;* ambulatory, itinerant, peripatetic, roving, rambling, gadding, discursive, vagrant, migratory, monadic; circumforanean†, circumforaneous†; noctivagrant†, mundivagrant; locomotive.

wayfaring, wayworn; travel-stained.

Adv. on foot, on horseback, on Shanks's mare; by the Marrowbone stage: in transitu &c 270 [Lat.]; en route &c 282.

Int. come along!,

267. *[Locomotion by water, or air.]* **Navigation** --
 N. navigation; aquatics; boating, yachting; ship &c 273; oar, paddle, screw, sail, canvas, aileron.

natation†, swimming; fin, flipper, fish's tail.

aerostation†, aerostatics†, aeronautics; balloonery†; balloon &c 273; ballooning, aviation, airmanship; flying, flight, volitation†; wing, pinion; rocketry, space travel, astronautics, orbital mechanics, orbiting.

voyage, sail, cruise, passage, circumnavigation, periplus†; headway, sternway, leeway; fairway.

mariner &c 269.

flight, trip; shuttle, run, airlift.

V. sail; put to sea &c *(depart)* 293; take ship, get under way; set sail, spread sail, spread canvas; gather way, have way on; make sail, carry sail; plow the waves, plow the deep, plow the main, plow the ocean; walk the waters.

navigate, warp, luff†, scud, boom, kedge; drift, course, cruise, coast; hug the shore, hug the land; circumnavigate.

ply the oar, row, paddle, pull, scull, punt, steam.

swim, float; buffet the waves, ride the storm, skim, effleurer *[Fr.]*, dive, wade.

fly, be wafted, hover, soar, flutter, jet, orbit, rocket; take wing, take a flight, take off, ascend, blast off, land, alight; wing one's flight, wing one's way; aviate; parachute, jump, glide.

Adj. sailing &c *v.;* volant†, aerostatic†; seafaring, nautical, maritime, naval; seagoing, coasting; afloat; navigable; aerial, aeronautic; grallatory†.

Adv. under way, under sail, under canvas, under steam; on the wing, in flight, in orbit.

Phr. bon voyage; spread the thin oar and catch the driving gale [Pope].

268. Traveler -- N. traveler, wayfarer, voyager, itinerant, passenger, commuter.

tourist, excursionist, explorer, adventurer, mountaineer, hiker, backpacker, Alpine Club; peregrinator†, wanderer, rover, straggler, rambler; bird of passage; gadabout, gadling†; vagrant, scatterling†, landloper†, waifs and estrays†, wastrel, foundling; loafer; tramp, tramper; vagabond, nomad, Bohemian, gypsy, Arab†, Wandering Jew, Hadji, pilgrim, palmer; peripatetic; somnambulist, emigrant, fugitive, refugee; beach comber, booly†; globegirdler†, globetrotter; vagrant, hobo *[U.S.]*, night walker, sleep walker; noctambulist, runabout, straphanger, swagman, swagsman *[Austral.]*; trecker†, trekker, zingano†, zingaro†.

runner, courier; Mercury, Iris, Ariel†, comet.

pedestrian, walker, foot passenger; cyclist; wheelman.

rider, horseman, equestrian, cavalier, jockey, roughrider, trainer, breaker.

driver, coachman, whip, Jehu, charioteer, postilion, postboy†, carter, wagoner, drayman†; cabman, cabdriver; voiturier†, vetturino†, condottiere†; engine driver; stoker, fireman, guard; chauffeur, conductor, engineer, gharry-wallah†, gari-wala†, hackman, syce†, truckman†.

Phr. on the road

269. Mariner -- N. sailor, mariner, navigator; seaman, seafarer, seafaring man; dock walloper *[Slang]*; tar, jack tar, salt, able seaman, A. B.; man-of-war's man, bluejacket, galiongee†, galionji†, marine, jolly, midshipman, middy; skipper; shipman†, boatman, ferryman, waterman†, lighterman†, bargeman, longshoreman; bargee†, gondolier; oar, oarsman; rower; boatswain, cockswain†; coxswain; steersman, pilot; crew.

aerial navigator, aeronaut, balloonist, Icarus; aeroplanist†, airman, aviator, birdman, man-bird, wizard of the air, aviatrix, flier, pilot, test pilot, glider pilot, bush pilot, navigator, flight attendant, steward, stewardess, crew; astronaut, cosmonaut; parachutist, paratrooper.

270. Transference -- N. transfer, transference; translocation, elocation†; displacement; metastasis, metathesis; removal; remotion†, amotion†; relegation; deportation, asportation†; extradition, conveyance, draft, carrying, carriage; convection, conduction, contagion; transfer &c *(of property)* 783.

transit, transition; passage, ferry, gestation; portage, porterage†, carting, cartage; shoveling &c *v.;* vection†, vecture†, vectitation†; shipment, freight, wafture†; transmission, transport, transportation, importation, exportation, transumption†, transplantation, translation; shifting, dodging; dispersion &c 73; transposition &c *(interchange)* 148; traction &c 285.

[Thing transferred] drift.

V. transfer, transmit, transport, transplace†, transplant, translocate; convey, carry, bear, fetch and carry; carry over, ferry over; hand pass, forward; shift; conduct, convoy, bring, fetch, reach; tote *[U.S.]*; port, import, export.

send, delegate, consign, relegate, turn over to, deliver; ship, embark; waft; shunt; transpose &c *(interchange)* 148; displace &c 185; throw &c 284; drag &c 285; mail, post.

shovel, ladle, decant, draft off, transfuse, infuse, siphon.

Adj. transferred &c *v.;* drifted, movable; portable, portative†; mailable *[U.S.]*; contagious.

Adv. from hand to hand, from pillar to post.

on the way, by the way; on the road, on the wing, under way, in transit, on course; as one goes; in transitu *[Lat.]*, en route, chemin faisant *[Fr.]*, en passant *[Fr.]*, in mid progress, in mid course.

271. Carrier -- **N.** carrier, porter, bearer, tranter[†], conveyer; cargador[†]; express, expressman; stevedore, coolie; conductor, locomotive, motor.

beast, beast of burden, cattle, horse, nag, palfrey, Arab[†], blood horse, thoroughbred, galloway[†], charger, courser, racer, hunter, jument[†], pony, filly, colt, foal, barb, roan, jade, hack, bidet, pad, cob, tit, punch, roadster, goer[†]; racehorse, pack horse, draft horse, cart horse, dray horse, post horse; ketch; Shetland pony, shelty, sheltie; garran[†], garron[†]; jennet, genet[†], bayard[†], mare, stallion, gelding; bronco, broncho[†], cayuse *[U.S.]*; creature, critter *[U.S.]*; cow pony, mustang, Narraganset, waler[†]; stud.

Pegasus, Bucephalus, Rocinante.

ass, donkey, jackass, mule, hinny; sumpter horse, sumpter mule; burro, cuddy[†], ladino *[U.S.]*; reindeer; camel, dromedary, llama, elephant; carrier pigeon.

[object used for carrying] pallet, brace, cart, dolley; support &c 215; fork lift.

carriage &c *(vehicle)* 272; ship &c 273.

Adj. equine, asinine.

272. Vehicle -- N. vehicle, conveyance, carriage, caravan, van; common carrier; wagon, waggon†, wain, dray, cart, lorry.

truck, tram; cariole, carriole†; limber, tumbrel, pontoon; barrow; wheel barrow, hand barrow; perambulator; Bath chair, wheel chair, sedan chair; chaise; palankeen†, palanquin; litter, brancard†, crate, hurdle, stretcher, ambulance; black Maria; conestoga wagon, conestoga wain; jinrikisha, ricksha, brett†, dearborn *[U.S.]*, dump cart, hack, hackery†, jigger, kittereen†, mailstate†, manomotor†, rig, rockaway†, prairie schooner *[U.S.]*, shay, sloven, team, tonga†, wheel; hobbyhorse, go-cart; cycle; bicycle, bike, two-wheeler; tricycle, velocipede, quadricycle†.

equipage, turn-out; coach, chariot, phaeton, break, mail phaeton, wagonette, drag, curricle†, tilbury†, whisky, landau, barouche, victoria, brougham, clarence†, calash, caleche *[Fr.]*, britzka†, araba†, kibitka†; berlin; sulky, desobligeant *[Fr.]*, sociable, vis-a-vis, dormeuse *[Fr.]*; jaunting car, outside car; dandi†; doolie†, dooly†; munchil†, palki†; roller skates, skate; runabout; ski; tonjon†; vettura†.

post chaise, diligence, stage; stage coach, mail coach, hackney coach, glass coach; stage wagon, car, omnibus, fly, cabriolet†, cab, hansom, shofle†, four-wheeler, growler, droshki†, drosky†.

dogcart, trap, whitechapel, buggy, four-in-hand, unicorn, random, tandem; shandredhan†, char-a-bancs *[Fr.]*.

motor car, automobile, limousine, car, auto, jalopy, clunker, lemon, flivver, coupe, sedan, two-door sedan, four-door sedan, luxury sedan; wheels *[Coll.]*, sports car, roadster, gran turismo*[It]*, jeep, four-wheel drive vehicle, electric car, steamer; golf cart, electric wagon; taxicab, cab, taxicoach†, checker cab, yellow cab; station wagon, family car; motorcycle, motor bike, side car; van, minivan, bus, minibus, microbus; truck, wagon, pick-up wagon, pick-up, tractor-trailer, road train, articulated vehicle; racing car, racer, hot rod, stock car, souped-up car.

bob, bobsled, bobsleigh†; cutter; double ripper, double runner *[U.S.]*; jumper, sled, sledge, sleigh, toboggan.

train; accommodation train, passenger train, express trail, special train, corridor train, parliamentary train, luggage train, freight train, goods train; 1st class train, 2nd class train, 3rd class train, 1st class carriage, 2nd class carriage, 3rd class carriage, 1st class compartment, 2nd class compartment, 3rd class compartment; rolling stock; horse box, cattle truck; baggage car, express car, freight car, parlor car, dining car, Pullman car, sleeping car, sleeper, dome car; surface car, tram car, trolley car; box car, box wagon; horse car *[U.S.]*; bullet train, shinkansen*[Jap.]*, cannonball, the Wabash cannonball, lightning express; luggage van; mail, mail car, mail van.

shovel, spool, spatula, ladle, hod, hoe; spade, spaddle†, loy†; spud; pitchfork; post hole digger.

[powered construction vehicles] tractor, steamshovel, backhoe, fork lift, earth mover, dump truck, bulldozer, grader, caterpillar, trench digger, steamroller; pile driver; crane, wrecking crane.

273. Ship -- **N.** ship, vessel, sail; craft, bottom.

navy, marine, fleet, flotilla; shipping.

man of war &c *(combatant)* 726; transport, tender, storeship†; merchant ship, merchantman; packet, liner; whaler, slaver, collier, coaster, lighter; fishing boat, pilot boat; trawler, hulk; yacht; baggala†; floating hotel, floating palace; ocean greyhound.

ship, bark, barque, brig, snow, hermaphrodite brig; brigantine, barkantine†; schooner; topsail schooner, for and aft schooner, three masted schooner; chasse-maree *[Fr.]*; sloop, cutter, corvette, clipper, foist, yawl, dandy, ketch, smack, lugger, barge, hoy†, cat, buss; sailer, sailing vessel; windjammer; steamer, steamboat, steamship, liner, ocean liner, cruiseship, ship of the line; mail steamer, paddle steamer, screw steamer; tug; line of steamers &c. destroyer, cruiser, frigate; landing ship, LST; aircraft carrier, carrier, flattop *[Coll.]*, nuclear powered carrier; submarine, submersible, atomic submarine.

boat, pinnace, launch; life boat, long boat, jolly boat, bum boat, fly boat, cock boat, ferry boat, canal boat; swamp boat, ark, bully, battery, bateau *[Can.]*, broadhorn†, dory, droger†, drogher; dugout, durham boat, flatboat, galiot†; shallop†, gig, funny, skiff, dingy, scow, cockleshell, wherry, coble†, punt, cog, kedge, lerret†; eight oar, four oar, pair oar; randan†; outrigger; float, raft, pontoon; prame†; iceboat, ice canoe, ice yacht.

catamaran, hydroplane, hovercraft, coracle, gondola, carvel†, caravel; felucca, caique†, canoe, birch bark canoe, dugout canoe; galley, galleyfoist†; bilander†, dogger†, hooker, howker†; argosy, carack†; galliass†, galleon; polacca†, polacre†, tartane†, junk, lorcha†, praam†, proa†, prahu†, saick†, sampan, xebec, dhow; dahabeah†; nuggah†; kayak, keel boat *[U.S.]*, log canoe, pirogue; quadrireme†, trireme; sternwheeler *[U.S.]*; wanigan†, wangan *[U.S.]*, wharf boat.

balloon; airship, aeroplane; biplane, monoplane, triplane†; hydroplane; aerodrome; air balloon, pilot balloon, fire balloon, dirigible, zeppelin; aerostat, Montgolfier; kite, parachute.

jet plane, rocket plane, jet liner, turbojet, prop-jet, propeller plane; corporate plane, corporate jet, private plane, private aviation; airline, common carrier; fighter, bomber, fighter-bomber, escort plane, spy plane; supersonic aircraft, subsonic aircraft.

Adv. afloat, aboard; on board, on ship board; hard a lee, hard a port, hard a starboard, hard a weather.

2. DEGREES OF MOTION

274. Velocity -- **N.** velocity, speed, celerity; swiftness &c *adj.;* rapidity, eagle speed; expedition &c *(activity)* 682; pernicity†; acceleration; haste &c 684.

spurt, rush, dash, race, steeple chase; smart rate, lively rate, swift rate &c *adj.;* rattling rate, spanking rate, strapping rate, smart pace, lively pace, swift pace, rattling pace, spanking pace, strapping pace; round pace; flying, flight.

lightning, greased lightning, light, electricity, wind; cannon ball, rocket, arrow, dart, hydrargyrum *[Lat.]*, quicksilver; telegraph, express train; torrent.

eagle, antelope, courser, race horse, gazelle, greyhound, hare, doe, squirrel, camel bird, chickaree†, chipmunk, hackee *[U.S.]*, ostrich, scorcher *[Slang]*.

Mercury, Ariel[†], Camilla[†], Harlequin.

[Measurement of velocity] log, log line; speedometer, odometer, tachometer, strobe, radar speed detector, radar trap, air speed gauge, wind sock, wind speed meter; pedometer.

V. move quickly, trip, fisk[†]; speed, hie, hasten, post, spank, scuttle; scud, scuddle[†]; scour, scour the plain; scamper; run like mad, beat it; fly, race, run a race, cut away, shot, tear, whisk, zoom, swoosh, sweep, skim, brush; cut along, bowl along, barrel along, barrel; scorch, burn up the track; rush &c *(be violent)* 173; dash on, dash off, dash forward; bolt; trot, gallop, amble, troll, bound, flit, spring, dart, boom; march in quick time, march in double time; ride hard, get over the ground.

hurry &c *(hasten)* 684; accelerate, put on; quicken; quicken one's pace, mend one's pace; clap spurs to one's horse; make haste, make rapid strides, make forced marches, make the best of one's way; put one's best leg foremost, stir one's stumps, wing one's way, set off at a score; carry sail, crowd sail; go off like a shot, go like a shot, go ahead, gain ground; outstrip the wind, fly on the wings of the wind.

keep up with, keep pace with; outstrip &c 303; outmarch[†].

Adj. fast, speedy, swift, rapid, quick, fleet; aliped[†]; nimble, agile, expeditious; express; active &c 682;

flying, galloping &c *v.;* light footed, nimble footed; winged, eagle winged, mercurial, electric, telegraphic; light-legged, light of heel; swift as an arrow &c *n.;* quick as lightning &c *n.,* quick as a thought.

Adv. swiftly &c *adj.;* with speed &c *n.;* apace; at a great rate, at full speed, at railway speed; full drive, full gallop; posthaste, in full sail, tantivy†; trippingly; instantaneously &c 113.

under press of sail, under press of canvas, under press of sail and steam; velis et remis *[Lat.]*, on eagle's wing, in double quick time; with rapid strides, with giant strides; a pas de geant*[Fr.]*; in seven league boots; whip and spur; ventre a terre *[Fr.]*; as fast as one's legs will carry one, as fast as one's heels will carry one; as fast as one can lay legs to the ground, at the top of one's speed; by leaps and bounds; with haste &c 684.

Phr. vires acquirit eundo *[Lat.]*; I'll put a girdle about the earth in forty minutes [M.N.D.]; swifter than arrow from the Tartar's bow [M.N.D.]; go like a bat out of hell; tempus fugit *[Lat.]*.

275. Slowness -- N. slowness &c *adj.;* languor &c *(inactivity)* 683; drawl; creeping &c *v.,* lentor†.

retardation; slackening &c v.; delay &c *(lateness)* 133; claudication†.

jog trot, dog trot; mincing steps; slow march, slow time.

slow goer†, slow coach, slow back; lingerer, loiterer, sluggard, tortoise, snail; poke *[U.S.]*; dawdle &c *(inactive)* 683.

V. move slowly &c *adv.;* creep, crawl, lag, slug, drawl, linger, loiter, saunter; plod, trudge, stump along, lumber; trail, drag; dawdle &c *(be inactive)* 683; grovel, worm one's way, steal along; job on, rub on, bundle on; toddle, waddle, wabble†, slug, traipse, slouch, shuffle, halt, hobble, limp, caludicate†, shamble; flag, falter, trotter, stagger; mince, step short; march in slow time, march in funeral procession; take one's time; hang fire &c *(be late)* 133.

retard, relax; slacken, check, moderate, rein in, curb; reef; strike sail, shorten sail, take in sail; put on the drag, apply the brake; clip the wings; reduce the speed; slacken speed, slacken one's pace; lose ground.

Adj. slow, slack; tardy; dilatory &c *(inactive)* 683; gentle, easy; leisurely; deliberate, gradual; insensible, imperceptible; glacial, languid, sluggish, slow paced, tardigrade†, snail-like; creeping &c *v.;* reptatorial†.

Adv. slowly &c *adj.;* leisurely; piano, adagio; largo, larghetto; at half speed, under easy sail; at a foots pace, at a snail's pace, at a funeral pace; in slow time, with mincing steps, with clipped wings; haud passibus aequis *[Lat.]* [Vergil].

gradually &c *adj.;* gradatim *[Lat.]*; by degrees, by slow degrees, by inches, by little and little; step by step, one step at a time; inch by inch, bit by bit, little by little, seriatim; consecutively.

Phr. dum Roma deliberat Saguntum perit *[Lat.]*; at a glacial pace.

3. MOTION CONJOINED WITH FORCE

276. Impulse -- **N.** impulse, impulsion, impetus; momentum; push, pulsion†, thrust, shove, jog, jolt, brunt, booming, boost *[U.S.]*, throw; explosion &c *(violence)* 173; propulsion &c 284.

percussion, concussion, collision, occursion†, clash, encounter, cannon, carambole†, appulse†, shock, crash, bump; impact; elan; charge &c *(attack)* 716; beating &c *(punishment)* 972.

blow, dint, stroke, knock, tap, rap, slap, smack, pat, dab; fillip; slam, bang; hit, whack, thwack; cuff &c 972; squash, dowse, swap, whap†, punch, thump, pelt, kick, punce†, calcitration†; ruade†; arietation†; cut, thrust, lunge, yerk†; carom, carrom†, clip *[Slang]*, jab, plug *[Slang]*, sidewinder *[U.S.]*, sidewipe†, sideswipe *[U.S.]*.

hammer, sledge hammer, mall, maul, mallet, flail; ram, rammer†; battering ram, monkey, pile-driving engine, punch, bat; cant hook; cudgel &c *(weapon)* 727; ax &c *(sharp)* 253.

[Science of mechanical forces] dynamics; seismometer, accelerometer, earthquake detector.

V. give an impetus &c *n.;* impel, push; start, give a start to, set going; drive, urge, boom; thrust, prod, foin *[Fr.]*; cant; elbow, shoulder, jostle, justle†, hustle, hurtle, shove, jog, jolt, encounter; run against, bump against, butt against; knock one's head against, run one's head against; impinge; boost *[U.S.]*; bunt, carom, clip y; fan, fan out; jab, plug *[Slang]*.

strike, knock, hit, tap, rap, slap, flap, dab, pat, thump, beat, blow, bang, slam, dash; punch, thwack, whack; hit hard, strike hard; swap, batter, dowse†, baste; pelt, patter, buffet, belabor; fetch one a blow; poke at, pink, lunge, yerk†; kick, calcitrate†; butt, strike at &c *(attack)* 716; whip &c *(punish)* 972.

come into a collision, enter into collision; collide; sideswipe; foul; fall foul of, run foul of; telescope.

throw &c *(propel)* 284.

Adj. impelling &c *v.;* impulsive, impellent†; booming; dynamic, dynamical; impelled &c *v..*

Phr. a hit, a very palpable hit [Hamlet].

277. Recoil -- **N.** recoil; reaction, retroaction; revulsion; bounce, rebound, ricochet; repercussion, recalcitration†; kick, contrecoup *[Fr.]*; springing back &c *v.;* elasticity &c 325; reflection, reflexion *[Brit.]*, reflex, reflux; reverberation &c *(resonance)* 408; rebuff, repulse; return.

ducks and drakes; boomerang; spring, reactionist†.

elastic collision, coefficient of restitution.

V. recoil, react; spring back, fly back, bounce back, bound back; rebound, reverberate, repercuss†, recalcitrate†; echo, ricochet.

Adj. recoiling &c *v.;* refluent†, repercussive, recalcitrant, reactionary; retroactive.

Adv. on the rebound, on the recoil &c *n..*

Phr. for every action there is a reaction, equal in force and opposite in direction [Newton].

4. MOTION WITH REFERENCE TO DIRECTION

278. Direction -- **N.** direction, bearing, course, vector; set, drift, tenor; tendency &c 176; incidence; bending, trending &c *v.;* dip, tack, aim, collimation; steering steerage.

point of the compass, cardinal points; North East, South, West; N by E, ENE, NE by N, NE, &c; rhumb†, azimuth, line of collimation.

line, path, road, range, quarter, line of march; alignment, allignment†; air line, beeline; straight shoot.

V. tend towards, bend towards, point towards; conduct to, go to; point to, point at; bend, trend, verge, incline, dip, determine.

steer for, steer towards, make for, make towards; aim at, level at; take aim; keep a course, hold a course; be bound for; bend one's steps towards; direct one's course, steer one's course, bend one's course, shape one's course; align one's march, allign one's march†; to straight, go straight to the point; march on, march on a point.

ascertain one's direction &c *n.;* s'orienter *[Fr.]*, see which way the wind blows; box the compass; take the air line.

Adj. directed &c *v..* directed towards; pointing towards &c *v.;* bound for; aligned, with alligned with†; direct, straight; undeviating, unswerving; straightforward; North, Northern, Northerly, &c *n..*

Adv. towards; on the road, on the high road to; en avant; versus, to; hither, thither, whither; directly; straight as an arrow, forwards as an arrow; point blank; in a bee line to, in a direct line to, as the crow flies, in a straight line to, in a bee line for, in a direct line for, in a straight line for, in a bee line with, in a direct line with, in a straight line with; in a line with; full tilt at, as the crow flies.

before the wind, near the wind, close to the wind, against the wind; windwards, in the wind's eye.

through, via, by way of; in all directions, in all manner of ways; quaquaversum *[Lat.]*, from the four winds.

Phr. the shortest distance between two points is a straight line.

279. Deviation -- **N.** deviation; swerving &c *v.;* obliquation†, warp, refraction; flection†, flexion; sweep; deflection, deflexure†; declination.

diversion, digression, depart from, aberration; divergence &c 291; zigzag; detour &c *(circuit)* 629; divagation.

[Desultory motion] wandering &c v.; vagrancy, evagation†; bypaths and crooked ways; byroad.

[Motion sideways, oblique motion] sidling &c v.; knight's move at chess.

V. alter one's course, deviate, depart from, turn, trend; bend, curve &c 245; swerve, heel, bear off; gybe†, wear.

intervert†; deflect; divert, divert from its course; put on a new scent, shift, shunt, draw aside, crook, warp.

stray, straggle; sidle; diverge &c 291; tralineate†; digress, wander; wind, twist, meander; veer, tack; divagate; sidetrack; turn aside, turn a corner, turn away from; wheel, steer clear of; ramble, rove, drift; go astray, go adrift; yaw, dodge; step aside, ease off, make way for, shy.

fly off at a tangent; glance off; wheel about, face about; turn to the right about, face to the right about; waddle &c *(oscillate)* 314; go out of one's way &c *(perform a circuit)* 629; lose one's way.

Adj. deviating &c v.; aberrant, errant; excursive, discursive; devious, desultory, loose; rambling; stray, erratic, vagrant, undirected, circuitous, indirect, zigzag; crab-like.

Adv. astray from, round about, wide of the mark; to the right about; all manner of ways; circuitously &c 629.

obliquely, sideling, like the move of the knight on a chessboard.

280. *[Going before.]* **Precession** -- **N.** precession, leading, heading; precedence &c 62; priority &c 116; the lead, le pas; van &c *(front)* 234; precursor &c 64.

V. go before, go ahead, go in the van, go in advance; precede, forerun; usher in, introduce, herald, head, take the lead; lead the way, lead the dance; get the start, have the start; steal a march; get before, get ahead, get in front of; outstrip &c 303; take precedence &c *(first in order)* 62.

Adj. leading, precedent &c *v.*.

Adv. in advance, before, ahead, in the van, in the lead; foremost, headmost[†]; in front; at the head, out in front; way out in front, far ahead.

Phr. seniores priores *[Lat.]*, ahead of his time.

281. *[Going after.]* **Sequence** -- **N.** sequence; coming after &c *(order)* 63; *(time)* 117; following pursuit &c 622.

follower, attendant, satellite, shadow, dangler, train.

V. follow; pursue &c 622; go after, fly after.

attend, beset, dance attendance on, dog; tread in the steps of, tread close upon; be in the wake of, be in the trail of, be in the rear of, go in the wake of, go in the trail of, go in the rear of, follow in the wake of, follow in the trail of, follow in the rear of; follow as a shadow, hang on the skirts of; tread on the heels of, follow on the heels of; camp on the trail.

Adj. subsequent, next, succeeding; following &c *v.*.

Adv. behind; in the rear &c 235, in the train of, in the wake of; after &c *(order)* 63, *(time)* 117.

282. *[Motion forward; progressive motion.]* **Progression** -- **N.** progress, progression, progressiveness; advancing &c *v.;* advance, advancement; ongoing; flood, tide, headway; march &c 266; rise; improvement &c 658.

V. advance; proceed, progress; get on, get along, get over the ground; gain ground; forge ahead; jog on, rub on, wag on; go with the stream; keep one's course, hold on one's course; go on, move on, come one, get on, pass on, push on, press on, go forward, move forward, come forward, get forward, pass forward, push forward, press forward, go forwards, move forwards, come forwards, get forwards, pass forwards, push forwards, press forwards, go ahead, move ahead, come ahead, get ahead, pass ahead, push ahead, press ahead; make one's way, work one's way, carve one's way, push one's way, force one's way, edge one's way, elbow one's way; make progress, make head, make way, make headway, make advances, make strides, make rapid strides &c *(velocity)* 274; go ahead, shoot ahead; distance; make up leeway.

Adj. advancing &c *v.;* progressive, profluent†; advanced.

Adv. forward, onward; forth, on, ahead, under way, en route for, on one's way, on the way, on the road, on the high road, on the road to; in progress; in mid progress; in transitu &c 270 [Lat.].

Phr. vestigia nulla retrorsum *[Lat.]*; westward the course of empire takes its way [Berkeley].

283. *[Motion backwards.]* **Regression** -- **N.** regress, regression; retrocession†, retrogression, retrograduation†, retroaction; reculade†; retreat, withdrawal, retirement, remigration†; recession &c *(motion from)* 287; recess; crab-like motion.

refluence†, reflux; backwater, regurgitation, ebb, return; resilience reflection,
reflexion *[Brit.] (recoil)* 277; flip-flop, volte-face *[Fr.]*.

counter motion, retrograde motion, backward movement, motion in reverse, counter movement, counter march; veering, tergiversation, recidivation†, backsliding, fall; deterioration &c 659; recidivism, recidivity†.

reversal, relapse, turning point &c *(reversion)* 145.

V. recede, regrade, return, revert, retreat, retire; retrograde, retrocede; back out; back down; balk; crawfish *[U.S.]*, crawl *[Slang]*; withdraw; rebound &c 277; go back, come back, turn back, hark back, draw back, fall back, get back, put back, run back; lose ground; fall astern, drop astern; backwater, put about; backtrack, take the back track; veer round; double, wheel, countermarch; ebb, regurgitate; jib, shrink, shy.

turn tail, turn round, turn upon one's heel, turn one's back upon; retrace one's steps, dance the back step; sound a retreat, beat a retreat; go home.

Adj. receding &c *v.;* retrograde, retrogressive; regressive, refluent†, reflex, recidivous, resilient; crab-like; balky; reactionary &c 277.

Adv. back, backwards; reflexively, to the right about; a reculons *[Fr.]*, a rebours *[Fr.]*.

Phr. revenons a nos moutons *[Fr.]*, as you were.

284. *[Motion given to an object situated in front.]* **Propulsion** -- **N.** propulsion, projection; propelment†; vis a tergo *[Lat.]*, force from behind; push, shove &c *(impulse)* 276; ejaculate; ejection &c 297; throw, fling, toss, shot, discharge, shy; launch, release.

[Science of propulsion] projectiles, ballistics, archery.

[devices to give propulsion] propeller, screw, twin screws, turbine, jet engine.

[objects propelled] missile, projectile, ball, discus, quoit, brickbat, shot; *[weapons which propel]* arrow, gun, ballista &c *(arms)* 727 [Obs.].

[preparation for propulsion] countdown, windup.

shooter; shot; archer, toxophilite†; bowman, rifleman, marksman; good shot, crack shot; sharpshooter &c *(combatant)* 726.

V. propel, project, throw, fling, cast, pitch, chuck, toss, jerk, heave, shy, hurl; flirt, fillip.

dart, lance, tilt; ejaculate, jaculate†; fulminate, bolt, drive, sling, pitchfork.

send; send off, let off, fire off; discharge, shoot; launch, release, send forth, let fly; put in orbit, send into orbit, launch into orbit dash.

put in motion, set in motion; set agoing†, start; give a start, give an impulse to; impel &c 276; trundle &c *(set in rotation)* 312; expel &c 297.

carry one off one's legs; put to flight.

Adj. propelled &c *v.;* propelling &c *v.;* propulsive, projectile.

285. *[Motion given to an object situated behind.]* **Traction** -- **N.** traction; drawing &c *v.;* draught, pull, haul; rake; a long pull a strong pull and a pull all together; towage†, haulage.

V. draw, pull, haul, lug, rake, drag, tug, tow, trail, train; take in tow.

wrench, jerk, twitch, touse†; yank *[U.S.]*.

Adj. drawing &c *v.;* tractile†, tractive.

286. *[Motion towards.]* **Approach** -- **N.** approach, approximation, appropinquation†; access; appulse†; afflux†, affluxion†; advent &c *(approach of time)* 121; pursuit &c 622.

V. approach, approximate, appropinquate†; near; get near, go near, draw near; come to close quarters, come near; move towards, set in towards; drift; make up to; gain upon; pursue &c 622; tread on the heels of; bear up; make the land; hug the shore, hug the land.

Adj. approaching &c *v.;* approximative†; affluent; impending, imminent &c *(destined)* 152.

Adv. on the road.

Int. come hither!, approach!, here!, come!, come near!, forward!,

287. *[Motion from.]* **Recession** -- **N.** recession, retirement, withdrawal; retreat; retrocession &c 283 [Obs.]; departure, &c 293; recoil &c 277; flight &c *(avoidance)* 623.

V. recede, go, move back, move from, retire; withdraw, shrink, back off; come away, move away, back away, go away, get away, drift away; depart &c 293; retreat &c 283; move off, stand off, sheer off; fall back, stand aside; run away &c *(avoid)* 623.

remove, shunt, distance.

Adj. receding &c *v.*.

Phr. distance oneself from a person.

288. *[Motion towards, actively; force causing to draw closer.]* **Attraction** -- **N.** attraction, attractiveness; attractivity†; drawing to, pulling towards, adduction†.

electrical attraction, electricity, static electricity, static, static cling; magnetism, magnetic attraction; gravity, attraction of gravitation.

[objects which attract by physical force] lodestone, loadstone, lodestar, loadstar†; magnet, permanent magnet, siderite, magnetite; electromagnet; magnetic coil, voice coil; magnetic dipole; motor coil, rotor, stator.

electrical charge; positive charge, negative charge.

magnetic pole; north pole, south pole; magnetic monopole.

V. attract, draw; draw towards, pull towards, drag towards; adduce.

Adj. attracting &c *v.*; attrahent†, attractive, adducent†, adductive†.

centrifugal.

Phr. ubi mel ibi apes *[Lat.]* [Plautus].

289. [*Motion from, actively; force driving apart.*] **Repulsion** -- N. repulsion; driving from &c v.; repulse, abduction.

magnetic repulsion, magnetic levitation; antigravity.

V. repel, push from, drive apart, drive from &c 276; chase, dispel; retrude†; abduce†, abduct; send away; repulse.

keep at arm's length, turn one's back upon, give the cold shoulder; send off, send away with a flea in one's ear.

Adj. repelling &c v.; repellent, repulsive; abducent†, abductive†.

centripetal

Phr. like charges repel; opposite charges attract; like poles repel, opposite poles attract.

290. [*Motion nearer to.*] **Convergence** --
 N. convergence, confluence, concourse, conflux†, congress, concurrence, concentration; convergency; appulse†, meeting; corradiation†.

assemblage &c 72; resort &c *(focus)* 74; asymptote.

V. converge, concur, come together, unite, meet, fall in with; close with, close in upon; center round, center in; enter in; pour in.

gather together, unite, concentrate, bring into a focus.

Adj. converging &c *v.;* convergent, confluent, concurrent; centripetal; asymptotical, asymptotic; confluxible†.

291. *[Motion further off.]* **Divergence** --
 N. divergence, divergency†; divarication, ramification, forking; radiation; separation &c *(disjunction)* 44; dispersion &c 73; deviation &c 279; aberration.

V. diverge, divaricate, radiate; ramify; branch off, glance off, file off; fly off, fly off at a tangent; spread, scatter, disperse &c 73; deviate &c 279; part &c *(separate)* 44.

Adj. diverging &c *v.;* divergent, radiant, centrifugal; aberrant.

292. *[Terminal motion at.]* **Arrival** -- **N.** arrival, advent; landing; debarkation, disembarkation; reception, welcome, vin d'honneur *[Fr.]*.

home, goal, goalpost; landing place, landing stage; bunder[†]; resting place; destination, harbor, haven, port, airport, spaceport; terminus, halting place, halting ground, landing strip, runway, terminal; journey's end; anchorage &c *(refuge)* 666.

return, remigration[†]; meeting; rencounter[†], encounter.

completion &c 729.

recursion *[Comp.]*.

V. arrive; get to, come to; come; reach, attain; come up with, come up to; overtake, make, fetch; complete &c 729; join, rejoin.

light, alight, dismount; land, go ashore; debark, disembark; put in, put into; visit, cast anchor, pitch one's tent; sit down &c *(be located)* 184; get to one's journey's end; make the land; be in at the death; come back, get back, come home, get home; return; come in &c *(ingress)* 294; make one's appearance &c *(appear)* 446; drop in; detrain, deplane; outspan; de-orbit.

come to hand; come at, come across; hit; come upon, light upon, pop upon, bounce upon, plump upon, burst upon, pitch upon; meet; encounter, rencounter†; come in contact.

Adj. arriving &c *v.;* homeward bound.

Adv. here, hither.

Int. welcome!, hail!, all Hail!, good-day, good morrow!,

Phr. any port in a storm.

293. *[Initial motion from.]* **Departure** --
 N. departure, decession†, decampment; embarkation; outset, start; removal; exit &c *(egress)* 295; exodus, hejira, flight.

leave taking, valediction, adieu, farewell, goodbye, auf wiedersehen *[G.]*, sayonara, dosvidanya *[Rus.]*, ciao, aloha, hasta la vista *[Sp.]*; stirrup cup; valedictorian.

starting point, starting post; point of departure, point of embarkation, place of departure, place of embarkation; port of embarkation; airport, take-off point, taxiing runway, runway, launching pad, spaceport.

V. depart; go away; take one's departure, set out; set off, march off, put off, start off, be off, move off, get off, whip off, pack off, go off, take oneself off; start, issue, march out, debouch; go forth, sally forth; sally, set forward; be gone; hail from.

leave a place, quit, vacate, evacuate, abandon; go off the stage, make one's exit; retire, withdraw, remove; vamoose *[Slang]*, vamose *[U.S.]*; go one's way, go along, go from home; take flight, take wing; spring, fly, flit, wing one's flight; fly away, whip away; embark; go on board, go aboard; set sail' put to sea, go to sea; sail, take ship; hoist blue Peter; get under way, weigh anchor; strike tents, decamp; walk one's chalks, cut one's stick; take leave; say good bye, bid goodbye &c *n.;* disappear &c 449; abscond &c *(avoid)* 623; entrain; inspan†.

Adj. departing &c *v.;* valedictory; outward bound.

Adv. whence, hence, thence; with a foot in the stirrup; on the wing, on the move.

Int. begone!, &c *(ejection)* 297; farewell!, adieu!, goodbye!, good day!, au revoir! *[Fr.]*, fare you well!, God bless you!, God speed!, all aboard!, auf wiedersehen! *[G.]*, au plaisir de vous revoir! *[Fr.]*, bon voyage!, gluckliche Reise! *[G.]*, vive valeque! *[Fr.]*,

294. *[Motion into.]* **Ingress** -- **N.** ingress; entrance, entry; introgression; influx, intrusion, inroad, incursion, invasion, irruption; ingression; penetration, interpenetration; illapse†, import, infiltration; immigration; admission &c *(reception)* 296; insinuation &c *(interjacence)* 228 [Obs.]; insertion &c 300.

inlet; way in; mouth, door, &c *(opening)* 260; barway†; path &c *(way)* 627; conduit &c 350; immigrant.

V. have the entree; enter; go into, go in, come into, come in, pour into, pour in, flow into, flow in, creep into, creep in, slip into, slip in, pop into, pop in, break into, break in, burst into, burst in; set foot on; ingress; burst in upon, break in upon; invade, intrude; insinuate itself; interpenetrate, penetrate; infiltrate; find one's way into, wriggle into, worm oneself into.

give entrance to &c *(receive)* 296; insert &c 300.

Adj. incoming.

295. *[Motion out of.]* **Egress** -- **N.** egress, exit, issue; emersion, emergence; outbreak, outburst; eruption, proruption†; emanation; egression; evacuation; exudation, transudation; extravasation *[Med.]*, perspiration, sweating, leakage, percolation, distillation, oozing; gush &c *(water in motion)* 348; outpour, outpouring; effluence, effusion; effluxion†, drain; dribbling &c *v.;* defluxion†; drainage; outcome, output; discharge &c *(excretion)* 299.

export, expatriation; emigration, remigration†; debouch, debouche; emunctory†; exodus &c *(departure)* 293; emigrant.

outlet, vent, spout, tap, sluice, floodgate; pore; vomitory, outgate†, sally port; way out; mouth, door &c *(opening)* 260; path &c *(way)* 627; conduit &c 350; airpipe &c 351 [Obs.].

V. emerge, emanate, issue; egress; go out of, come out of, move out of, pass out of, pour out of, flow out of; pass out of, evacuate.

exude, transude; leak, run through, out through; percolate, transcolate†; egurgitate†; strain, distill; perspire, sweat, drain, ooze; filter, filtrate; dribble, gush, spout, flow out; well, well out; pour, trickle, &c *(water in motion)* 348; effuse, extravasate *[Med.]*, disembogue†, discharge itself, debouch; come forth, break forth; burst out, burst through; find vent; escape &c 671.

Adj. effused &c *v.;* outgoing.

296. *[Motion into, actively.]* **Reception** --
 N. reception; admission, admittance, entree, importation; introduction, intromission; immission†, ingestion, imbibation†, introception†, absorption, ingurgitation†, inhalation; suction, sucking; eating, drinking &c *(food)* 298; insertion &c 300; interjection &c 228; introit.

V. give entrance to, give admittance to, give the entree; introduce, intromit; usher, admit, receive, import, bring in, open the door to, throw in, ingest, absorb, imbibe, inhale, breathe in; let in, take in, suck in, draw in; readmit, resorb, reabsorb; snuff up, swallow, ingurgitate†; engulf, engorge; gulp; eat, drink &c *(food)* 298.

Adj. admitting &c *v.*, admitted &c *v.*; admissable; absorbent.

297. *[Motion out of, actively]* **Ejection** --
N. ejection, emission, effusion, rejection, expulsion, exportation, eviction, extrusion, trajection†; discharge.

emesis, vomiting, vomition†.

egestion†, evacuation; ructation†, eructation; bloodletting, venesection *[Med.]*, phlebotomy, paracentesis†; expuition, exspuition; tapping, drainage; clearance, clearage†.

deportation; banishment &c *(punishment)* 972; rouge's march; relegation, extradition; dislodgment.

bouncer *[U.S.]*, chucker-out *[Slang]*.

[material vomited] vomit, vomitus *[Med.]*, puke, barf *[Coll.]*.

V. give exit, give vent to; let out, give out, pour out, squeeze out, send out; dispatch, despatch; exhale, excern†, excrete; embogue†; secrete, secern†; extravasate *[Med.]*, shed, void, evacuation; emit; open the sluices, open the floodgates; turn on the tap; extrude, detrude†; effuse, spend, expend; pour forth; squirt, spirt†, spurt, spill, slop; perspire &c *(exude)* 295; breathe, blow &c *(wind)* 349.

tap, draw off; bale out, lade out; let blood, broach.

eject, reject; expel, discard; cut, send to coventry, boycott; chasser *[Fr.]*; banish &c *(punish)* 972; bounce *[U.S.]*; fire *[Slang]*, fire out *[Slang]*; throw &c 284, throw out, throw up, throw off, throw away, throw aside; push &c 276; throw out, throw off, throw away, throw aside; shovel out, shovel away, sweep out, sweep away; brush off, brush away, whisk off, whisk away, turn off, turn away, send off, send away; discharge; send adrift, turn adrift, cast adrift; turn out, bundle out; throw overboard; give the sack to; send packing, send about one's business, send to the right about; strike off the roll &c *(abrogate)* 756; turn out neck and heels, turn out head and shoulders, turn out neck and crop; pack off; send away with a flea in the ear; send to Jericho; bow out, show the door to, turn out of doors, turn out of house and home; evict, oust; unhouse, unkennel; dislodge; unpeople†, dispeople†; depopulate; relegate, deport.

empty; drain to the dregs; sweep off; clear off, clear out, clear away; suck, draw off; clean out, make a clean sweep of, clear decks, purge.

embowel†, disbowel†, disembowel; eviscerate, gut; unearth, root out, root up; averuncate†; weed out, get out; eliminate, get rid of, do away with, shake off; exenterate†.

vomit, throw up, regurgitate, spew, puke, keck†, retch, heave, upchuck, chuck up, barf; belch out; cast up, bring up, be sick, get sick, worship the porcelain god.

disgorge; expectorate, clear the throat, hawk, spit, sputter, splutter, slobber, drivel, slaver, slabber†; eructate; drool.

unpack, unlade, unload, unship, offload; break bulk; dump.

be let out.

spew forth, erupt, ooze &c *(emerge)* 295.

Adj. emitting, emitted, &c *v*..

Int. begone!, get you gone!, get away, go away, get along, go along, get along with you, go along with you!, go your way!, away with!, off with you!, get the hell out of here! *[Vulg.]*, go about your business!, be off!, avaunt!†, aroynt!†, allez-vous-en! *[Fr.]*, jao!†, va-t'en! *[Fr.]*,

298. *[Eating.]* **Food** -- N. eating &c v.; deglutition, gulp, epulation†, mastication, manducation†, rumination; gluttony &c 957.

[eating specific foods] hippophagy†, ichthyophagy†.

[Eating anatomy:] *(appetite)* &c 865; mouth, jaws, mandible, mazard†, gob *[Slang]*, chops.

drinking &c v.; potation, draught, libation; carousal &c *(amusement)* 840; drunkenness &c 959.

food, pabulum; aliment, nourishment, nutriment; sustenance, sustentation, sustention; nurture, subsistence, provender, corn, feed, fodder, provision, ration, keep, commons, board; commissariat &c *(provision)* 637; prey, forage, pasture, pasturage; fare, cheer; diet, dietary; regimen; belly timber, staff of life; bread, bread and cheese.

comestibles, eatables, victuals, edibles, ingesta; grub, grubstake, prog†, meat; bread, bread stuffs; cerealia†; cereals; viands, cates†, delicacy, dainty, creature comforts, contents of the larder, fleshpots; festal board; ambrosia; good cheer, good living.

beef, bisquit†, bun; cornstarch *[U.S.]*; cookie, cooky *[U.S.]*; cracker, doughnut; fatling†; hardtack, hoecake *[U.S.]*, hominy *[U.S.]*; mutton, pilot bread; pork; roti†, rusk, ship biscuit; veal; joint, piece de resistance *[Fr.]*, roast and boiled; remove, entremet†, releve *[Fr.]*, hash, rechauffe *[Fr.]*, stew, ragout, fricassee, mince; pottage, potage†, broth, soup, consomme, puree, spoonmeat†; pie, pasty, volauvent†; pudding, omelet; pastry; sweets &c 296; kickshaws†; condiment &c 393.

appetizer, hors d'oeuvre *[Fr.]*.

main course, entree.

alligator pear, apple &c, apple slump; artichoke; ashcake†, griddlecake, pancake, flapjack; atole†, avocado, banana, beche de mer *[Fr.]*, barbecue, beefsteak; beet root; blackberry, blancmange, bloater, bouilli†, bouillon, breadfruit, chop suey *[U.S.]*; chowder, chupatty†, clam, compote, damper, fish, frumenty†, grapes, hasty pudding, ice cream, lettuce, mango, mangosteen, mince pie, oatmeal, oyster, pineapple, porridge, porterhouse steak, salmis†, sauerkraut, sea slug, sturgeon ("Albany beef"), succotash *[U.S.]*, supawn *[U.S.]*, trepang†, vanilla, waffle, walnut.

table, cuisine, bill of fare, menu, table d'hote *[Fr.]*, ordinary, entree.

meal, repast, feed, spread; mess; dish, plate, course; regale; regalement†, refreshment, entertainment; refection, collation, picnic, feast, banquet, junket; breakfast; lunch, luncheon; dejeuner*[Fr.]*, bever†, tiffin†, dinner, supper, snack, junk food, fast food, whet, bait, dessert; potluck, table d'hote *[Fr.]*, dejeuner a la fourchette *[Fr.]*; hearty meal, square meal, substantial meal, full meal; blowout *[Slang]*; light refreshment; bara†, chotahazri†; bara khana†.

mouthful, bolus, gobbet†, morsel, sop, sippet†.

drink, beverage, liquor, broth, soup; potion, dram, draught, drench, swill *[Slang]*; nip, sip, sup, gulp.

wine, spirits, liqueur, beer, ale, malt liquor, Sir John Barleycorn, stingo†, heavy wet; grog, toddy, flip, purl, punch, negus†, cup, bishop, wassail; gin &c *(intoxicating liquor)* 959; coffee, chocolate, cocoa, tea, the cup that cheers but not inebriates; bock beer, lager beer, Pilsener beer, schenck beer†; Brazil tea, cider, claret, ice water, mate, mint julep *[U.S.]*; near beer, 3.2 beer, non-alcoholic beverage.

eating house &c 189.

[person who eats] diner; hippophage; glutton &c 957.

V. eat, feed, fare, devour, swallow, take; gulp, bolt, snap; fall to; despatch, dispatch; discuss; take down, get down, gulp down; lay in, tuck in *[Slang]*; lick, pick, peck; gormandize &c 957; bite, champ, munch, cranch†, craunch†, crunch, chew, masticate, nibble, gnaw, mumble.

live on; feed upon, batten upon, fatten upon, feast upon; browse, graze, crop, regale; carouse &c *(make merry)* 840; eat heartily, do justice to, play a good knife and fork, banquet.

break bread, break one's fast; breakfast, lunch, dine, take tea, sup.

drink in, drink up, drink one's fill; quaff, sip, sup; suck, suck up; lap; swig; swill *[Slang]*, chugalug *[Slang]*, tipple &c *(be drunken)* 959; empty one's glass, drain the cup; toss off, toss one's glass; wash down, crack a bottle, wet one's whistle.

purvey &c 637.

Adj. eatable, edible, esculent†, comestible, alimentary; cereal, cibarious†; dietetic; culinary; nutritive, nutritious; gastric; succulent; potable, potulent†; bibulous.

omnivorous, carnivorous, herbivorous, granivorous, graminivorous, phytivorous; ichthyivorous; omophagic, omophagous; pantophagous, phytophagous, xylophagous.

Phr. across the walnuts and the wine [Tennyson]; blessed hour of our dinners! [O.

Meredith]; now good digestion wait on appetite, and health on both! [Macbeth]; who can cloy the hungry edge of appetite? [Richard II],

299. Excretion -- **N.** excretion, discharge, emanation; exhalation, exudation, extrusion, secretion, effusion, extravasation *[Med.]*, ecchymosis *[Med.]*; evacuation, dejection, faeces, excrement, shit, stools, crap *[Vulg.]*; bloody flux; cacation[†]; coeliac-flux, coeliac-passion; dysentery; perspiration, sweat; subation[†], exudation; diaphoresis; sewage; eccrinology *[Med.]*.

saliva, spittle, rheum; ptyalism[†], salivation, catarrh; diarrhoea; ejecta, egesta *[Biol.]*, sputa; excreta; lava; exuviae &c *(uncleanness)* 653 [Lat.].

hemorrhage, bleeding; outpouring &c *(egress)* 295.

V. excrete &c *(eject)* 297; emanate &c *(come out)* 295.

300. *[Forcible ingress.]* **Insertion** -- **N.** insertion, implantation, introduction; insinuation &c *(intervention)* 228; planting, &c *v.*; injection, inoculation, importation, infusion; forcible ingress &c 294; immersion; submersion, submergence, dip, plunge; bath &c *(water)* 337; interment &c 363.

clyster *[Med.]*, enema, glyster[†], lavage, lavement[†].

V. insert; introduce, intromit; put into, run into; import; inject; interject &c 298; infuse, instill, inoculate, impregnate, imbue, imbrue.

graft, ingraft†, bud, plant, implant; dovetail.

obtrude; thrust in, stick in, ram in, stuff in, tuck in, press, in, drive in, pop in, whip in, drop in, put in; impact; empierce† &c *(make a hole)* 260 [Obs.].

imbed; immerse, immerge, merge; bathe, soak &c *(water)* 337; dip, plunge &c 310.

bury &c *(inter)* 363.

insert itself, lodge itself &c; plunge in medias res.

Adj. inserted &c *v.*.

301. *[Forcible egress.]* **Extraction** -- **N.** extraction; extracting &c *v.*; removal, elimination, extrication, eradication, evolution.

evulsion†, avulsion†; wrench; expression, squeezing; extirpation, extermination; ejection &c 297; export &c *(egress)* 295.

extractor, corkscrew, forceps, pliers.

V. extract, draw; take out, draw out, pull out, tear out, pluck out, pick out, get out; wring from, wrench; extort; root up, weed up, grub up, rake up, root out, weed out, grub out, rake out; eradicate; pull up by the roots, pluck up by the roots; averruncate†; unroot†; uproot, pull up, extirpate, dredge.

remove; educe, elicit; evolve, extricate; eliminate &c *(eject)* 297; eviscerate &c 297.

express, squeeze out, press out.

Adj. extracted &c *v.*.

302. *[Motion through.]* **Passage** -- **N.** passage, transmission; permeation; penetration, interpenetration; transudation, infiltration; endosmose exosmose†; endosmosis *[Chem]*; intercurrence†; ingress &c 294; egress &c 295; path &c 627; conduit &c 350; opening &c 260; journey &c 266; voyage &c 267.

V. pass, pass through; perforate &c *(hole)* 260; penetrate, permeate, thread, thrid†, enfilade; go through, go across; go over, pass over; cut across; ford, cross; pass and repass, work; make one's way, thread one's way, worm one's way, force one's way; make a passage form a passage; cut one's way through; find its way, find its vent; transmit, make way, clear the course; traverse, go over the ground.

Adj. passing &c *v.;* intercurrent†; endosmosmic†, endosmotic *[Chem]*.

Adv. en passant &c *(transit)* 270 [Fr.].

303. *[Motion beyond]* **Transcursion** --
  N. transcursion†, transiliency†, transgression; trespass; encroachment, infringement; extravagation†, transcendence; redundancy &c 641.

  V. transgress, surpass, pass; go beyond, go by; show in front, come to the front; shoot ahead of; steal a march upon, steal a gain upon.

  overstep, overpass, overreach, overgo†, override, overleap, overjump†, overskip†, overlap, overshoot the mark; outstrip, outleap, outjump, outgo, outstep†, outrun, outride, outrival, outdo; beat, beat hollow; distance; leave in the lurch, leave in the rear; throw into the shade; exceed, transcend, surmount; soar &c *(rise)* 305.

  encroach, trespass, infringe, trench upon, entrench on, intrench on†; strain; stretch a point, strain a point; cross the Rubicon.

  Adj. surpassing &c *v.*.

  Adv. beyond the mark, ahead.

304. *[motion short of]* **Shortcoming** --
  N. shortcoming, failure; falling short &c *v.*; default, defalcation; leeway; labor in vain, no go.

incompleteness &c 53; imperfection &c 651; insufficiency &c 640; noncompletion &c 730; failure &c 732.

V. 303, come short of, fall short of, stop short of, come short, fall short, stop short; not reach; want; keep within bounds, keep within the mark, keep within the compass.

break down, stick in the mud, collapse, flat out *[U.S.]*, come to nothing; fall through, fall to the ground; cave in, end in smoke, miss the mark, fail; lose ground; miss stays.

Adj. unreached; deficient; short, short of; minus; out of depth; perfunctory &c *(neglect)* 460.

Adv. within the mark, within the compass, within the bounds; behindhand; re infecta *[Lat.]*; to no purpose; for from it.

Phr. the bubble burst.

305. *[Motion upwards]* **Ascent** -- **N.** ascent, ascension; rising &c 309; acclivity, hill &c 217; flight of steps, flight of stairs; ladder rocket, lark; sky rocket, sky lark; Alpine Club.

V. ascend, rise, mount, arise, uprise; go up, get up, work one's way up, start up; shoot up, go into orbit; float up; bubble up; aspire.

climb, clamber, ramp, scramble, escalade†, surmount; shin, shinny, shinney; scale, scale the heights.

[cause to go up] raise, elevate &c 307.

go aloft, fly aloft; tower, soar, take off; spring up, pop up, jump up, catapult upwards, explode upwards; hover, spire, plane, swim, float, surge; leap &c 309.

Adj. rising &c *v..* scandent†, buoyant; supernatant, superfluitant†; excelsior.

Adv. uphill.

306. *[Motion downwards]* **Descent** -- **N.** descent, descension†, declension, declination; fall; falling &c *v.;* slump; drop, plunge, plummet, cadence; subsidence, collapse, lapse; downfall, tumble, slip, tilt, trip, lurch; cropper, culbute†; titubation†, stumble; fate of Icarus.

avalanche, debacle, landslip, landslide.

declivity, dip, hill.

[equipment for descending by rappeling] rappel.

V. descend; go down, drop down, come down; fall, gravitate, drop, slip, slide, rappel, settle; plunge, plummet, crash; decline, set, sink, droop, come down a peg; slump.

dismount, alight, light, get down; swoop; stoop &c 308; fall prostrate, precipitate oneself; let fall &c 308.

tumble, trip, stumble, titubate†, lurch, pitch, swag, topple, topple over, tumble over, topple down, tumble down; tilt, sprawl, plump down, come down a cropper.

Adj. descending &c *v.;* descendent; decurrent†, decursive†; labent†, deciduous; nodding to its fall.

Adv. downhill, downwards.

Phr. the bottom fell out.

307. Elevation -- **N.** elevation; raising &c *v.;* erection, lift; sublevation†, upheaval; sublimation, exaltation; prominence &c *(convexity)* 250.

lever &c 633; crane, derrick, windlass, capstan, winch; dredge, dredger, dredging machine.

dumbwaiter, elevator, escalator, lift.

V. heighten, elevate, raise, lift, erect; set up, stick up, perch up, perk up, tilt up; rear, hoist, heave; uplift, upraise, uprear, upbear†, upcast†, uphoist†, upheave; buoy, weigh mount, give a lift; exalt; sublimate; place on a pedestal, set on a pedestal.

escalate &c *(increase)* 35 102 194.

take up, drag up, fish up; dredge.

stand up, rise up, get up, jump up; spring to one's feet; hold oneself, hold one's head up; drawn oneself up to his full height.

Adj. elevated &c *v.;* stilted, attollent†, rampant.

Adv. on stilts, on the shoulders of, on one's legs, on one's hind legs.

308. Depression -- **N.** lowering &c *v.;* depression; dip &c *(concavity)* 252; abasement; detrusion†; reduction.

overthrow, overset†, overturn; upset; prostration, subversion, precipitation.

bow; courtesy, curtsy; genuflexion†, genuflection, kowtow, obeisance, salaam.

V. depress, lower, let down, take down, let down a peg, take down a peg; cast; let drop, let fall; sink, debase, bring low, abase, reduce, detrude†, pitch, precipitate.

overthrow, overturn, overset†; upset, subvert, prostate, level, fell; cast down, take down, throw down, fling down, dash down, pull down, cut down, knock down, hew down; raze, raze to the ground, rase to the ground†; trample in the dust, pull about one's ears.

sit, sit down; couch, squat, crouch, stoop, bend, bow; courtesy, curtsy; bob, duck, dip, kneel; bend the knee, bow the knee, bend the head, bow the head; cower; recline &c *(be horizontal)*213.

Adj. depressed &c *v.;* at a low ebb; prostrate &c *(horizontal)* 213; detrusive†.

Phr. facinus quos inquinat aequat *[Lat.]* [Lucan].

309. Leap -- N. leap, jump, hop, spring, bound, vault, saltation†.

ance, caper; curvet, caracole; gambade†, gambado†; capriole, demivolt†; buck, buck jump; hop skip and jump; falcade†.

kangaroo, jerboa; chamois, goat, frog, grasshopper, flea; buckjumper†; wallaby.

V. leap; jump up, jump over the moon; hop, spring, bound, vault, ramp, cut capers, trip, skip, dance, caper; buck, buck jump; curvet, caracole; foot it, bob, bounce, flounce, start; frisk

&c *(amusement)* 840; jump about
&c *(agitation)* 315; trip it on the light fantastic toe, trip the light fantastic, dance oneself off one's legs, dance off one's shoes.

Adj. leaping &c *v.;* saltatory†, frisky.

Adv. on the light fantastic toe.

Phr. di salto in salto *[It]*.

310. Plunge -- **N.** plunge, dip, dive, header; ducking &c *v.;* diver.

V. plunge, dip, souse, duck; dive, plump; take a plunge, take a header; make a plunge; bathe &c *(water)* 337.

submerge, submerse; immerse; douse, sink, engulf, send to the bottom.

get out of one's depth; go to the bottom, go down like a stone, drop like a lead balloon; founder, welter, wallow.

311. *[Curvilinear motion.]* **Circuition** --
 N. circuition†, circulation; turn, curvet; excursion, circumvention, circumnavigation, circumambulation; northwest passage; circuit &c 629.

turning &c v.; wrench; evolution; coil, corkscrew.

V. turn, bend, wheel; go about, put about; heel; go round to the right about, turn round to the right about; turn on one's heel; make a circle, make a complete circle, describe a circle, describe a complete circle; go through 180 degrees, go through 360 degrees, pass through 180 degrees, pass through 360 degrees.

circumnavigate, circumambulate, circumvent; put a girdle round about the earth [M.N.D.]; go the round, make the round of.

wind, circulate, meander; whisk, twirl; twist &c *(convolution)* 248; make a detour &c *(circuit)* 629.

Adj. turning &c v.; circuitous; circumforaneous†, circumfluent†.

Adv. round about.

312. *[Motion in a continued circle.]* **Rotation** --
 N. rotation, revolution, spinning, gyration, turning about an axis, turning aound an axis, circulation, roll; circumrotation†, circumvolution, circumgyration†; volutation†, circination†, turbination†, pirouette, convolution.

verticity†, whir, whirl, eddy, vortex, whirlpool, gurge†; countercurrent; Maelstrom, Charybdis; Ixion.

[rotating air] cyclone; tornado, whirlwind; dust devil.

[rotation of an automobile] spin-out.

axis, axis of rotation, swivel, pivot, pivot point; axle, spindle, pin, hinge, pole, arbor, bobbin, mandrel; axle shaft; gymbal; hub, hub of rotation.

[rotation and translation together] helix, helical motion.

[measure of rotation] angular momentum, angular velocity; revolutions per minute, RPM.

[result of rotation] centrifugal force; surge; vertigo, dizzy round; coriolis force.

[things that go around] carousel, merry-go-round; Ferris wheel; top, dreidel†, teetotum; gyroscope; turntable, lazy suzan; screw, whirligig, rollingstone†, water wheel, windmill; wheel, pulley wheel, roulette wheel, potter's wheel, pinwheel, gear; roller; flywheel; jack; caster; centrifuge, ultracentrifuge, bench centrifuge, refrigerated centrifuge, gas centrifuge, microfuge; drill, augur, oil rig; wagon wheel, wheel, tire, tyre *[Brit.]*.

[Science of rotary motion] trochilics†.

[person who rotates] whirling dervish.

V. rotate; roll along; revolve, spin; turn round; circumvolve†; circulate; gyre, gyrate, wheel, whirl, pirouette; twirl, trundle, troll, bowl.

roll up, furl; wallow, welter; box the compass; spin like a top, spin like a teetotum†.

[of an automobile] spin out.

Adj. rotating &c *v.;* rotary, rotary; circumrotatory†, trochilic†, vertiginous, gyratory; vortical, vorticose†.

Adv. head over heels, round and round, like a horse in a mill.

313. *[Motion in the reverse circle.]* **Evolution** --
 N. evolution, unfolding, development; evolvement; unfoldment; eversion &c *(inversion)* 218.

V. evolve; unfold, unroll, unwind, uncoil, untwist, unfurl, untwine, unravel; untangle, disentangle; develop.

Adj. evolving &c *v.;* evolved &c *v.*.

314. *[Reciprocating motion, motion to and fro.]* **Oscillation** -- **N.** oscillation; vibration, libration; motion of a pendulum; nutation; undulation; pulsation; pulse.

alternation; coming and going &c *v.;* ebb and flow, flux and reflux, ups and down.

fluctuation; vacillation &c *(irresolution)* 605.

wave, vibratiuncle†, swing, beat, shake, wag, seesaw, dance, lurch, dodge; logan†, loggan†, rocking-stone, vibroscope†.

V. oscillate; vibrate, librate†; alternate, undulate, wave; rock, swing; pulsate, beat; wag, waggle; nod, bob, courtesy, curtsy; tick; play; wamble†, wabble†; dangle, swag.

fluctuate, dance, curvet, reel, quake; quiver, quaver; shake, flicker; wriggle; roll, toss, pitch; flounder, stagger, totter; move up and down, bob up and down &c *adv.;* pass and repass, ebb and flow, come and go; vacillate &c 605; teeter *[U.S.].*

brandish, shake, flourish.

Adj. oscillating &c *v.;* oscillatory, undulatory, pulsatory†, libratory, rectilinear; vibratory, vibratile†; pendulous.

Adv. to and fro, up and down, backwards and forwards, hither and yon, seesaw, zigzag, wibble-wabble†, in and out, from side to side, like buckets in a well.

315. *[Irregular motion]* **Agitation** -- N. agitation, stir, tremor, shake, ripple, jog, jolt, jar, jerk, shock, succussion†, trepidation, quiver, quaver, dance; jactitation†, quassation†; shuffling &c *v.;* twitter, flicker, flutter.

turbulence, perturbation; commotion, turmoil, disquiet; tumult, tumultuation†; hubbub, rout, bustle, fuss, racket, subsultus†, staggers, megrims, epilepsy, fits; carphology†, chorea, floccillation†, the jerks, St. Vitus's dance, tilmus†.

spasm, throe, throb, palpitation, convulsion.

disturbance, chaos &c *(disorder)* 59; restlessness &c *(changeableness)* 149.

ferment, fermentation; ebullition, effervescence, hurly-burly, cahotage†; tempest, storm, ground swell, heavy sea, whirlpool, vortex &c 312; whirlwind &c *(wind)* 349.

V. be agitated &c*;* shake; tremble, tremble like an aspen leaf; quiver, quaver, quake, shiver, twitter, twire†, writhe, toss, shuffle, tumble, stagger, bob, reel, sway, wag, waggle; wriggle, wriggle like an eel; dance, stumble, shamble, flounder, totter, flounce, flop, curvet, prance, cavort *[U.S.]*; squirm.

throb, pulsate, beat, palpitate, go pitapat; flutter, flitter, flicker, bicker; bustle.

ferment, effervesce, foam; boil, boil over; bubble up; simmer.

toss about, jump about; jump like a parched pea; shake like an aspen leaf; shake to its center, shake to its foundations; be the sport of the winds and waves; reel to and fro like a drunken man; move from post to pillar and from pillar to post, drive from post to pillar and from pillar to post, keep between hawk and buzzard.

agitate, shake, convulse, toss, tumble, bandy, wield, brandish, flap, flourish, whisk, jerk, hitch, jolt; jog, joggle, jostle, buffet, hustle, disturb, stir, shake up, churn, jounce, wallop, whip, vellicate[†].

Adj. shaking &c v.; agitated tremulous; desultory, subsultory[†]; saltatoric[†]; quasative[†]; shambling; giddy-paced, saltatory[†], convulsive, unquiet, restless, all of a twitter.

Adv. by fits and starts; subsultorily[†] &c *adj.*[†]; per saltum *[Lat.]*; hop skip and jump; in convulsions, in fits.

Phr. tempete dans un verre d'eau *[Fr.]*.

CLASS III

WORDS RELATING TO MATTER

SECTION I.

MATTER IN GENERAL

316. Materiality -- N. materiality, materialness; corporeity†, corporality†; substantiality, substantialness, flesh and blood, plenum; physical condition.

matter, body, substance, brute matter, stuff, element, principle, parenchyma *[Biol.]*, material, substratum, hyle†, corpus, pabulum; frame.

object, article, thing, something; still life; stocks and stones; materials &c 635.

[Science of matter] physics; somatology†, somatics; natural philosophy, experimental philosophy; physicism†; physical science, philosophie positive *[Fr.]*, materialism; materialist; physicist; somatism†, somatist†.

Adj. material, bodily; corporeal, corporal; physical; somatic, somatoscopic†; sensible, tangible, ponderable, palpable, substantial.

objective, impersonal, nonsubjective†, neuter, unspiritual, materialistic.

317. Immateriality

N. immateriality, immaterialness; incorporeity†, spirituality; inextension†; astral plane.

personality; I, myself, me; ego, spirit &c *(soul)* 450; astral body; immaterialism†; spiritualism, spiritualist.

V. disembody, spiritualize.

Adj. immaterial, immateriate†; incorporeal, incorporal†; incorporate, unfleshly†; supersensible†; asomatous†, unextended†; unembodied†, disembodied; extramundane, unearthly; pneumatoscopic†; spiritual &c *(psychical)* 450 [Obs.].

personal, subjective, nonobjective.

318. World

N. world, creation, nature, universe; earth, globe, wide world; cosmos; kosmos†; terraqueous globe†, sphere; macrocosm, megacosm†; music of the spheres.

heavens, sky, welkin†, empyrean; starry cope, starry heaven, starry host; firmament; Midgard;

supersensible regions†; varuna; vault of heaven, canopy of heaven; celestial spaces.

heavenly bodies, stars, asteroids; nebulae; galaxy, milky way, galactic circle, via lactea *[Lat.]*, ame no kawa *[Jap.]*.

sun, orb of day, Apollo†, Phoebus; photosphere, chromosphere; solar system; planet, planetoid; comet; satellite, moon, orb of night, Diana, silver-footed queen; aerolite†, meteor; planetary ring; falling star, shooting star; meteorite, uranolite†.

constellation, zodiac, signs of the zodiac, Charles's wain, Big Dipper, Little Dipper, Great Bear, Southern Cross, Orion's belt, Cassiopea's chair, Pleiades.

colures†, equator, ecliptic, orbit.

[Science of heavenly bodies] astronomy; uranography, uranology†; cosmology, cosmography†, cosmogony; eidouranion†, orrery; geodesy &c *(measurement)* 466; star gazing, star gazer†; astronomer; observatory; planetarium.

Adj. cosmic, cosmical†; mundane, terrestrial, terrestrious†, terraqueous†, terrene, terreous†, telluric, earthly, geotic†, under the sun; sublunary†, subastral†.

solar, heliacal†; lunar; celestial, heavenly, sphery†; starry, stellar; sidereal, sideral†; astral; nebular; uranic.

Adv. in all creation, on the face of the globe, here below, under the sun.

Phr. die Weltgeschichte ist das Weltergesicht *[G.]*; earth is but the frozen echo of the silent voice of God [Hageman]; green calm below, blue quietness above [Whittier]; hanging in a golden chain this pendant World [Paradise Lost]; nothing in nature is unbeautiful [Tennyson]; silently as a dream the fabric rose [Cowper]; some touch of nature's genial glow [Scott]; this majestical roof fretted with golden fire [Hamlet]; through knowledge we behold the World's creation [Spenser].

319. Gravity -- N. gravity, gravitation; weight; heaviness &c *adj.;* specific gravity; pondorosity†, pressure, load; burden, burthen†; ballast, counterpoise; lump of, mass of, weight of.

lead, millstone, mountain, Ossa on Pelion.

weighing, ponderation†, trutination†; weights; avoirdupois weight, troy weight, apothecaries' weight; grain, scruple, drachma†, ounce, pound, lb, arroba†, load, stone, hundredweight, cwt, ton, long ton, metric ton, quintal, carat, pennyweight, tod†.

[metric weights] gram, centigram, milligram, microgram, kilogram; nanogram, picogram, femtogram, attogram.

[Weighing Instrument] balance, scale, scales, steelyard, beam, weighbridge†; spring balance, piezoelectric balance, analytical balance, two-pan balance, one-pan balance; postal scale, baby scale.

[Science of gravity] statics.

V. be heavy &c *adj.;* gravitate, weigh, press, cumber, load.

[Measure the weight of] weigh, poise.

Adj. weighty; weighing &c *v.;* heavy as lead; ponderous, ponderable; lumpish†, lumpy, cumbersome, burdensome; cumbrous, unwieldy, massive.

incumbent, superincumbent†.

320. Levity -- **N.** levity; lightness &c *adj.;* imponderability, buoyancy, volatility.

feather, dust, mote, down, thistle, down, flue, cobweb, gossamer, straw, cork, bubble, balloon; float, buoy; ether, air.

leaven, ferment, barm†, yeast.

lighter-than-air balloon, helium balloon, hydrogen balloon, hot air balloon.

convection, thermal draft, thermal.

V. be light &c *adj.;* float, rise, swim, be buoyed up.

render light &c *adj.;* lighten, leaven.

Adj. light, subtile, airy; imponderous[†], imponderable; astatic[†], weightless, ethereal, sublimated; gossamery; suberose[†], suberous[†]; uncompressed, volatile; buoyant, floating &c *v.;* portable.

light as a feather, light as a thistle, light as air; lighter than air; rise like a balloon, float like a balloon

SECTION II.

INORGANIC MATTER

1. SOLID MATTER

321. Density -- **N.** density, solidity; solidness &c *adj.;* impenetrability, impermeability;

incompressibility; imporosity†; cohesion &c 46; constipation, consistence, spissitude†.

specific gravity; hydrometer, areometer†.

condensation; caseation†; solidation†, solidification; consolidation; concretion, coagulation; petrification &c *(hardening)* 323; crystallization, precipitation; deposit, precipitate; inspissation†; gelation, thickening &c *v*.. indivisibility, indiscerptibility†, insolubility, indissolvableness.

solid body, mass, block, knot, lump; concretion, concrete, conglomerate; cake, clot, stone, curd, coagulum; bone, gristle, cartilage; casein, crassamentum†; legumin†.

superdense matter, condensed states of matter; dwarf star, neutron star.

V. be dense &c *adj.;* become solid, render solid &c *adj.;* solidify, solidate†; concrete, set, take a set, consolidate, congeal, coagulate; curd, curdle; lopper; fix, clot, cake, candy, precipitate, deposit, cohere, crystallize; petrify &c *(harden)* 323.

condense, thicken, gel, inspissate†, incrassate†; compress, squeeze, ram down, constipate.

Adj. dense, solid; solidified &c *v.;* caseous; pukka†; coherent, cohesive &c 46; compact, close, serried, thickset; substantial, massive, lumpish†; impenetrable, impermeable, nonporous, imporous†;

incompressible; constipated; concrete &c *(hard)* 323; knotted, knotty; gnarled; crystalline, crystallizable; thick, grumous†, stuffy.

undissolved, unmelted†, unliquefied†, unthawed†.

indivisible, indiscerptible†, infrangible†, indissolvable†, indissoluble, insoluble, infusible.

322. Rarity -- **N.** rarity, tenuity; absence of solidity &c 321; subtility†; subtilty†, subtlety; sponginess, compressibility.

rarefaction, expansion, dilatation, inflation, subtilization†.

vaporization, evaporation, diffusion, gassification†.

ether &c *(gas)* 334.

V. rarefy, expand, dilate, subtilize†.

Adj. rare, subtile, thin, fine, tenuous, compressible, flimsy, slight; light &c 320; cavernous, spongy &c *(hollow)* 252.

rarefied &c *v.;* unsubstantial; uncompact†, incompressed†; rarefiable†.

323. Hardness -- **N.** hardness &c *adj.;* rigidity; renitence†, renitency; inflexibility, temper, callosity, durity†.

induration, petrifaction; lapidification†, lapidescence†; vitrification, ossification; crystallization.

stone, pebble, flint, marble, rock, fossil, crag, crystal, quartz, granite, adamant; bone, cartilage; hardware; heart of oak, block, board, deal board; iron, steel; cast iron, decarbonized iron, wrought iron; nail; brick, concrete; cement.

V. render hard &c *adj.;* harden, stiffen, indurate, petrify, temper, ossify, vitrify; accrust†.

Adj. hard, rigid, stubborn, stiff, firm; starch, starched; stark, unbending, unlimber, unyielding; inflexible, tense; indurate, indurated; gritty, proof.

adamant, adamantine, adamantean†; concrete, stony, granitic, calculous, lithic†, vitreous; horny, corneous†; bony; osseous, ossific†; cartilaginous; hard as a rock &c *n.;* stiff as buckram, stiff as a poker; stiff as starch, stiff as as board.

324. Softness -- **N.** softness, pliableness &c *adj.;* flexibility; pliancy, pliability; sequacity†, malleability; ductility, tractility†; extendibility, extensibility; plasticity; inelasticity, flaccidity, laxity.

penetrability.

clay, wax, butter, dough, pudding; alumina, argil; cushion, pillow, feather bed, down, padding, wadding; foam.

mollification; softening &c *v.*.

V. render soft &c *adj.;* soften, mollify, mellow, relax, temper; mash, knead, squash.

bend, yield, relent, relax, give.

plasticize'.

Adj. soft, tender, supple; pliant, pliable; flexible, flexile; lithe, lithesome; lissom, limber, plastic; ductile; tractile†, tractable; malleable, extensile, sequacious†, inelastic; aluminous†; remollient†.

yielding &c *v.;* flabby, limp, flimsy.

doughy, spongy, penetrable, foamy, cushiony†.

flaccid, flocculent, downy; edematous, oedematous†, medullary *[Anat.]*, argillaceous, mellow.

soft as butter, soft as down, soft as silk; yielding as wax, tender as chicken.

325. Elasticity -- **N.** elasticity, springiness, spring, resilience, renitency, buoyancy.

rubber, India rubber, Indian rubber, latex, caoutchouc, whalebone, gum elastic, baleen, natural rubber; neoprene, synthetic rubber, Buna-S, plastic.

flexibility, Young's modulus.

V. stretch, flex, extend, distend, be elastic &c *adj.;* bounce, spring back &c *(recoil)* 277.

Adj. elastic, flexible, tensile, spring, resilient, renitent, buoyant; ductile, stretchable, extendable.

Phr. the stress is proportional to the strain.

326. Inelasticity -- **N.** want of elasticity, absence of elasticity &c 325; inelasticity &c *(softness)* 324,

Adj. unyielding, inelastic, inflexible &c *(soft)* 324; irresilient[†].

327. Tenacity -- **N.** {ant.

328} tenacity, toughness, strength; *(cohesion)* 46; grip, grasp, stickiness, *(cohesion)* 46; sequacity[†];

stubbornness &c *(obstinacy);;* glue, cement, glutinousness†, sequaciousness†, viscidity, *(semiliquidity)* 352.

leather; white leather, whitleather†; gristle, cartilage.

unbreakability, tensile strength.

V. be tenacious &c *adj.;* resist fracture.

grip, grasp, stick *(cohesion)* 46.

Adj. tenacious, tough, strong, resisting, sequacious†, stringy, gristly cartilaginous, leathery, coriaceous†, tough as whitleather†; stubborn &c *(obstinate)* 606.

unbreakable, indivisible; atomic.

328. Brittleness -- N. {ant.

327} brittleness &c *adj.;* fragility, friability, frangibility, fissibility†; house of cards, house of glass.

V. be brittle &c *adj.;* live in a glass house.

break, crack, snap, split, shiver, splinter, crumble, break short, burst, fly, give way; fall to pieces; crumble to, crumble into dust.

Adj. brittle, brash *[U.S.]*, breakable, weak, frangible, fragile, frail, gimcrack†, shivery, fissile; splitting &c *v.;* lacerable†, splintery, crisp, crimp, short, brittle as glass.

329. *[Structure.]* **Texture** -- **N.** structure *(form)* 240, organization, anatomy, frame, mold, fabric, construction; framework, carcass, architecture; stratification, cleavage.

substance, stuff, compages†, parenchyma *[Biol.]*; constitution, staple, organism.

[Science of structures] organography†, osteology, myology, splanchnology†, neurology, angiography†, adeology†; angiography†, adenography†.

texture, surface texture; intertexture†, contexture†; tissue, grain, web, surface; warp and woof, warp and weft; tooth, nap &c *(roughness)* 256;
flatness *(smoothness)* 255; fineness of grain; coarseness of grain, dry goods.

silk, satin; muslin, burlap.

[Science of textures] histology.

Adj. structural, organic; anatomic, anatomical.

textural, textile; fine grained, coarse grained; fine, delicate, subtile, gossamery, filmy, silky, satiny; coarse; homespun.

rough, gritty; smooth.

smooth as silk, smooth as satin.

330. Pulverulence -- **N.** powderiness† *[State of powder.]*, pulverulence†; sandiness &c *adj.;* efflorescence; friability.

powder, dust, sand, shingle; sawdust; grit; meal, bran, flour, farina, rice, paddy, spore, sporule†; crumb, seed, grain; particle &c *(smallness)* 32; limature†, filings, debris, detritus, tailings, talus slope, scobs†, magistery†, fine powder; flocculi *[Lat.]*.

smoke; cloud of dust, cloud of sand, cloud of smoke; puff of smoke, volume of smoke; sand storm, dust storm.

[Reduction to powder] pulverization, comminution†, attenuation, granulation, disintegration, subaction†, contusion, trituration *[Chem]*, levigation†, abrasion, detrition, multure†; limitation; tripsis†; filing &c *v.*. *[Instruments for pulverization]* mill, arrastra†, gristmill, grater, rasp, file, mortar and pestle, nutmeg grater, teeth, grinder, grindstone, kern†, quern†, koniology†.

V. come to dust; be disintegrated, be reduced to powder &c reduce to powder, grind to powder; pulverize, comminute, granulate, triturate, levigate†; scrape, file, abrade, rub down, grind, grate, rasp, pound, bray, bruise; contuse, contund†; beat, crush, cranch†, craunch†, crunch, scranch†, crumble, disintegrate; attenuate &c 195.

Adj. powdery, pulverulent†, granular, mealy, floury, farinaceous, branny†, furfuraceous†, flocculent, dusty, sandy, sabulous†, psammous†; arenose†, arenarious†, arenaceous†; gritty, efflorescent, impalpable; lentiginous†, lepidote†, sabuline†; sporaceous†, sporous†.

pulverizable; friable, crumbly, shivery; pulverized &c *v.*; attrite†; in pieces.

331. Friction -- **N.** friction, attrition; rubbing, abrasion, scraping &c *v.*; confrication†, detrition, contrition†, affriction†, abrasion, arrosion†, limature†, frication†, rub; elbow grease; rosin; massage; roughness &c 256.

rolling friction, sliding friction, starting friction.

V. rub, scratch, scrape, scrub, slide, fray, rasp, graze, curry, scour, polish, rub out, wear down, gnaw; file, grind &c *(reduce to powder)* 330.

set one's teeth on edge; rosin.

Adj. anatriptic†; attrite†.

332. *[Absence of friction. Prevention of friction.]* **Lubrication** -- **N.** smoothness &c 255; unctuousness &c 355.

lubrication, lubrification†; anointment; oiling &c *v.*. synovia *[Anat.]*; glycerine, oil, lubricating oil, grease &c 356; saliva; lather.

teflon.

V. lubricate, lubricitate†; oil, grease, lather, soap; wax.

Adj. lubricated &c *v.;* lubricous.

2. FLUID MATTER

1. Fluids in General

333. Fluidity -- **N.** fluidity, liquidity; liquidness &c *adj.*†*;* gaseity &c 334 [Obs.].

fluid, inelastic fluid; liquid, liquor; lymph, humor, juice, sap, serum, blood, serosity†, gravy, rheum, ichor†, sanies†; chyle *[Med.]*.

solubility, solubleness†.

[Science of liquids at rest] hydrology, hydrostatics, hydrodynamics.

V. be fluid &c *adj.;* flow &c *(water in motion)* 348; liquefy, melt, condense &c 335.

Adj. liquid, fluid, serous, juicy, succulent, sappy; ichorous†; fluent &c *(flowing)* 348.

liquefied &c 335; uncongealed; soluble.

334. Gaseity -- **N.** gaseity†; vaporousness &c *adj.;* flatulence, flatulency; volatility; aeration, aerification.

elastic fluid, gas, air, vapor, ether, steam, essence, fume, reek, effluvium, flatus; cloud &c 353; ammonia, ammoniacal gas†; volatile alkali; vacuum, partial vacuum.

[Science of elastic fluids] pneumatics, pneumatostatics†; aerostatics†, aerodynamics.

gasmeter†, gasometer†; air bladder, swimming bladder, sound, (of a fish).

V. vaporize, evaporate, evanesce, gasify, emit vapor &c 336; diffuse.

Adj. gaseous, aeriform†, ethereal, aerial, airy, vaporous, volatile, evaporable†, flatulent.

335. Liquefaction -- **N.** liquefaction; liquescence†, liquescency†; melting &c *(heat)* 384; colliquation†, colliquefaction†; thaw; liquation†, deliquation†, deliquescence; lixiviation†, dissolution.

solution, apozem†, lixivium†, infusion, flux.

solvent, menstruum, alkahest†.

V. render liquid &c 333; liquefy, run; deliquesce; melt &c *(heat)* 384; solve; dissolve, resolve; liquate†; hold in solution; condense, precipitate, rain.

Adj. liquefied &c *v.,* liquescent, liquefiable; deliquescent, soluble, colliquative†.

336. Vaporization -- **N.** vaporization, volatilization; gasification, evaporation, vaporation†; distillation, cupellation *[Chem]*, cohobation, sublimination†, exhalation; volatility.

vaporizer, still, retort; fumigation, steaming; bay salt, chloride of sodium†.

mister, spray.

bubble, effervescence.'

V. render gaseous &c 334; vaporize, volatilize; distill, sublime; evaporate, exhale, smoke, transpire, emit vapor, fume, reek, steam, fumigate; cohobate†; finestill†.

bubble, sparge, effervesce, boil.

Adj. volatilized &c *v.;* reeking &c *v.;* volatile; evaporable†, vaporizable.

bubbly, effervescent, boiling.

2. Specific Fluids

337. Water -- **N.** water; serum, serosity†; lymph; rheum; diluent; agua *[Sp.]*, aqua, pani†.

dilution, maceration, lotion; washing &c *v.;* immersion†, humectation†, infiltration, spargefaction†, affusion†, irrigation, douche, balneation†, bath.

deluge &c *(water in motion)* 348; high water, flood tide.

V. be watery &c *adj.;* reek.

add water, water, wet; moisten &c 339; dilute, dip, immerse; merge; immerge, submerge; plunge, souse, duck, drown; soak, steep, macerate, pickle, wash, sprinkle, lave, bathe, affuse†, splash, swash, douse, drench; dabble, slop, slobber, irrigate, inundate, deluge; syringe, inject, gargle.

Adj. watery, aqueous, aquatic, hydrous, lymphatic; balneal†, diluent; drenching &c v.; diluted &c v.; weak; wet &c *(moist)* 339.

Phr. the waters are out.

338. Air -- N. air &c *(gas)* 334; common air, atmospheric air; atmosphere; aerosphere†.

open air; sky, welkin; blue sky; cloud &c 353.

weather, climate, rise and fall of the barometer, isobar.

[Science of air] aerology, aerometry†, aeroscopy†, aeroscopy†, aerography†; meteorology, climatology; pneumatics; eudioscope†, baroscope†, aeroscope†, eudiometer†, barometer, aerometer†; aneroid, baroscope†; weather gauge, weather glass, weather cock.

exposure to the air, exposure to the weather; ventilation; aerostation†, aeronautics, aeronaut.

V. air, ventilate, fan &c *(wind)* 349.

Adj. containing air, flatulent, effervescent; windy &c 349.

atmospheric, airy; aerial, aeriform†; meteorological; weatherwise†.

Adv. in the open air, a la belle etoile *[Fr.]*, al fresco; sub jove dio *[Lat.]*.

339. Moisture -- N. moisture; moistness &c *adj.;* humidity, humectation†; madefaction†, dew; serein†; marsh &c 345; hygrometry, hygrometer.

V. moisten, wet; humect†, humectate†; sponge, damp, bedew; imbue, imbrue, infiltrate, saturate; soak, drench &c *(water)* 337.

be moist &c *adj.;* not have a dry thread; perspire &c *(exude)* 295.

Adj. moist, damp; watery &c 337; madid†, roric†; undried†, humid, sultry, wet, dank, luggy†, dewy; roral†, rorid†; roscid†; juicy.

wringing wet, soaking wet; wet through to the skin; saturated &c *v..* swashy†, soggy, dabbled; reeking, dripping, soaking, soft, sodden, sloppy, muddy; swampy &c *(marshy)* 345; irriguous†.

340. Dryness -- **N.** dryness &c *adj.;* siccity[†], aridity, drought, ebb tide, low water.

exsiccation[†], desiccation; arefaction[†], dephlegmation[†], drainage; drier.

[chemical subs. which renders dry] desiccative, dessicator.

[device to render dry] dessicator; hair drier, clothes drier, gas drier, electric drier; vacuum oven, drying oven, kiln; lyophilizer.

clothesline.

V. be dry &c *adj..* render dry &c *adj.;* dry; dry up, soak up; sponge, swab, wipe; drain.

desiccate, dehydrate, exsiccate[†]; parch.

kiln dry; vacuum dry, blow dry, oven dry; hang out to dry.

mummify.

be fine, hold up.

Adj. dry, anhydrous, arid; adust[†], arescent[†]; dried &c *v.;* undamped; juiceless[†], sapless; sear; husky; rainless, without rain, fine; dry as a bone, dry as dust, dry as a stick, dry as a mummy, dry as a biscuit.

water proof, water tight.

dehydrated, dessicated.

341. Ocean -- **N.** sea, ocean, main, deep, brine, salt water, waves, billows, high seas, offing, great waters, watery waste, vasty deep; wave, tide, &c *(water in motion)* 348.

hydrography, hydrographer; Neptune, Poseidon, Thetis, Triton, Naiad, Nereid; sea nymph, Siren; trident, dolphin.

Adj. oceanic; marine, maritime; pelagic, pelagian; seagoing; hydrographic; bathybic†, cotidal†.

Adv. at sea, on sea; afloat.

342. Land -- **N.** land, earth, ground, dry land, terra firma.

continent, mainland, peninsula, chersonese *[Fr.]*, delta; tongue of land, neck of land; isthmus, oasis; promontory &c *(projection)* 250; highland &c *(height)* 206.

coast, shore, scar, strand, beach; playa; bank, lea; seaboard, seaside, seabank†, seacoast, seabeach†;

ironbound coast; loom of the land; derelict; innings; alluvium, alluvion†; ancon.

riverbank, river bank, levee.

soil, glebe, clay, loam, marl, cledge†, chalk, gravel, mold, subsoil, clod, clot; rock, crag.

acres; real estate &c *(property)* 780; landsman†.

V. land, come to land, set foot on the soil, set foot on dry land; come ashore, go ashore, debark.

Adj. earthy, continental, midland, coastal, littoral, riparian; alluvial; terrene &c *(world)* 318; landed, predial†, territorial; geophilous†; ripicolous.

Adv. ashore; on shore, on land.

343. Gulf. Lake -- N. land covered with water, gulf, gulph†, bay, inlet, bight, estuary, arm of the sea, bayou *[U.S.]*, fiord, armlet; frith†, firth, ostiary†, mouth; lagune†, lagoon; indraught†; cove, creek; natural harbor; roads; strait; narrows; Euripus; sound, belt, gut, kyles†; continental slope, continental shelf.

lake, loch, lough†, mere, tarn, plash, broad, pond, pool, lin†, puddle, slab, well, artesian well; standing water, dead water, sheet of water; fish pond, mill pond; ditch, dike, dyke, dam; reservoir

&c *(store)* 636; alberca†, barachois†, hog wallow *[U.S.]*.

Adj. lacustrine†.

344. Plain -- **N.** plain, table-land, face of the country; open country, champaign country†; basin, downs, waste, weary waste, desert, wild, steppe, pampas, savanna, prairie, heath, common, wold†, veldt; moor, moorland; bush; plateau &c *(level)* 213; campagna†; alkali flat, llano; mesa, mesilla *[U.S.]*, playa; shaking prairie, trembling prairie; vega *[Sp.]*.

meadow, mead, haugh†, pasturage, park, field, lawn, green, plat, plot, grassplat†, greensward, sward, turf, sod, heather; lea, ley, lay; grounds; maidan†, agostadero†.

Adj. champaign†, alluvial; campestral†, campestrial†, campestrian†, campestrine†.

345. Marsh -- **N.** marsh, swamp, morass, marish†, moss, fen, bog, quagmire, slough, sump, wash; mud, squash, slush; baygall *[U.S.]*, cienaga†, jhil†, vlei†.

Adj. marsh, marshy; swampy, boggy, plashy†, poachy†, quaggy†, soft; muddy, sloppy, squashy; paludal†; moorish, moory; fenny.

346. Island -- **N.** island, isle, islet, eyot†, ait†, holf†, reef, atoll, breaker; archipelago; islander.

Adj. insular, seagirt; archipelagic†.

3. Fluids in Motion

347. *[Fluid in motion.]* **Stream** -- **N.** stream &c *(of water)* 348, *(of air)* 349.

flowmeter.

V. flow &c 348; blow &c 349.

348. *[Water in motion.]* **River** -- **N.** running water.

jet, spirt†, spurt, squirt, spout, spray, splash, rush, gush, jet d'eau *[Fr.]*; sluice.

water spout, water fall; cascade, force, foss†; lin†, linn†; ghyll†, Niagara; cataract, rapids, white water, catadupe†, cataclysm; debacle, inundation, deluge; chute, washout.

rain, rainfall; serein†; shower, scud; downpour; driving rain, drenching rain, cloudburst; hyetology†, hyetography†; predominance of Aquarius†, reign of St.

Swithin; mizzle†, drizzle, stillicidum†, plash; dropping &c *v.;* falling weather; northeaster, hurricane, typhoon.

stream, course, flux, flow, profluence†; effluence &c *(egress)* 295; defluxion†; flowing &c *v.;* current, tide, race, coulee.

spring, artesian well, fount, fountain; rill, rivulet, gill, gullet, rillet†; streamlet, brooklet; branch *[U.S.]*; runnel, sike†, burn, beck, creek, brook, bayou, stream, river; reach, tributary.

geyser, spout, waterspout.

body of water, torrent, rapids, flush, flood, swash; spring tide, high tide, full tide; bore, tidal bore, eagre†, hygre†; fresh, freshet; indraught†, reflux, undercurrent, eddy, vortex, gurge†, whirlpool, Maelstrom, regurgitation, overflow; confluence, corrivation†.

wave, billow, surge, swell, ripple; anerythmon gelasma *[Gr.]*; beach comber, riffle *[U.S.]*, rollers, ground swell, surf, breakers, white horses, whitecaps; rough sea, heavy sea, high seas, cross sea, long sea, short sea, chopping sea.

[Science of fluids in motion] hydrodynamics; hydraulics, hydraulicostatics†; rain gauge, flowmeter; pegology†.

irrigation &c *(water)* 337; pump; watering pot, watering cart; hydrant, syringe; garden hose, lawn spray; bhisti†, mussuk†.

V. flow, run; meander; gush, pour, spout, roll, jet, well, issue; drop, drip, dribble, plash, spirtle†, trill, trickle, distill, percolate; stream, overflow, inundate, deluge, flow over, splash, swash; guggle†, murmur, babble, bubble, purl, gurgle, sputter, spurt, spray, regurgitate; ooze, flow out &c *(egress)* 295.

rain hard, rain in torrents, rain cats and dogs, rain pitchforks; pour with rain, drizzle, spit, set in; mizzle†.

flow into, fall into, open into, drain into; discharge itself, disembogue†.

[Cause a flow] pour; pour out &c *(discharge)* 297; shower down, irrigate, drench &c *(wet)* 337; spill, splash.

[Stop a flow] stanch; dam, up &c *(close)* 261; obstruct &c 706.

Adj. fluent; diffluent†, profluent†, affluent; tidal; flowing &c *v.;* meandering, meandry†, meandrous†; fluvial, fluviatile; streamy†, showery, rainy, pluvial, stillicidous†; stillatitious†.

Phr. for men may come and men may go but I go on forever [Tennyson]; that old man river, he just keeps rolling along [Showboat].

349. *[Air in motion]* **Wind** -- N. wind, draught, flatus, afflatus, efflation†, eluvium†; air; breath, breath of air; puff, whiff, zephyr; blow, breeze, drift; aura; stream, current, jet stream; undercurrent.

gust, blast, squall, gale, half a gale, storm, tempest, hurricane, whirlwind, tornado, samiel, cyclone, anticyclone, typhoon; simoon†, simoom; harmattan†, monsoon, trade wind, sirocco, mistral, bise†, tramontane, levanter; capful of wind; fresh breeze, stiff breeze; keen blast; blizzard, barber *[Can.]*, candelia†, chinook, foehn, khamsin†, norther, vendaval†, wuther†.

windiness &c *adj.;* ventosity†; rough weather, dirty weather, ugly weather, stress of weather; dirty sky, mare's tail; thick squall, black squall, white squall.

anemography†, aerodynamics; wind gauge, weathercock, vane, weather-vane, wind sock; anemometer, anemoscope†.

sufflation†, insufflation†, perflation†, inflation, afflation†; blowing, fanning &c *v.;* ventilation.

sneezing &c *v.;* errhine†; sternutative†, sternutatory†; sternutation; hiccup, hiccough; catching of the breath.

Eolus, Boreas, Zephyr, cave of Eolus.

air pump, air blower, lungs, bellows, blowpipe, fan, ventilator, punkah†; branchiae†, gills, flabellum†, vertilabrum†.

whiffle ball.

V. blow, waft; blow hard, blow great guns, blow a hurricane &c *n.;* wuther†; stream, issue.

respire, breathe, puff; whiff, whiffle; gasp, wheeze; snuff, snuffle; sniff, sniffle; sneeze, cough.

fan, ventilate; inflate, perflate†; blow up.

Adj. blowing &c *v.;* windy, flatulent; breezy, gusty, squally; stormy, tempestuous, blustering; boisterous &c *(violent)* 173.

pulmonic *[Med.]*, pulmonary.

Phr. lull'd by soft zephyrs [Pope]; the storm is up and all is on the hazard [Julius Caesar]; the winds were wither'd in the stagnant air [Byron]; while mocking winds are piping loud [Milton]; winged with red lightning and tempestuous rage [Paradise Lost].

350. *[Channel for the passage of water.]* **Conduit --**
 N. conduit, channel, duct, watercourse, race; head race, tail race; abito†, aboideau†, aboiteau *[Fr.]*, bito†; acequia†, acequiador†, acequiamadre†; arroyo;

adit†, aqueduct, canal, trough, gutter, pantile; flume, ingate†, runner; lock-weir, tedge†; vena†; dike, main, gully, moat, ditch, drain, sewer, culvert, cloaca, sough, kennel, siphon; piscina†; pipe &c *(tube)* 260; funnel; tunnel &c *(passage)* 627; water pipe, waste pipe; emunctory†, gully hole, artery, aorta, pore, spout, scupper; adjutage†, ajutage†; hose; gargoyle; gurgoyle†; penstock, weir; flood gate, water gate; sluice, lock, valve; rose; waterworks.

pipeline.

Adj. vascular &c *(with holes)* 260.

351. *[Channel for the passage of air.]* **Airpipe** -- **N.** air pipe, air tube; airhole†, blowhole, breathinghole†, venthole; shaft, flue, chimney, funnel, vent, nostril, nozzle, throat, weasand†, trachea; bronchus, bronchia *[Med.]*; larynx, tonsils, windpipe, spiracle; ventiduct†, ventilator; louvre, jalousie, Venetian blinds; blowpipe &c *(wind)* 349; pipe &c *(tube)* 260; jhilmil†; smokestack.

screen, window screen.' artificial lung, iron lung, heart and lung machine.

3. IMPERFECT FLUIDS

352. Semiliquidity -- N. semiliquidity; stickiness &c *adj.;* viscidity, viscosity; gummosity†, glutinosity†, mucosity†; spissitude†, crassitude†; lentor†; adhesiveness &c *(cohesion)* 46.

inspissation†, incrassation†; thickening.

jelly, mucilage, gelatin, gluten; carlock†, fish glue; ichthyocol†, ichthycolla†; isinglass; mucus, phlegm, goo; pituite†, lava; glair†, starch, gluten, albumen, milk, cream, protein†; treacle; gum, size, glue *(tenacity)* 327; wax, beeswax.

emulsion, soup; squash, mud, slush, slime, ooze; moisture &c 339; marsh &c 345.

V. inspissate†, incrassate†; thicken, mash, squash, churn, beat up.

sinter.

Adj. semifluid, semiliquid; tremellose†; half melted, half frozen; milky, muddy &c *n.;* lacteal, lactean†, lacteous†, lactescent†, lactiferous†; emulsive, curdled, thick, succulent, uliginous†.

gelatinous, albuminous, mucilaginous, glutinous; glutenous, gelatin, mastic, amylaceous†, ropy, clammy, clotted; viscid, viscous; sticky, tacky, gooey; slab, slabby†; lentous†, pituitous†; mucid†, muculent†, mucous; gummy.

353. *[Mixture of air and water.]* **Bubble** *[Cloud.]* --
N. bubble, foam, froth, head, spume, lather, suds, spray, surf, yeast, barm†, spindrift.

cloud, vapor, fog, mist, haze, steam, geyser; scud, messenger, rack, nimbus; cumulus, woolpack†, cirrus, stratus; cirrostratus, cumulostratus; cirrocumulus; mackerel sky, mare's tale, dirty sky; curl cloud; frost smoke; thunderhead.

[Science of clouds] nephelognosy†; nephograph†, nephology†.

effervescence, fermentation; bubbling &c *v..* nebula; cloudiness &c *(opacity)* 426 [Obs.]; nebulosity &c *(dimness)* 422.

V. bubble, boil, foam, froth, mantle, sparkle, guggle†, gurgle; effervesce, ferment, fizzle.

Adj. bubbling &c *v.;* frothy, nappy†, effervescent, sparkling, mousseux *[Fr.]*, frothy *[Fr.Tr.]*, up.

cloudy &c *n.;* thunderheaded†; vaporous, nebulous, overcast.

Phr. the lowring element scowls o'er the darkened landscip [Paradise Lost].

354. Pulpiness -- **N.** pulpiness &c *adj.;* pulp, taste, dough, curd, pap, rob, jam, pudding, poultice, grume†.

mush, oatmeal, baby food.

Adj. pulpy &c *n.;* pultaceous†, grumous†; baccate†.

355. Unctuousness -- **N.** unctuousness &c *adj.;* unctuosity†, lubricity; ointment &c *(oil)* 356; anointment; lubrication &c 332.

V. oil &c *(lubricate)* 332.

Adj. unctuous, oily, oleaginous, adipose, sebaceous; unguinous†; fat, fatty, greasy; waxy, butyraceous, soapy, saponaceous†, pinguid, lardaceous†; slippery.

356. Oil -- **N.** oil, fat, butter, cream, grease, tallow, suet, lard, dripping exunge†, blubber; glycerin, stearin, elaine *[Chem]*, oleagine†; soap; soft soap, wax, cerement; paraffin, spermaceti, adipocere†; petroleum, mineral, mineral rock, mineral crystal, mineral oil; vegetable oil, colza oil†, olive oil, salad oil, linseed oil, cottonseed oil, soybean oil, nut oil; animal oil, neat's foot oil, train oil; ointment, unguent, liniment; aceite†, amole†, Barbados tar†; fusel oil, grain oil, rape oil, seneca oil; hydrate of amyl, ghee†; heating oil, #2 oil, No.

2 oil, distillate, residual oils, kerosene, jet fuel, gasoline, naphtha; stearin.

356a. Resin -- **N.** resin, rosin; gum; lac, sealing wax; amber, ambergris; bitumen, pitch, tar; asphalt, asphaltum; camphor; varnish, copal†, mastic, magilp†, lacquer, japan.

artificial resin, polymer; ion-exchange resin, cation-exchange resin, anion exchange resin, water softener, Amberlite†, Dowex *[Chem]*, Diaion.

V. varnish &c *(overlay)* 223.

Adj. resiny†, resinous; bituminous, pitchy, tarry; asphaltic, asphaltite.

SECTION III.

ORGANIC MATTER

1. VITALITY
   1. Vitality in general

357. Organization -- N. organized world, organized nature; living nature, animated nature; living beings; organic remains, fossils.

protoplasm, cytoplasm, protein; albumen; structure &c 329; organization, organism.

[Science of living beings] biology; natural history, organic chemistry, anatomy, physiology; zoology &c 368; botany; microbiology, virology, bacteriology, mycology &c 369; naturalist.

archegenesis &c *(production)* 161 [Obs.]; antherozoid†, bioplasm†, biotaxy†, chromosome, dysmeromorph†; ecology, oecology; erythroblast *[Physio.]*, gametangium†, gamete, germinal matter, invagination *[Biol.]*; isogamy†, oogamy†; karyaster†; macrogamete†, microgamete†; metabolism, anabolism, catabolism; metaplasm†, ontogeny, ovary, ovum, oxidation, phylogeny, polymorphism, protozoa, spermary†, spermatozoon, trophoplasm†, vacuole, vertebration†, zoogloea†, zygote.

Darwinism, neo-Darwinism, Lamarkism, neoLamarkism, Weismannism.

morphology, taxonomy.

Adj. organic, organized; karyoplasmic†, unsegmentic†, vacuolar, zoogloeic†, zoogloeoid†.

358. Inorganization -- **N.** mineral world, mineral kingdom; unorganized matter, inorganic matter, brute matter, inanimate matter.

[Science of the mineral kingdom] mineralogy, geology, geognosy†, geoscopy†; metallurgy, metallography†; lithology; oryctology†, oryctography†.

V. turn to dust; mineralize, fossilize.

Adj. inorganic, inanimate, inorganized†; lithoidal†; azoic; mineral.

359. Life -- **N.** life, vitality, viability; animation; vital spark, vital flame, soul, spirit.

respiration, wind; breath of life, breath of one's nostrils; oxygen, air.

[devices to sustain respiration] respirator, artificial respirator, heart and lung machine, iron lung; medical devices &c 662.

lifeblood; Archeus†; existence &c 1.

vivification; vital force; vitalization; revivification &c 163; Prometheus; life to come &c *(destiny)* 152.

[Science of life] physiology, biology; animal ecology.

nourishment, staff of life &c *(food)* 298.

genetics, heredity, inheritance, evolution, natural selection, reproduction *(production)* 161.

microbe, aerobe, anaerobe, facultative anaerobe, obligate aerobe, obligate anaerobe, halophile *[Micro.]*, methanogen *[Micro.]*, archaebacteria *[Micro.]*, microaerophile *[Micro.]*.

animal &c 366; vegetable &c 367.

artificial life, robot, robotics, artificial intelligence.

[vital signs] breathing, breathing rate, heartbeat, pulse, temperature.

preservation of life, healing *(medicine)* 662.

V. be alive &c *adj.*; live, breathe, respire; subsist &c *(exist)* 1; walk the earth, strut and fret one's hour upon the stage [Macbeth]; be spared.

see the light, be born, come into the world, fetch breath, draw breath, fetch the breath of life, draw the breath of life; quicken; revive; come to life.

give birth to &c *(produce)* 161; bring to life, put into life, vitalize; vivify, vivificate†; reanimate &c *(restore)* 660; keep alive, keep body and soul together, keep the wolf from the door; support life.

hive nine lives like a cat.

Adj. living, alive; in life, in the flesh, in the land of the living; on this side of the grave, above ground, breathing, quick, animated; animative[†]; lively &c *(active)* 682; all alive and kicking; tenacious of life; full of life, yeasty.

vital, vitalic[†]; vivifying, vivified, &c *v.;* viable, zoetic[†]; Promethean.

Adv. vivendi causa *[Lat.]*.

Phr. atqui vivere militare est *[Lat.]* [Seneca]; non est vivere sed valere vita *[Lat.]* [Marial].

360. Death -- **N.** death; decease, demise; dissolution, departure, obit, release, rest, quietus, fall; loss, bereavement; mortality, morbidity.

end of life &c 67, cessation of life &c 142, loss of life, extinction of life, ebb of life &c 359.

death warrant, death watch, death rattle, death bed; stroke of death, agonies of death, shades of death, valley of death, jaws of death, hand of death; last breath, last gasp, last agonies; dying day, dying breath, dying agonies; chant du cygne *[Fr.]*; rigor mortis *[Lat.]*; Stygian shore.

King of terrors, King Death; Death; doom &c *(necessity)* 601; Hell's grim Tyrant [Pope].

euthanasia; break up of the system; natural death, natural decay; sudden death, violent death; untimely end, watery grave; debt of nature; suffocation, asphyxia; fatal disease &c *(disease)* 655; death blow &c *(killing)* 361.

necrology, bills of mortality, obituary; death song &c *(lamentation)* 839.

V. die, expire, perish; meet one's death, meet one's end; pass away, be taken; yield one's breath, resign one's breath; resign one's being, resign one's life; end one's days, end one's life, end one's earthly career; breathe one's last; cease to live, cease to breathe; depart this life; be no more &c *adj.;* go off, drop off, pop off; lose one's life, lay down one's life, relinquish one's life, surrender one's life; drop into the grave, sink into the grave; close one's eyes; fall dead, drop dead, fall down dead, drop down dead; break one's neck; give up the ghost, yield up the ghost; be all over with one.

pay the debt to nature, shuffle off this mortal coil, take one's last sleep; go the way of all flesh; hand in one's checks, pass in one's checks, hand in one's chips, pass in one's chips *[U.S.]*; join the greater number, join the majority; come to dust, turn to dust; cross the Stygian ferry, cross the bar; go to one's long account, go to one's last home, go to Davy Jones's locker, go to the wall; receive one's death warrant, make one's will, step out, die a natural death, go out like the snuff of a candle; come to an untimely end; catch one's death; go off the hooks, kick the bucket, buy the farm, hop the twig, turn up one's toes; die a violent death &c *(be killed)* 361.

Adj. dead, lifeless; deceased, demised, departed, defunct, extinct; late, gone, no more; exanimate†, inanimate; out of the world, taken off, released; departed this life &c *v.;* dead and gone; dead as a doornail, dead as a doorpost†, dead as a mutton, dead as a herring, dead as nits; launched into eternity, gone to one's eternal reward, gone to meet one's maker, pushing up daisies, gathered to one's fathers, numbered with the dead.

dying &c *v.;* moribund, morient†; hippocratic; in articulo, in extremis; in the jaws of death, in the agony of death; going off; aux abois *[Fr.]*; one one's last legs, on one's death bed; at the point of death, at death's door, at the last gasp; near one's end, given over, booked; with one foot in the grave, tottering on the brink of the grave.

stillborn; mortuary; deadly &c *(killing)* 361.

Adv. post obit, post mortem *[Lat.]*.

Phr. life ebbs, life fails, life hangs by a thread; one's days are numbered, one's hour is come, one's race is run, one's doom is sealed; Death knocks at the door, Death stares one in the face; the breath is out of the body; the grave closes over one; sic itur ad astra *[Lat.]* [Vergil]; de mortuis nil nisi bonum *[Lat.]*; dulce et decorum est pro patria mori *[Lat.]* [Horace]; honesta mors turpi vita potior *[Lat.]* [Tacitus]; in adamantine chains shall death be bound [Pope]; mors ultima linea rerum est *[Lat.]* [Girace]; ominia mors aequat *[Lat.]* [Claudianus]; Spake the grisly Terror [Paradise Lost]; the lone couch of this everlasting sleep [Shelley]; nothing is certain but death and taxes.

361. *[Destruction of life; violent death.]* **Killing** -- N. killing &c v.; homicide, manslaughter, murder, assassination, trucidation†, iccusion†; effusion of blood; blood, blood shed; gore, slaughter, carnage, butchery; battue†.

massacre; fusillade, noyade†; thuggery, Thuggism†.

deathblow, finishing stroke, coup de grace, quietus; execution &c *(capital punishment)* 972; judicial murder; martyrdom.

butcher, slayer, murderer, Cain, assassin, terrorist, cutthroat, garroter, bravo, Thug, Moloch, matador, sabreur†; guet-a-pens; gallows, executioner &c *(punishment)* 975; man-eater, apache†, hatchet man *[U.S.]*, highbinder *[U.S.]*.

regicide, parricide, matricide, fratricide, infanticide, feticide, foeticide†, uxoricide†, vaticide†.

suicide, felo de se†, hara-kiri, suttee, Juggernath†; immolation, auto da fe, holocaust.

suffocation, strangulation, garrote; hanging &c v.; lapidation†.

deadly weapon &c *(arms)* 727; Aceldama†.

[Destruction of animals] slaughtering; phthisozoics†; sport, sporting; the chase, venery; hunting, coursing, shooting, fishing; pig-sticking; sportsman, huntsman, fisherman; hunter, Nimrod; slaughterhouse, meat packing plant, shambles, abattoir.

fatal accident, violent death, casualty.

V. kill, put to death, slay, shed blood; murder, assassinate, butcher, slaughter, victimize, immolate; massacre; take away life, deprive of life; make away with, put an end to; despatch, dispatch; burke, settle, do for.

strangle, garrote, hang, throttle, choke, stifle, suffocate, stop the breath, smother, asphyxiate, drown.

saber; cut down, cut to pieces, cut the throat; jugulate†; stab, run through the body, bayonet, eviscerate; put to the sword, put to the edge of the sword.

shoot dead; blow one's brains out; brain, knock on the head; stone, lapidate†; give a deathblow; deal a deathblow; give a quietus, give a coupe de grace.

behead, bowstring, electrocute, gas &c *(execute)* 972.

hunt, shoot &c *n.*. cut off, nip in the bud, launch into eternity, send to one's last account, sign one's death warrant, strike the death knell of.

give no quarter, pour out blood like water; decimate; run amuck; wade knee deep in blood, imbrue one's hands in blood.

die a violent death, welter in one's blood; dash out one's brains, blow out one's brains; commit suicide; kill oneself, make away with oneself, put an end to oneself, put an end to it all.

Adj. killing &c *v.;* murderous, slaughterous; sanguinary, sanguinolent†; blood stained, blood thirsty; homicidal, red handed; bloody, bloody minded; ensanguined†, gory; thuggish.

mortal, fatal, lethal; dead, deadly; mortiferous†, lethiferous†; unhealthy &c 657; internecine; suicidal.

sporting; piscatorial, piscatory†.

Adv. in at the death.

Phr. assassination has never changed the history of the world [Disraeli].

362. Corpse -- **N.** corpse, corse†, carcass, cadaver, bones, skeleton, dry bones; defunct, relics, reliquiae *[Lat.]*, remains, mortal remains, dust, ashes, earth, clay; mummy; carrion; food for worms, food for fishes; tenement of clay this mortal coil.

shade, ghost, manes.

organic remains, fossils.

Adj. cadaverous, corpse-like; unburied &c 363; sapromyiophyllous†.

363. Interment -- **N.** interment, burial, sepulture†; inhumation†; obsequies, exequies†; funeral, wake, pyre, funeral pile; cremation.

funeral, funeral rite, funeral solemnity; kneel, passing bell, tolling; dirge &c *(lamentation)* 839; cypress; orbit, dead march, muffled drum; mortuary, undertaker, mute; elegy; funeral, funeral oration, funeral sermon; epitaph.

graveclothes†, shroud, winding sheet, cerecloth; cerement.

coffin, shell, sarcophagus, urn, pall, bier, hearse, catafalque, cinerary urn†.

grave, pit, sepulcher, tomb, vault, crypt, catacomb, mausoleum, Golgotha, house of death, narrow house; cemetery, necropolis; burial place, burial ground; grave yard, church yard; God's acre; tope, cromlech, barrow, tumulus, cairn; ossuary; bone house, charnel house, dead house; morgue; lich gate†; burning ghat†; crematorium, crematory; dokhma†, mastaba†, potter's field, stupa†, Tower of Silence.

sexton, gravedigger.

monument, cenotaph, shrine; grave stone, head stone, tomb stone; memento mori *[Lat.]*; hatchment†, stone; obelisk, pyramid.

exhumation, disinterment; necropsy, autopsy, post mortem examination *[Lat.]*; zoothapsis†.

V. inter, bury; lay in the grave, consign to the grave, lay in the tomb, entomb, in tomb; inhume; lay out, perform a funeral, embalm, mummify; toll the knell; put to bed with a shovel; inurn†.

exhume, disinter, unearth.

Adj. burried &c v.; burial, funereal, funebrial†; mortuary, sepulchral, cinerary†; elegiac; necroscopic†.

Adv. in memoriam; post obit, post mortem *[Lat.]*; beneath the sod.

Phr. hic jacet *[Lat.]*, ci-git *[Fr.]*; RIP; requiescat in pace *[Lat.]*; the lone couch of his everlasting sleep [Shelley]; without a grave-unknell'd, uncoffin'd, and unknown [Byron]; in the dark union of insensate dust [Byron]; the deep cold shadow of the tomb [Moore].

2. Special Vitality

364. Animality -- **N.** animal life; animation, animality†, animalization†; animalness, corporeal nature, human system; breath.

flesh, flesh and blood; physique; strength &c 159.

Adj. fleshly, human, corporeal.

365. Vegetability† -- **N.** vegetable life; vegetation, vegetability†; vegetality†.

V. vegetate, grow roots, put down roots.

Adj. rank, lush; vegetable, vegetal, vegetive†.

366. Animal -- N. animal, animal kingdom; fauna; brute creation.

beast, brute, creature, critter *[U.S.]*; wight, created being; creeping thing, living thing; dumb animal, dumb creature; zoophyte.

[major divisions of animals] mammal, bird, reptile, amphibian, fish, crustacean, shellfish, mollusk, worm, insect, arthropod, microbe.

[microscopic animals] microbe, animalcule &c 193.

[reptiles] alligator, crocodile; saurian; dinosaur (extinct); snake, serpent, viper, eft; asp, aspick[†].

[amphibians] frog, toad.

[fishes] trout, bass, tuna, muskelunge, sailfish, sardine, mackerel.

[insects] ant, mosquito, bee, honeybee.

[arthropods] tardigrade, spider.

[classification by number of feet] biped, quadruped; *[web-footed animal]* webfoot.

flocks and herds, live stock; domestic animals, wild animals; game, ferae naturae *[Lat.]*; beasts of the field, fowls of the air, denizens of the sea; black game, black grouse; blackcock†, duck, grouse, plover, rail, snipe.

[domesticated mammals] horse &c *(beast of burden)* 271; cattle, kine†, ox; bull, bullock; cow, milch cow, calf, heifer, shorthorn; sheep; lamb, lambkin†; ewe, ram, tup; pig, swine, boar, hog, sow; steer, stot†; tag, teg†; bison, buffalo, yak, zebu, dog, cat.

[dogs] dog, hound; pup, puppy; whelp, cur, mongrel; house dog, watch dog, sheep dog, shepherd's dog, sporting dog, fancy dog, lap dog, toy dog, bull dog, badger dog; mastiff; blood hound, grey hound, stag hound, deer hound, fox hound, otter hound; harrier, beagle, spaniel, pointer, setter, retriever; Newfoundland; water dog, water spaniel; pug, poodle; turnspit; terrier; fox terrier, Skye terrier; Dandie Dinmont; collie.

[cats--generally] feline, puss, pussy; grimalkin†; gib cat, tom cat.

[wild mammals] fox, Reynard, vixen, stag, deer, hart, buck, doe, roe; caribou, coyote, elk, moose, musk ox, sambar†.

[birds] bird; poultry, fowl, cock, hen, chicken, chanticleer, partlet†, rooster, dunghill cock, barn

door fowl; feathered tribes, feathered songster; singing bird, dicky bird; canary, warbler; finch; aberdevine†, cushat†, cygnet, ringdove†, siskin, swan, wood pigeon.

[undesirable animals] vermin, varmint *[U.S.]*, pest.

Adj. animal, zoological equine, bovine, vaccine, canine, feline, fishy; piscatory†, piscatorial; molluscous†, vermicular; gallinaceous, rasorial†, solidungulate†, soliped†.

367. Vegetable -- N. vegetable, vegetable kingdom; flora, verdure.

plant; tree, shrub, bush; creeper; herb, herbage; grass.

annual; perennial, biennial, triennial; exotic.

timber, forest; wood, woodlands; timberland; hurst†, frith†, holt, weald†, park, chase, greenwood, brake, grove, copse, coppice, bocage†, tope, clump of trees, thicket, spinet, spinney; underwood, brushwood; scrub; boscage, bosk†, ceja *[Sp.]*, chaparal, motte *[U.S.]*; arboretum &c 371.

bush, jungle, prairie; heath, heather; fern, bracken; furze, gorse, whin; grass, turf; pasture, pasturage; turbary†; sedge, rush, weed; fungus, mushroom, toadstool; lichen, moss, conferva†, mold; growth;

alfalfa, alfilaria†, banyan; blow, blowth†; floret†, petiole; pin grass, timothy, yam, yew, zinnia.

foliage, branch, bough, ramage†, stem, tigella†; spray &c 51; leaf.

flower, blossom, bine†; flowering plant; timber tree, fruit tree; pulse, legume.

Adj. vegetable, vegetal, vegetive†, vegitous†; herbaceous, herbal; botanic†; sylvan, silvan†; arborary†, arboreous†, arborescent†, arborical†; woody, grassy; verdant, verdurous; floral, mossy; lignous†, ligneous; wooden, leguminous; vosky†, cespitose†, turf-like, turfy; endogenous, exogenous.

Phr. green-robed senators of mighty woods [Keats]; this is the forest primeval [Longfellow].

368. *[The science of animals.]* **Zoology** --
N. zoology, zoonomy†, zoography†, zootomy†; anatomy; comparative anatomy; animal physiology, comparative physiology; morphology; mammalogy.

anthropology, ornithology, ichthyology, herpetology, ophiology†, malacology†, helminthology *[Med.]*, entomology, oryctology†, paleontology, mastology†, vermeology†; ornithotomy†, ichthyotomy†, &c; taxidermy.

zoologist &c

Adj. zoological &c *n*..

369. *[The science of plants.]* **Botany** -- **N.** botany; physiological botany, structural botany, systematic botany; phytography†, phytology†, phytotomy†; vegetable physiology, herborization†, dendrology, mycology, fungology†, algology†; flora, romona; botanic garden &c *(garden)* 371 [Obs.]; hortus siccus *[Lat.]*, herbarium, herbal.

botanist &c; herbist†, herbarist†, herbalist, herborist†, herbarian†.

V. botanize, herborize†.

Adj. botanical &c *n.;* botanic†.

370. *[The economy or management of animals.]* **Husbandry** -- **N.** husbandry, taming &c *v.;* circuration†, zoohygiantics†; domestication, domesticity; manege *[Fr.]*, veterinary art; farriery†; breeding, pisciculture.

menagerie, vivarium, zoological garden; bear pit; aviary, apiary, alveary†, beehive; hive; aquarium, fishery; duck pond, fish pond.

phthisozoics &c *(killing)* 361 [Obs.] *[Destruction of animals];* euthanasia, sacrifice, humane destruction.

neatherd[†], cowherd, shepherd; grazier, drover, cowkeeper[†]; trainer, breeder; apiarian[†], apiarist; bull whacker *[U.S.]*, cowboy, cow puncher *[U.S.]*, farrier; horse leech, horse doctor; vaquero, veterinarian, vet, veterinary surgeon.

cage &c *(prison)* 752; hencoop[†], bird cage, cauf[†]; range, sheepfold, &c *(inclosure)* 232.

V. tame, domesticate, acclimatize, breed, tend, break in, train; cage, bridle, &c *(restrain)* 751.

Adj. pastoral, bucolic; tame, domestic.

371. *[The economy or management of plants.]* **Agriculture -- N.** agriculture, cultivation, husbandry, farming; georgics, geoponics[†]; tillage, agronomy, gardening, spade husbandry, vintage; horticulture, arboriculture[†], floriculture; landscape gardening; viticulture.

husbandman, horticulturist, gardener, florist; agricultor[†], agriculturist; yeoman, farmer, cultivator, tiller of the soil, woodcutter, backwoodsman; granger, habitat, vigneron[†], viticulturist; Triptolemus.

field, meadow, garden; botanic garden[†], winter garden, ornamental garden, flower garden, kitchen garden, market garden, hop garden; nursery; green house, hot house; conservatory, bed, border, seed plot; grassplot†, grassplat†, lawn; park &c *(pleasure ground)* 840; parterre, shrubbery, plantation, avenue, arboretum, pinery†, pinetum†, orchard; vineyard, vinery; orangery†; farm &c *(abode)* 189.

V. cultivate; till the soil; farm, garden; sow, plant; reap, mow, cut; manure, dress the ground, dig, delve, dibble, hoe, plough, plow, harrow, rake, weed, lop and top; backset *[U.S.]*.

Adj. agricultural, agrarian, agrestic†.

arable, predial†, rural, rustic, country; horticultural.

372. Mankind -- **N.** man, mankind; human race, human species, human kind, human nature; humanity, mortality, flesh, generation.

[Science of man] anthropology, anthropogeny†, anthropography†, anthroposophy†; ethnology, ethnography; humanitarian.

human being; person, personage; individual, creature, fellow creature, mortal, body, somebody; one; such a one, some one; soul, living soul; earthling; party, head, hand; dramatis personae*[Lat.]*; quidam *[Lat.]*.

people, persons, folk, public, society, world; community, community at large; general public; nation, nationality; state, realm; commonweal, commonwealth; republic, body politic; million &c *(commonalty)* 876; population &c *(inhabitant)* 188.

tribe, clan *(paternity)* 166; family *(consanguinity)* 11.

cosmopolite; lords of the creation; ourselves.

Adj. human, mortal, personal, individual, national, civic, public, social; cosmopolitan; anthropoid.

Phr. am I not a man and a brother? [Wedgwood].

373. Man -- N. man, male, he, him; manhood &c *(adolescence)* 131; gentleman, sir, master; sahib; yeoman, wight[†], swain, fellow, blade, beau, elf, chap, gaffer, good man; husband &c*(married man)* 903; Mr., mister; boy &c *(youth)* 129.

[Male animal] cock, drake, gander, dog, boar, stag, hart, buck, horse, entire horse, stallion; gibcat[†], tomcat; he goat, Billy goat; ram, tup; bull, bullock; capon, ox, gelding, steer, stot[†].

androgen.

homosexual, gay, queen *[Slang]*.

V. masculinize

Adj. male, he-, masculine; manly, virile; unwomanly, unfeminine.

Pron.

he, him, his.

Phr. hominem pagina nostra sapit *[Lat.]* [Martial]; homo homini aut deus aut lupus *[Lat.]* [Erasmus]; homo vitae commodatus non donatus est *[Lat.]* [Syrus].

374. Woman -- **N.** woman, she, her, female, petticoat.

feminality†, muliebrity†; womanhood &c *(adolescence)* 131.

womankind; the sex, the fair; fair sex, softer sex; weaker vessel.

dame, madam, madame, mistress, Mrs.

lady, donna belle *[Sp.]*, matron, dowager, goody, gammer†; Frau *[G.]*, frow†, Vrouw *[Du.]*, rani; good woman, good wife; squaw; wife &c *(marriage)* 903; matronage, matronhood†.

bachelor girl, new woman, feminist, suffragette, suffragist.

nymph, wench, grisette†; girl &c *(youth)* 129.

[Effeminacy] sissy, betty, cot betty *[U.S.]*, cotquean†, henhussy†, mollycoddle, muff, old woman.

[Female animal] hen, bitch, sow, doe, roe, mare; she goat, Nanny goat, tabita; ewe, cow; lioness, tigress; vixen.

gynecaeum†.

estrogen, oestrogen.

consanguinity &c 166 *[Female relatives]*, paternity &c 11.

lesbian, dyke *[Slang]*.

V. feminize.

Adj. female, she-; feminine, womanly, ladylike, matronly, maidenly, wifely; womanish, effeminate, unmanly; gynecic†, gynaecic†.

Pron.

she, her, hers.'

Phr. a perfect woman nobly planned [Wordsworth]; a lovely lady garmented in white [Shelley]; das Ewig-Weibliche zieht uns hinan [Goethe]; earth's noblest thing, a woman perfected [Lowell]; es de vidrio la mujer *[Sp.]*; she moves a goddess and she looks a queen [Pope]; the beauty of a lovely woman is like music [G.

Eliot]; varium et mutabile semper
femina *[Lat.]* [Vergil]; woman is the lesser man [Tennyson].

374a. Sexuality *[human]* -- **N.** sex, sexuality, gender; male, masculinity, maleness &c 373; female, femininity &c 374.

sexual intercourse, copulation, mating, coitus, sex; lovemaking, marital relations, sexual union; sleeping together, carnal knowledge.

sex instinct, sex drive, libido, lust, concupiscence; hots, horns *[Coll.]*; arousal, heat, rut, estrus, oestrus; tumescence; erection, hard-on, boner.

masturbation, self-gratification, autoeroticism, onanism, self-abuse.

orgasm, climax, ejaculation.

sexiness, attractiveness; sensuality, voluptuousness.

[sexual intercourse outside of marriage] fornication, adultery.

[person who is sexy] sex symbol, sex goddess; stud, hunk.

one-night stand.

pornography, porn, porno; hardcore pornography, softcore pornography; pin-up, cheesecake; beefcake; *[magazines with sexual photos],* Playboy, Esquire, Hustler.

[unorthodox sexual activity] perversion, deviation, sexual abnormality; fetish, fetishism; homosexuality, lesbianism, bisexuality; sodomy, buggery; pederasty; sadism.

masochism, sado-masochism; incest.

V. mate, copulate; make love, have intercourse, fornicate, have sex, do it, sleep together, fuck *[Vulg.]*; sleep around, play the field.

masturbate, jerk off *[Coll.]*, jack off *[Coll.]*, play with oneself.

have the hots *[Coll.]*; become aroused, get hot; have an erection, get it up.

come, climax, ejaculate.

Adj. sexy, erotic, sexual, carnal, sensual.

hot, horny, randy, rutting; passionate, lusty, hot-blooded, libidinous; up, in the mood.

homosexual, gay, lesbian, bisexual.

2. SENSATION

1. Sensation in general

375. Physical Sensibility -- **N.** sensibility; sensitiveness &c *adj.;* physical sensibility, feeling, impressibility, perceptivity, aesthetics; moral sensibility &c 822.

sensation, impression; consciousness &c *(knowledge)* 490.

external senses.

V. be sensible of &c *adj.;* feel, perceive.

render sensible &c *adj.;* sharpen, cultivate, tutor.

cause sensation, impress; excite an impression, produce an impression.

Adj. sensible, sensitive, sensuous; aesthetic, perceptive, sentient; conscious &c *(aware)* 490.

acute, sharp, keen, vivid, lively, impressive, thin-skinned.

Adv. to the quick.

Phr. the touch'd needle trembles to the pole [Pope].

376. Physical Insensibility -- **N.** insensibility, physical insensibility; obtuseness &c *adj.;* palsy, paralysis, paraesthesia *[Med.]*, anaesthesia; sleep &c 823; hemiplegia[†], motor paralysis; vegetable state; coma.

anaesthetic agent, opium, ether, chloroform, chloral; nitrous oxide, laughing gas; exhilarating gas, protoxide of nitrogen; refrigeration.

V. be insensible &c *adj.;* have a thick skin, have a rhinoceros hide.

render insensible &c *adj.;* anaesthetize[†], blunt, pall, obtund[†], benumb, paralyze; put under the influence of chloroform &c *n.;* stupefy, stun.

Adj. insensible, unfeeling, senseless, impercipient[†], callous, thick-skinned, pachydermatous; hard, hardened; case hardened; proof, obtuse, dull; anaesthetic; comatose, paralytic, palsied, numb, dead.

377. Physical Pleasure -- **N.** pleasure; physical pleasure, sensual pleasure, sensuous pleasure; bodily enjoyment, animal gratification, hedonism, sensuality; luxuriousness &c *adj.;* dissipation, round of pleasure, titillation, gusto, creature comforts, comfort, ease; pillow &c *(support)* 215; luxury, lap of luxury; purple and fine linen; bed of downs, bed of roses; velvet, clover; cup of Circe &c *(intemperance)* 954.

treat; refreshment, regale; feast; delice *[Fr.]*; dainty &c 394; bonne bouche *[Fr.]*.

source of pleasure &c 829; happiness &c *(mental enjoyment)* 827.

V. feel pleasure, experience pleasure, receive pleasure; enjoy, relish; luxuriate in, revel in, riot in, bask in, swim in, drink up, eat up, wallow in; feast on; gloat over, float on; smack the lips.

live on the fat of the land, live in comfort &c *adv.;* bask in the sunshine, faire ses choux gras *[Fr.]*.

give pleasure &c 829.

Adj. enjoying &c *v.;* luxurious, voluptuous, sensual, comfortable, cosy, snug, in comfort, at ease.

pleasant, agreeable &c 829.

Adv. in comfort &c *n.;* on a bed of roses &c *n.;* at one's ease.

Phr. ride si sapis *[Lat.]* [Martial]; voluptales commendat rarior usus *[Lat.]* [Juvenal].

378. Physical Pain -- N. pain; suffering, sufferance, suffrance†; bodily pain, physical pain, bodily suffering, physical suffering, body pain; mental suffering &c 828; dolour, ache; aching &c *v.;* smart; shoot, shooting; twinge, twitch, gripe, headache, stomach ache, heartburn, angina, angina pectoris *[Lat.]*; hurt, cut; sore, soreness; discomfort, malaise; cephalalgia *[Med.]*, earache, gout, ischiagra†, lumbago, neuralgia, odontalgia†, otalgia†, podagra†, rheumatism, sciatica; tic douloureux *[Fr.]*, toothache, tormina†, torticollis†.

spasm, cramp; nightmare, ephialtes†; crick, stitch; thrill, convulsion, throe; throb &c *(agitation)* 315; pang; colic; kink.

sharp pain, piercing pain, throbbing pain, shooting pain, sting, gnawing pain, burning pain; excruciating pain.

anguish, agony; torment, torture; rack; cruciation†, crucifixion; martyrdom, toad under a harrow, vivisection.

V. feel pain, experience pain, suffer pain, undergo pain &c *n.;* suffer, ache, smart, bleed; tingle, shoot; twinge, twitch, lancinate†; writhe, wince, make a wry face; sit on thorns, sit on pins and needles.

give pain, inflict pain; lacerate; pain, hurt, chafe, sting, bite, gnaw, gripe; pinch, tweak; grate, gall, fret, prick, pierce, wring, convulse; torment, torture; rack, agonize; crucify; cruciate†, excruciate†; break on the wheel, put to the rack; flog &c *(punish)* 972; grate on the ear &c *(harsh sound)* 410.

Adj. in pain &c *n.*, in a state of pain; pained &c *v.*; gouty, podagric†, torminous†.

painful; aching &c *v.*; sore, raw.

2. Special Sensation

(1) Touch

379. *[Sensation of pressure]* **Touch** -- **N.** touch; tact, taction†, tactility; feeling; palpation, palpability; contrectation†; manipulation; massage.

[Organ of touch] hand, finger, forefinger, thumb, paw, feeler, antenna; palpus†.

V. touch, feel, handle, finger, thumb, paw, fumble, grope, grabble; twiddle, tweedle; pass the fingers over, run the fingers over; manipulate, wield; throw out a feeler.

Adj. tactual, tactile; tangible, palpable; lambent.

380. Sensations of Touch -- **N.** itching, pruritis *[Med.]* &c *v.*; titillation, formication†, aura; stereognosis†.

V. itch, tingle, creep, thrill, sting; prick, prickle; tickle, titillate.

Adj. itching &c *v.;* stereognostic†, titillative.

381. *[insensibility to touch.]* **Numbness** --
N. numbness &c *(physical insensibility)* 376; anaesthesia; pins and needles.

V. benumb &c 376.

Adj. numb; benumbed &c *v.;* deadened; intangible, impalpable.

(2) Heat

382. Heat -- **N.** heat, caloric; temperature, warmth, fervor, calidity†; incalescence†, incandescence; glow, flush; fever, hectic.

phlogiston; fire, spark, scintillation, flash, flame, blaze; bonfire; firework, pyrotechnics, pyrotechny†; wildfire; sheet of fire, lambent flame; devouring element; adiathermancy†; recalescence *[Phys.]*.

summer, dog days; canicular days†; baking &c 384; heat, white heat, tropical heat, Afric heat†, Bengal heat†, summer heat, blood heat; sirocco, simoom; broiling sun; insolation; warming &c 384.

sun &c *(luminary)* 423.

[Science of heat] pyrology†; thermology†, thermotics†, thermodynamics; thermometer &c 389.

[thermal units] calorie, gram-calorie, small calorie; kilocalorie, kilogram calorie, large calorie; British Thermal Unit, B.T.U.; therm, quad.

[units of temperature] degrees Kelvin, kelvins, degrees centigrade, degrees Celsius; degrees Fahrenheit.

V. be hot &c *adj.;* glow, flush, sweat, swelter, bask, smoke, reek, stew, simmer, seethe, boil, burn, blister, broil, blaze, flame; smolder; parch, fume, pant.

heat &c *(make hot)* 384; recalesce†; thaw, give.

Adj. hot, warm, mild, genial, tepid, lukewarm, unfrozen; thermal, thermic; calorific; fervent, fervid; ardent; aglow.

sunny, torrid, tropical, estival†, canicular†, steamy; close, sultry, stifling, stuffy, suffocating, oppressive; reeking &c *v.;* baking &c 384.

red hot, white hot, smoking hot, burning &c *v..* hot, piping hot; like a furnace, like an oven; burning, hot as fire, hot as pepper; hot enough to roast an ox, hot enough to boil an egg.

fiery; incandescent, incalescent†; candent†, ebullient, glowing, smoking; live; on fire; dazzling &c v.; in flames, blazing, in a blaze; alight, afire, ablaze; unquenched, unextinguished†; smoldering; in a heat, in a glow, in a fever, in a perspiration, in a sweat; sudorific†; sweltering, sweltered; blood hot, blood warm; warm as a toast, warm as wool.

volcanic, plutonic, igneous; isothermal†, isothermic†, isotheral†.

Phr. not a breath of air; whirlwinds of tempestuous fire [Paradise Lost].

383. Cold -- N. cold, coldness &c adj.; frigidity, inclemency, fresco.

winter; depth of winter, hard winter; Siberia, Nova Zembla; wind-chill factor.

[forms of frozen water] ice; snow, snowflake, snow crystal, snow drift; sleet; hail, hailstone; rime, frost; hoar frost, white frost, hard frost, sharp frost; barf; glaze *[U.S.]*, lolly *[U.S.]*; icicle, thick-ribbed ice; fall of snow, heavy fall; iceberg, icefloe; floe berg; glacier; nev_ee, serac†; pruina†.

[cold substances] freezing mixture, dry ice, liquid nitrogen, liquid helium.

[Sensation of cold] chilliness &c *adj.;* chill; shivering &c *v.;* goose skin, horripilation†; rigor; chattering of teeth; numbness, frostbite.

V. be cold &c *adj.;* shiver, starve, quake, shake, tremble, shudder, didder†, quiver; freeze, freeze to death, perish with cold.

freeze &c *(render cold)* 385; horripilate†, make the skin crawl, give one goose flesh.

Adj. cold, cool; chill, chilly; icy; gelid, frigid, algid†; fresh, keen, bleak, raw, inclement, bitter, biting, niveous†, cutting, nipping, piercing, pinching; clay-cold; starved &c *(made cold)* 385; chilled to the bone, shivering &c *v.;* aguish, transi de froid *[Fr.]*; frostbitten, frost-bound, frost-nipped.

cold as a stone, cold as marble, cold as lead, cold as iron, cold as a frog, cold as charity, cold as Christmas; cool as a cucumber, cool as custard.

icy, glacial, frosty, freezing, pruinose†, wintry, brumal†, hibernal†, boreal, arctic, Siberian, hyemal†; hyperborean, hyperboreal†; icebound; frozen out.

unwarmed†, unthawed†; lukewarm, tepid; isocheimal†, isocheimenal†, isocheimic†.

frozen, numb, frost-bitten.

Adv. coldly, bitterly &c *adj.;* pierre fendre *[Fr.]*;

384. Calefaction -- **N.** increase of temperature; heating &c *v.;* calefaction†, tepefaction†, torrefaction†; melting, fusion; liquefaction &c 335; burning &c *v.;* ambustion†, combustion; incension†, accension†; concremation†, cremation; scorification†; cautery, cauterization; ustulation†, calcination; cracking, refining; incineration, cineration†; carbonization; cupellation*[Chem]*.

ignition, inflammation, adustion†, flagration†; deflagration, conflagration; empyrosis†, incendiarism; arson; auto dafe *[Fr.]*.

boiling &c *v.;* coction†, ebullition, estuation†, elixation†, decoction; ebullioscope†; geyser; distillation *(vaporization)* 336.

furnace &c 386; blanket, flannel, fur; wadding &c *(lining)* 224; clothing &c 225.

still; refinery; fractionating column, fractionating tower, cracking tower.

match &c *(fuel)* 388; incendiary; petroleuse *[Fr.]*; *[biological effects resembling the effects of heat] [substances causing a burning sensation and damage on skin or tissue]* cauterizer†; caustic, lunar caustic, alkali, apozem†, moxa†; acid, aqua fortis *[Lat.]*, aqua regia; catheretic†, nitric acid, nitrochloro-hydric acid, nitromuriatic acid; radioactivity, gamma rays, alpha particles, beta rays,

X-rays, radiation, cosmic radiation, background radiation, radioactive isotopes, tritium, uranium, plutonium, radon, radium.

sunstroke, coup de soleil *[Fr.]*; insolation.

[artifacts requiring heat in their manufacture] pottery, ceramics, crockery, porcelain, china; earthenware, stoneware; pot, mug, terra cotta *[Sp.]*, brick, clinker.

[products of combustion] cinder, ash, scoriae, embers, soot; slag.

[products of heating organic materials] coke, carbon, charcoal; wood alcohol, turpentine, tea tree oil; gasoline, kerosene, naptha, fuel oil *(fuel)* 388; wax, paraffin; residue, tar.

inflammability, combustibility.

[Transmission of heat] diathermancy†, transcalency†, conduction; convection; radiation, radiant heat; heat conductivity, conductivity.

[effects of heat 2] thermal expansion; coefficient of expansion.

V. heat, warm, chafe, stive†, foment; make hot &c 382; sun oneself, sunbathe.

go up in flames, burn to the ground *(flame)* 382.

fire; set fire to, set on fire; kindle, enkindle, light, ignite, strike a light; apply the match to, apply the torch to; rekindle, relume†; fan the flame, add fuel to the flame; poke the fire, stir the fire, blow the fire; make a bonfire of.

melt, thaw, fuse; liquefy &c 335.

burn, inflame, roast, toast, fry, grill, singe, parch, bake, torrefy†, scorch; brand, cauterize, sear, burn in; corrode, char, calcine, incinerate; smelt, scorify†; reduce to ashes; burn to a cinder; commit to the flames, consign to the flames.

boil, digest, stew, cook, seethe, scald, parboil, simmer; do to rags.

take fire, catch fire; blaze &c *(flame)* 382.

Adj. heated &c *v.;* molten, sodden; r_echauff_e; heating &c *v.;* adust†.

inflammable, combustible; diathermal†, diathermanous†; burnt &c *v.;* volcanic, radioactive.

385. Refrigeration -- N. refrigeration, infrigidation†, reduction of temperature; cooling &c *v.;* congelation†, conglaciation†; ice &c 383; solidification &c *(density)* 321; ice box *(refrigerator)* 385.

extincteur *[Fr.]*; fire annihilator; amianth†, amianthus†; earth-flax, mountain-flax; flexible asbestos; fireman, fire brigade *(incombustibility)* 388.1.

incombustibility, incombustibleness &c *adj.*†. *(insulation)* 388.1.

air conditioning *[residential cooling]*, central air conditioning; air conditioner; fan, attic fan; dehumidifier.

V. cool, fan, refrigerate, refresh, ice; congeal, freeze, glaciate; benumb, starve, pinch, chill, petrify, chill to the marrow, regelate†, nip, cut, pierce, bite, make one's teeth chatter, damp, slack quench; put out, stamp out; extinguish; go out, burn out *(incombustibility)* 388.1.

Adj. cooled &c *v.;* frozen out; cooling &c *v.;* frigorific†.

386. Furnace -- N. furnace, stove, kiln, oven; cracker; hearth, focus, combustion chamber; athanor†, hypocaust†, reverberatory; volcano; forge, fiery furnace; limekiln; Dutch oven; tuyere, brasier†, salamander, heater, warming pan; boiler, caldron, seething caldron, pot; urn, kettle; chafing-dish; retort, crucible, alembic, still; waffle irons; muffle furnace, induction furnace; electric heater, electric furnace, electric resistance heat.

[steel-making furnace] open-hearth furnace.

fireplace, gas fireplace; coal fire, wood fire; fire-dog, fire-irons; grate, range, kitchener; caboose, camboose†; poker, tongs, shovel, ashpan, hob, trivet; andiron, gridiron; ashdrop; frying-pan, stew-pan, backlog.

[area near a fireplace] hearth, inglenook.

[residential heating methods] oil burner, gas burner, Franklin stove, pot-bellied stove; wood-burning stove; central heating, steam heat, hot water heat, gas heat, forced hot air, electric heat, heat pump; solar heat, convective heat.

hothouse, bakehouse†, washhouse†; laundry; conservatory; sudatory†; Turkish bath, Russian bath, vapor bath, steam bath, sauna, warm bath; vaporarium†.

387. Refrigerator -- N. refrigerator, refrigeratory†; frigidarium†; cold storage, cold room, cold laboratory; icehouse, icepail, icebag, icebox; cooler, damper, polyurethane cooler; wine cooler.

freezer, deep freeze, dry ice freezer, liquid nitrogen freezer, refrigerator-freezer.

freezing mixture *[refrigerating substances]*, ice, ice cubes, blocks of ice, chipped ice; liquid nitrogen, dry ice, dry ice-acetone, liquid helium.

388. Fuel -- N. fuel, firing, combustible.

[solid fuels] coal, wallsend†, anthracite, culm†, coke, carbon, charcoal, bituminous coal, tar shale; turf, peat, firewood, bobbing, faggot, log; cinder &c *(products of combustion)* 384; ingle, tinder, touchwood; sulphur, brimstone; incense; port-fire; fire-barrel, fireball, brand; amadou†, bavin†; blind coal, glance coal; German tinder, pyrotechnic sponge, punk, smudge *[U.S.]*; solid fueled rocket.

[fuels for candles and lamps] wax, paraffin wax, paraffin oil; lamp oil, whale oil.

[liquid fuels] oil, petroleum, gasoline, high octane gasoline, nitromethane, petrol, gas, juice *[Coll.]*, gasohol, alcohol, ethanol, methanol, fuel oil, kerosene, jet fuel, heating oil, number 2 oil, number 4 oil, naphtha; rocket fuel, high specific impulse fuel, liquid hydrogen, liquid oxygen, lox.

[gaseous fuels] natural gas, synthetic gas, synthesis gas, propane, butane, hydrogen.

brand, torch, fuse; wick; spill, match, light, lucifer, congreve†, vesuvian, vesta†, fusee, locofoco†; linstock†.

candle &c *(luminary)* 423; oil &c *(grease)* 356.

Adj. carbonaceous; combustible, inflammable; high octane, high specific impulse; heat of combustion,

388a. Insulation *[Fire extinction]* {ant. of 388} -- **N.** insulation, incombustible material, noncombustible material; fire retardant, flame retardant; fire wall, fire door.

incombustibility, incombustibleness
&c *adj.*. extincteur *[Fr.]*; fire annihilator; amianth†, amianthus†; earth-flax, mountain-flax; asbestos; fireman, fire fighter, fire eater, fire department, fire brigade, engine company; pumper, fire truck, hook and ladder, aerial ladder, bucket; fire hose, fire hydrant.

[forest fires] backfire, firebreak, trench; aerial water bombardment.

wet blanket; fire extinguisher, soda and acid extinguisher, dry chemical extinguisher, CO-two extinguisher, carbon tetrachloride, foam; sprinklers, automatic sprinkler system; fire bucket, sand bucket.

[warning of fire] fire alarm, evacuation alarm, *[laws to prevent fire]* fire code, fire regulations, fire; fire inspector; code violation, citation.

V. go out, die out, burn out; fizzle.

extinguish; damp, slack, quench, smother; put out, stamp out; douse, snuff, snuff out, blow out.

fireproof, flameproof.

Adj. incombustible; nonflammable, uninflammable, unflammable†; fireproof.

Phr. fight fire with fire

389. Thermometer -- N. thermometer, thermometrograph†, mercury thermometer, alcohol thermometer, clinical thermometer, dry-bulb thermometer, wet-bulb thermometer, Anschutz thermometer *[G.]*, gas thermometer, telethermometer; color-changing temperature indicator; thermopile, thermoscope†; pyrometer, calorimeter, bomb calorimeter; thermistor, thermocouple.

[temperature-control devices] thermostat, thermoregulator.

(3) Taste

390. Taste -- N. taste, flavor, gust, gusto, savor; gout, relish; sapor†, sapidity†; twang, smack, smatch†; aftertaste, tang.

tasting; degustation, gustation.

palate, tongue, tooth, stomach.

V. taste, savor, smatch[†], smack, flavor, twang; tickle the palate &c *(savory)* 394; smack the lips.

Adj. sapid, saporific[†]; gustable[†], gustatory; gustful[†]; strong, gamy; palatable &c 394.

391. Insipidity -- **N.** insipidity, blandness; tastelessness &c *adj..*

V. be tasteless &c *adj..*

Adj. bland, void of taste &c 390; insipid; tasteless, gustless[†], savorless; ingustible[†], mawkish, milk and water, weak, stale, flat, vapid, fade, wishy-washy, mild; untasted[†].

392. Pungency -- **N.** pungency, piquance, piquancy, poignancy haut-gout, strong taste, twang, race.

sharpness &c *adj.;* acrimony; roughness &c *(sour)* 392; unsavoriness &c 395.

mustard, cayenne, caviare; seasoning &c *(condiment)* 393; niter, saltpeter, brine *(saltiness)* 392.1; carbonate of ammonia; sal ammoniac†, sal volatile, smelling salts; hartshorn *(acridity)*401.1.

dram, cordial, nip.

nicotine, tobacco, snuff, quid, smoke; segar†; cigar, cigarette; weed; fragrant weed, Indian weed; Cavendish, fid†, negro head, old soldier, rappee†, stogy†.

V. be pungent &c *adj.;* bite the tongue.

render pungent &c *adj.;* season, spice, salt, pepper, pickle, brine, devil.

smoke, chew, take snuff.

Adj. pungent, strong; high-, full-flavored; high-tasted, high-seasoned; gamy, sharp, stinging, rough, piquant, racy; biting, mordant; spicy; seasoned &c *v.;* hot, hot as pepper; peppery, vellicating†, escharotic†, meracious†; acrid, acrimonious, bitter; rough &c *(sour)* 397; unsavory &c 395.

392a. Saltiness -- N. saltiness.

niter, saltpeter, brine.

Adj. salty, salt, saline, brackish, briny; salty as brine, salty as a herring, salty as Lot's wife.

salty, racy *(indecent)* 961.

Phr. take it with a grain of salt.

392b. Bitterness -- **N.** bitterness, acridness†, acridity, acrimony; caustic, alkali; acerbity; gall, wormwood; bitters, astringent bitters.

Angostura *[additive for alcoholic beverages]*, aromatic bitters.

sourness &c 397; pungency &c 392.

[bitter substances] alkaloids; turmeric.

Adj. bitter, bitterish, acrid, acerb, acerbic.

Phr. bitter as gall; bitter pill to take; sugar coating on a bitter pill.

393. Condiment -- **N.** condiment, seasoning, sauce, spice, relish, appetizer.

[Condiments] salt; mustard, grey poupon mustard; pepper, black pepper, white pepper, peppercorn, curry, sauce piquante *[Fr.]*; caviare, onion, garlic, pickle; achar†, allspice; bell pepper, Jamaica pepper, green pepper; chutney; cubeb†, pimento.

[capsicum peppers] capsicum, red pepper, chili peppers, cayenne.

nutmeg, mace, cinnamon, oregano, cloves, fennel.

[herbs] pot herbs, parsley, sage, rosemary, thyme, bay leaves, marjoram.

[fragrant woods and gums] frankincense, balm, myrrh.

[from pods] paprika.

[from flower stigmas] saffron.

[from roots] ginger, turmeric.

V. season, spice, flavor, spice up &c *(render pungent)* 392.

394. Savoriness -- N. savoriness &c *adj.;* good taste, deliciousness, delectability.

relish, zest; appetizer.

tidbit, titbit[†], dainty, delicacy, tasty morsel; appetizer, hors d'ouvres *[Fr.]*; ambrosia, nectar, bonne-bouche *[Fr.]*; game, turtle, venison; delicatessen.

V. be savory &c *adj.;* tickle the palate, tickle the appetite; flatter the palate.

render palatable &c *adj..* relish, like, smack the lips.

Adj. savory, delicious, tasty, well-tasted, to one's taste, good, palatable, nice, dainty, delectable; toothful†, toothsome; gustful†, appetizing, lickerish†, delicate, exquisite, rich, luscious, ambrosial, scrumptious, delightful.

Adv. per amusare la bocca *[It]*

Phr. cela se laisse manger *[Fr.]*.

395. Unsavoriness -- **N.** unsavoriness &c *adj.;* amaritude†; acrimony,
acridity *(bitterness)* 392.2; roughness &c *(sour)* 397; acerbity, austerity; gall and wormwood, rue, quassia†, aloes; marah†; sickener†.

V. be unpalatable &c *adj.;* sicken, disgust, nauseate, pall, turn the stomach.

Adj. unsavory, unpalatable, unsweetened, unsweet†; ill-flavored; bitter, bitter as gall; acrid, acrimonious; rough.

offensive, repulsive, nasty; sickening &c *v.;* nauseous; loathsome, fulsome; unpleasant &c 830.

396. Sweetness -- N. sweetness, dulcitude†.

sugar, syrup, treacle, molasses, honey, manna; confection, confectionary; sweets, grocery, conserve, preserve, confiture†, jam, julep; sugar-candy, sugar-plum; licorice, marmalade, plum, lollipop, bonbon, jujube, comfit, sweetmeat; apple butter, caramel, damson, glucose; maple sirup†, maple syrup, maple sugar; mithai†, sorghum, taffy.

nectar; hydromel†, mead, meade†, metheglin†, honeysuckle, liqueur, sweet wine, aperitif.

[sources of sugar] sugar cane, sugar beets.

[sweet foods] desert, pastry, pie, cake, candy, ice cream, tart, puff, pudding *(food)* 298.

dulcification†, dulcoration†.

sweetener, corn syrup, cane sugar, refined sugar, beet sugar, dextrose; artificial sweetener, saccharin, cyclamate, aspartame, Sweet'N Low.

V. be sweet &c *adj..* render sweet &c *adj.;* sweeten; edulcorate†; dulcorate†, dulcify†; candy; mull.

Adj. sweet; saccharine, sacchariferous†; dulcet, candied, honied†, luscious, lush, nectarious†, melliferous†; sweetened &c *v..* sweet as a nut, sweet as sugar, sweet as honey.

sickly sweet.

Phr. eau sucr_ee *[Fr.]*; sweets to the sweet [Hamlet].

397. Sourness -- **N.** sourness &c *adj.;* acid, acidity, low pH; acetous fermentation, lactic fermentation.

vinegar, verjuice†, crab, alum; acetic acid, lactic acid.

V. be sour; sour, turn sour &c *adj.;* set the teeth on edge.

render sour &c *adj.;* acidify, acidulate.

Adj. sour; acid, acidulous, acidulated; tart, crabbed; acetous, acetose†; acerb, acetic; sour as vinegar, sourish, acescent†, subacid *[Chem]*; styptic, hard, rough.

Phr. sour as a lemon.

(4) Odor

398. Odor -- **N.** odor, smell, odorament†, scent, effluvium; emanation, exhalation; fume, essence, trail, nidor†, redolence.

sense of smell; scent; act of smelling &c *v.;* olfaction, olfactories[†].

[pleasant odor] fragrance &c 400.

odorant.

[animal with acute sense of smell] bloodhound, hound.

[smell detected by a hound] spoor.

V. have an odor &c *n.;* smell, smell of, smell strong of; exhale; give out a smell &c *n.;* reek, reek of; scent.

smell, scent; snuff, snuff up; sniff, nose, inhale.

Adj. odorous, odoriferous; smelling, reeking, foul-smelling, strong-scented; redolent, graveolent[†], nidorous[†], pungent; putrid, foul.

[Relating to the sense of smell] olfactory, quick-scented.

399. Inodorousness -- **N.** inodorousness[†]; absence of smell, want of smell.

deodorant, deodorization, deodorizer.

V. be inodorous &c *adj.*[†]; not smell.

deodorize.

Adj. inodorous†, onodorate; scentless; without smell, wanting smell &c 398.

deodorized, deodorizing.

400. Fragrance -- N. fragrance, aroma, redolence, perfume, bouquet, essence, scent; sweet smell, aromatic perfume.

agalloch†, agallochium†; aloes wood; bay rum; calambac†, calambour†; champak†, horehound, lign-aloes†, marrubium†, mint, muskrat, napha water†, olibanum†, spirit of myrcia†.

essential oil.

incense; musk, frankincense; pastil†, pastille; myrrh, perfumes of Arabia†; otto†, ottar†, attar; bergamot, balm, civet, potpourri, pulvil†; nosegay; scentbag†; sachet, smelling bottle, vinaigrette; eau de Cologne *[Fr.]*, toilet water, lotion, after-shave lotion; thurification†.

perfumer.

[fragrant wood oils] eucalyptus oil, pinene.

V. be fragrant &c *adj.;* have a perfume &c *n.;* smell sweet.

scent *[render fragrant]*, perfume, embalm.

Adj. fragrant, aromatic, redolent, spicy, savory, balmy, scented, sweet-smelling, sweet-scented; perfumed, perfumatory†; thuriferous; fragrant as a rose, muscadine†, ambrosial.

401. Fetor -- **N.** fetor†; bad &c *adj.*. smell, bad odor; stench, stink; foul odor, malodor; empyreuma†; mustiness &c *adj.;* rancidity; foulness &c *(uncleanness)* 653.

stoat, polecat, skunk; assafoetida†; fungus, garlic; stinkpot; fitchet†, fitchew†, fourmart†, peccary.

acridity &c 401.1.

V. have a bad smell &c *n.;* smell; stink, stink in the nostrils, stink like a polecat; smell strong &c *adj.*, smell offensively.

Adj. fetid; strong-smelling; high, bad, strong, fulsome, offensive, noisome, rank, rancid, reasty†, tainted, musty, fusty, frouzy†; olid†, olidous†; nidorous†; smelling, stinking; putrid &c 653; suffocating, mephitic; empyreumatic†.

401a. Acridity -- **N.** acridity, astringency, bite.

[acrid substances] tear gas; smoke, acrid fumes.

Adj. acrid, biting, astringent, sharp, harsh; bitter &c 392.2.

(5) Sound

(i) SOUND IN GENERAL

402. Sound -- **N.** sound, noise, strain; accent, twang, intonation, tone; cadence; sonorousness &c *adj.;* audibility; resonance &c 408; voice &c 580; aspirate; ideophone†; rough breathing.

[Science, of sound] acoustics; phonics, phonetics, phonology, phonography†; diacoustics†, diaphonics†; phonetism†.

V. produce sound; sound, make a noise; give out sound, emit sound; resound &c 408.

Adj. sounding; soniferous†; sonorous, sonorific†; resonant, audible, distinct; stertorous; phonetic; phonic, phonocamptic†.

Phr. a thousand trills and quivering sounds [Addison]; forensis strepitus *[Lat.]*.

403. Silence -- **N.** silence; stillness &c *(quiet)* 265; peace, hush, lull; muteness &c 581; solemn silence, awful silence, dead silence, deathlike silence.

V. be silent &c *adj.;* hold one's tongue &c *(not speak)* 585.

render silent &c *adj.;* silence, still, hush; stifle, muffle, stop; muzzle, put to silence &c *(render mute)* 581.

Adj. silent; still, stilly; noiseless, soundless; hushed &c *v.;* mute &c 581.

soft, solemn, awful, deathlike, silent as the grave; inaudible &c *(faint)* 405.

Adv. silently &c *adj.;* sub silentio *[Lat.].*

Int. hush!, silence!, soft!, whist!, tush!, chut!†, tut!, pax! *[Lat.],* be quiet!, be silent!, be still!, shut up! *[Slang]*; chup!†, chup rao!†, tace! *[It],*

Phr. one might hear a feather drop, one might hear a pin drop, so quiet you could hear a pin drop; grosse Seelen dulden still *[G.]*; le silence est la vertu de ceux qui ne sont pas sages *[Fr.]*; le silence est le parti le plus sar de celui se d_efie de soi-meme *[Fr.]*; silence more musical than any song [C.G. Rossetti]; tacent satis laudant *[Lat.]*; better to be silent and thought a fool than to speak up and remove all doubt.

404. Loudness -- N. loudness, power; loud noise, din; blare; clang, clangor; clatter, noise, bombilation†, roar, uproar, racket, hubbub, bobbery†, fracas, charivari†, trumpet blast, flourish of trumpets, fanfare, tintamarre†, peal, swell, blast, larum†, boom; bang *(explosion)* 406; resonance &c 408.

vociferation, hullabaloo, &c 411; lungs; Stentor.

artillery, cannon; thunder.

V. be loud &c *adj.;* peal, swell, clang, boom, thunder, blare, fulminate, roar; resound &c 408.

speak up, shout &c *(vociferate)* 411; bellow &c *(cry as an animal)* 412.

rend the air, rend the skies; fill the air; din in the ear, ring in the ear, thunder in the ear; pierce the ears, split the ears, rend the ears, split the head; deafen, stun; faire le diable a quatre *[Fr.]*; make one's windows shake, rattle the windows; awaken the echoes, startle the echoes; wake the dead.

Adj. loud, sonorous; high-sounding, big-sounding; deep, full, powerful, noisy, blatant, clangorous, multisonous†; thundering, deafening &c *v.;* trumpet-tongued; ear-splitting, ear-rending, ear-deafening; piercing; obstreperous, rackety, uproarious; enough to wake the dead, enough to wake seven sleepers.

shrill &c 410 clamorous &c *(vociferous)* 411 stentorian, stentorophonic†.

Adv. loudly &c *adj.*. aloud; at the top of one's voice, at the top of one's lungs, lustily, in full cry.

Phr. the air rings with; the deep dread-bolted thunder [Lear].

405. Faintness -- N. faintness &c *adj.;* faint sound, whisper, breath; undertone, underbreath†; murmur, hum, susurration; tinkle; still small voice.

hoarseness &c *adj.;* raucity†.

V. whisper, breathe, murmur, purl, hum, gurgle, ripple, babble, flow; tinkle; mutter &c *(speak imperfectly)* 583; susurrate†.

steal on the ear; melt in the air, float on the air.

Adj. inaudible; scarcely audible, just audible; low, dull; stifled, muffled; hoarse, husky; gentle, soft, faint; floating; purling, flowing &c *v.;* whispered &c *v.;* liquid; soothing; dulcet &c *(melodious)* 413; susurrant†, susurrous†.

Adv. in a whisper, with bated breath, sotto voce *[Lat.]*, between the teeth, aside; piano, pianissimo; d la sourdine†; out of earshot inaudibly &c *adj.*.

(ii) SPECIFIC SOUNDS

406. *[Sudden and violent sounds.]* **Snap** -- **N.** snap &c *v.*; rapping &c *v.*; decrepitation, crepitation; report, thud; burst, explosion, blast, boom, discharge, detonation, firing, salvo, volley.

squib, cracker, firecracker, cherry bomb, M80, gun, cap, cap gun, popgun.

implosion.

bomb burst, atomic explosion, nuclear explosion *(arms)* 727.

[explosive substances] gunpowder, dynamite, gun cotton, nitroglycerine, nitrocellulose, plastic explosive, plastique, TNT, cordite, trinitrotoluene, picric acid, picrates, mercury fulminate *(arms)* 727.

whack, wham, pow.

V. rap, snap, tap, knock, ping; click; clash; crack, crackle; crash; pop; slam, bang, blast, boom, clap, clang, clack, whack, wham; brustle[†]; burst on the ear; crepitate, rump.

blow up, blow; detonate.

Adj. rapping &c *v.*.

Int. kaboom!, whamo!, Heewhack!, pow!,

407. *[Repeated and protracted sounds.]* **Roll** --
  N. roll &c v.; drumming &c v.; berloque†, bombination†, rumbling; tattoo, drumroll; dingdong; tantara†; rataplan†; whirr; ratatat, ratatat-tat; rubadub; pitapat; quaver, clutter, charivari†, racket; cuckoo; repetition &c 104; peal of bells, devil's tattoo; reverberation &c 408.

[sound of railroad train rolling on rails] clickety-clack.

hum, purr.

[animals that hum] hummingbird.

[animals that purr] cat, kitten *(animal sounds)* 412.

V. roll, drum, rumble, rattle, clatter, patter, clack; bombinate†.

hum, trill, shake; chime, peal, toll; tick, beat.

drum in the ear, din in the ear.

Adj. rolling &c v.; monotonous &c *(repeated)* 104; like a bee in a bottle.

408. Resonance -- **N.** resonance; ring &c v.; ringing, tintinabulation &c v.; reflexion *[Brit.]*, reflection, reverberation; echo, reecho; zap, zot *[Coll.]*; buzz *(hiss)* 409.

low note, base note, bass note, flat note, grave note, deep note; bass; basso, basso profondo *[It]*; baritone, barytone†; contralto.

[device to cause resonance] echo chamber, resonator.

[ringing in the ears] tinnitus *[Med.]*.

[devices which make a resonating sound] bell, doorbell, buzzer; gong, cymbals *(musical instruments)* 417.

[physical resonance] sympathetic vibrations; natural frequency, coupled vibration frequency; overtone; resonating cavity; sounding board, tuning fork.

[electrical resonance] tuning, squelch, frequency selection; resonator, resonator circuit; radio &c *[chemical resonance]* resonant structure, aromaticity, alternating double bonds, non-bonded resonance; pi clouds, unsaturation, double bond, (valence).

V. resound, reverberate, reecho, resonate; ring, jingle, gingle†, chink, clink; tink†, tinkle; chime; gurgle &c 405; plash, goggle, echo, ring in the ear.

Adj. resounding &c *v.;* resonant, reverberant, tinnient†, tintinnabulary; sonorous, booming, deep-toned, deep-sounding, deep-mouthed, vibrant; hollow, sepulchral; gruff &c *(harsh)* 410.

Phr. sweet bells jangled, out of time and harsh [Hamlet]; echoing down the mountain and through the dell.

408a. Nonresonance[†] -- **N.** thud, thump, dead sound; nonresonance[†]; muffled drums, cracked bell; damper; silencer.

V. sound dead; stop the sound, damp the sound, deaden the sound, deaden the reverberations, dampen the reverberations.

Adj. nonresonant[†], dead; dampened, muffled.

409. *[Hissing sounds.]* **Sibilation** -- **N.** sibilance, sibilation; zip; hiss &c v.; sternutation; high note &c 410.

[animals that hiss] goose, serpent, snake *(animal sounds)* 412.

[animals that buzz] insect, bug; bee, mosquito, wasp, fly.

[inanimate things that hiss] tea kettle, pressure cooker; air valve, pressure release valve, safety valve, tires, air escaping from tires, punctured tire; escaping steam, steam, steam radiator, steam release valve.

V. hiss, buzz, whiz, rustle; fizz, fizzle; wheeze, whistle, snuffle; squash; sneeze; sizzle, swish.

Adj. sibilant; hissing &c *v.;* wheezy; sternutative†.

410. *[Harsh sounds.]* **Stridor** -- **N.** creak &c *v.;* creaking &c *v.;* discord, &c 414; stridor; roughness, sharpness, &c *adj.;* cacophony; cacoepy†.

acute note, high note; soprano, treble, tenor, alto, falsetto, penny trumpet, voce di testa *[It]*.

V. creak, grate, jar, burr, pipe, twang, jangle, clank, clink; scream &c *(cry)* 411; yelp &c *(animal sound)* 412; buzz &c *(hiss)* 409.

set the teeth on edge, corcher les oreilles *[Fr.]*; pierce the ears, split the ears, split the head; offend the ear, grate upon the ear, jar upon the ear.

Adj. creaking &c *v.;* stridulous†, harsh, coarse, hoarse, horrisonous†, rough, gruff, grum†, sepulchral, hollow.

sharp, high, acute, shrill; trumpet-toned; piercing, ear-piercing, high-pitched, high-toned; cracked; discordant &c 414; cacophonous.

411. Cry -- **N.** cry &c *v.;* voice &c *(human)* 580; hubbub; bark &c *(animal)* 412.

vociferation, outcry, hullabaloo, chorus, clamor, hue and cry, plaint; lungs; stentor.

V. cry, roar, shout, bawl, brawl, halloo, halloa, hoop, whoop, yell, bellow, howl, scream, screech, screak[†], shriek, shrill, squeak, squeal, squall, whine, pule, pipe, yaup[†].

cheer; hoot; grumble, moan, groan.

snore, snort; grunt &c *(animal sounds)* 412.

vociferate; raise up the voice, lift up the voice; call out, sing out, cry out; exclaim; rend the air; thunder at the top of one's voice, shout at the top of one's voice, shout at the pitch of one's breath, thunder at the pitch of one's breath; s'_egosiller; strain the throat, strain the voice, strain the lungs; give a cry &c

Adj. crying &c *v.;* clamant[†], clamorous; vociferous; stentorian &c *(loud)* 404; open-mouthed.

412. *[Animal sounds.]* **Ululation** -- **N.** cry &c *v.;* crying &c *v.;* bowwow, ululation, latration[†], belling; reboation[†]; wood-note; insect cry, fritiniancy[†], drone; screech owl; cuckoo.

wailing *(lamentation)* 839.

V. cry, roar, bellow, blare, rebellow†; growl, snarl.

[specific animal sounds] bark [dog, seal]; bow-wow, yelp [dog]; bay, bay at the moon [dog, wolf]; yap, yip, yipe, growl, yarr†, yawl, snarl, howl [dog, wolf]; grunt, gruntle†; snort [pig, hog, swine, horse]; squeak, [swine, mouse]; neigh, whinny [horse]; bray [donkey, mule, hinny, ass]; mew, mewl [kitten]; meow [cat]; purr [cat]; caterwaul, pule [cats]; baa†, bleat [lamb]; low, moo [cow, cattle]; troat†, croak, peep [frog]; coo [dove, pigeon]; gobble [turkeys]; quack [duck]; honk, gaggle, guggle [goose]; crow, caw, squawk, screech, [crow]; cackle, cluck, clack [hen, rooster, poultry]; chuck, chuckle; hoot, hoo [owl]; chirp, cheep, chirrup, twitter, cuckoo, warble, trill, tweet, pipe, whistle [small birds]; hum [insects, hummingbird]; buzz [flying insects, bugs]; hiss [snakes, geese]; blatter†; ratatat [woodpecker].

Adj. crying &c *v.*; blatant, latrant†, remugient†, mugient†; deep-mouthed, full-mouthed; rebellowing†, reboant†.

Adv. in full cry.

(iii) MUSICAL SOUNDS

413. Melody. Concord -- N. melody, rhythm, measure; rhyme &c *(poetry)* 597.

pitch, timbre, intonation, tone.

scale, gamut; diapason; diatonic chromatic scale†, enharmonic scale†; key, clef, chords.

modulation, temperament, syncope, syncopation, preparation, suspension, resolution.

staff, stave, line, space, brace; bar, rest; appoggiato†, appoggiatura†; acciaccatura†.

note, musical note, notes of a scale; sharp, flat, natural; high note &c *(shrillness)* 410; low note &c 408; interval; semitone; second, third, fourth &c; diatessaron†.

breve, semibreve *[Mus.]*, minim, crotchet, quaver; semiquaver, demisemiquaver, hemidemisemiquaver; sustained note, drone, burden.

tonic; key note, leading note, fundamental note; supertonic†, mediant†, dominant; submediant†, subdominant†; octave, tetrachord†; major key, minor key, major scale, minor scale, major mode, minor mode; passage, phrase.

concord, harmony; emmeleia†; unison, unisonance†; chime, homophony; euphony, euphonism†; tonality; consonance; consent; part.

[Science of harmony] harmony, harmonics; thorough-bass, fundamental-bass; counterpoint; faburden†.

piece of music &c 415 [Fr.]; composer, harmonist†, contrapuntist *(musician)* 416.

V. be harmonious &c *adj.;* harmonize, chime, symphonize†, transpose; put in tune, tune, accord, string.

Adj. harmonious, harmonical†; in concord &c *n.*, in tune, in concert; unisonant†, concentual†, symphonizing†, isotonic, homophonous†, assonant; ariose†, consonant.

measured, rhythmical, diatonic†, chromatic, enharmonic†.

melodious, musical; melic†; tuneful, tunable; sweet, dulcet, canorous†; mellow, mellifluous; soft, clear, clear as a bell; silvery; euphonious, euphonic, euphonical†; symphonious; enchanting &c *(pleasure-giving)* 829; fine-toned, full-toned, silver-toned.

Adv. harmoniously, in harmony; as one &c *adj.*.

Phr. the hidden soul of harmony [Milton].

414. Discord -- N. discord, discordance; dissonance, cacophony, want of harmony, caterwauling; harshness &c 410.

[Confused sounds], Babel, Dutch concert, cat's concert; marrowbones and cleavers.

V. be discordant &c *adj.;* jar &c *(sound harshly)* 410.

Adj. discordant; dissonant, absonant†; out of tune, tuneless; unmusical, untunable†; unmelodious, immelodious†; unharmonious†, inharmonious; singsong; cacophonous; harsh &c 410; jarring.

415. Music -- N. music; concert; strain, tune, air; melody &c 413; aria, arietta†; piece of music *[Fr.]*, work, number, opus; sonata; rondo, rondeau *[Fr.]*; pastorale, cavatina†, roulade†, fantasia, concerto, overture, symphony, variations, cadenza; cadence; fugue, canon, quodlibet, serenade, notturno *[It]*, dithyramb; opera, operetta; oratorio; composition, movement; stave; passamezzo *[It]*, toccata, Vorspiel *[G.]*.

instrumental music; full score; minstrelsy, tweedledum and tweedledee, band, orchestra; concerted piece *[Fr.]*, potpourri, capriccio.

vocal music, vocalism†; chaunt, chant; psalm, psalmody; hymn; song &c *(poem)* 597; canticle, canzonet†, cantata, bravura, lay, ballad, ditty, carol, pastoral, recitative, recitativo†, solfeggio†.

Lydian measures; slow music, slow movement; adagio &c *adv.;* minuet; siren strains, soft music, lullaby; dump; dirge &c *(lament)* 839; pibroch†;

martial music, march; dance music; waltz &c *(dance)* 840.

solo, duet, duo, trio; quartet, quartett[†]; septett[†]; part song, descant, glee, madrigal, catch, round, chorus, chorale; antiphon[†], antiphony; accompaniment, second, bass; score; bourdon[†], drone, morceau[†], terzetto[†].

composer &c 413; musician &c 416.

V. compose, perform &c 416; attune.

Adj. musical; instrumental, vocal, choral, lyric, operatic; harmonious &c 413; Wagnerian.

Adv. adagio; largo, larghetto, andante, andantino[†]; alla capella *[It]*; maestoso[†], moderato; allegro, allegretto; spiritoso[†], vivace[†], veloce[†]; presto, prestissimo[†]; con brio; capriccioso[†]; scherzo, scherzando[†]; legato, staccato, crescendo, diminuendo, rallentando[†], affettuoso[†]; obbligato; pizzicato; desto[†].

Phr. in notes by distance made more sweet [Collins]; like the faint exquisite music of a dream [Moore]; music arose with its voluptuous swell [Byron]; music is the universal language of mankind [Longfellow]; music's golden tongue [Keats]; the speech of angels [Carlyle]; will sing the savageness out of a bear [Othello]; music hath charms to soothe the savage beast.

416. Musician *[Performance of Music.]* --
 N. musician, artiste, performer, player, minstrel; bard &c *(poet)* 597; *[specific types of musicians]* accompanist, accordionist, instrumentalist, organist, pianist, violinist, flautist; harper, fiddler, fifer†, trumpeter, piper, drummer; catgut scraper.

band, orchestral waits.

vocalist, melodist; singer, warbler; songster, chaunter†, chauntress†, songstress; cantatrice†.

choir, quire, chorister; chorus, chorus singer; liedertafel *[G.]*.

nightingale, philomel†, thrush; siren; bulbul, mavis; Pierides; sacred nine; Orpheus, Apollo†, the Muses Erato, Euterpe, Terpsichore; tuneful nine, tuneful quire.

composer &c 413.

performance, execution, touch, expression, solmization†.

V. play, pipe, strike up, sweep the chords, tweedle, fiddle; strike the lyre, beat the drum; blow the horn, sound the horn, wind the horn; doodle; grind the organ; touch the guitar &c *(instruments)* 417; thrum, strum, beat time.

execute, perform; accompany; sing a second, play a second; compose, set to music, arrange.

sing, chaunt, chant, hum, warble, carol, chirp, chirrup, lilt, purl, quaver, trill, shake, twitter, whistle; sol-fa†; intone.

have an ear for music, have a musical ear, have a correct ear.

Adj. playing &c *v.;* musical.

Adv. adagio, andante &c *(music)* 415.

417. Musical Instruments -- **N.** musical instruments; band; string-band, brass-band; orchestra; orchestrina†.

[Stringed instruments], monochord†, polychord†; harp, lyre, lute, archlute†; mandola†, mandolin, mandoline†; guitar; zither; cither†, cithern†; gittern†, rebeck†, bandurria†, bandura, banjo; bina†, vina†; xanorphica†.

viol, violin, fiddle, kit; viola, viola d'amore *[Fr.],* viola di gamba *[It];* tenor, cremona, violoncello, bass; bass viol, base viol; theorbo†, double base, contrabasso†, violone†, psaltery *[Slang];* bow, fiddlestick†.

piano, pianoforte; harpsichord, clavichord, clarichord†, manichord†; clavier, spinet, virginals, dulcimer, hurdy-gurdy, vielle†, pianino†, Eolian harp.

[Wind instruments]; organ, harmonium, harmoniphon†; American organ†, barrel organ, hand organ; accordion, seraphina†, concertina; humming top.

flute, fife, piccolo, flageolet; clarinet, claronet†; basset horn, corno di bassetto *[It]*, oboe, hautboy, cor Anglais *[Fr.]*, corno Inglese†, bassoon, double bassoon, contrafagotto†, serpent, bass clarinet; bagpipes, union pipes; musette, ocarina, Pandean pipes; reed instrument; sirene†, pipe, pitch-pipe; sourdet†; whistle, catcall; doodlesack†, harmoniphone†.

horn, bugle, cornet, cornet-a-pistons, cornopean†, clarion, trumpet, trombone, ophicleide†; French horn, saxophone, sax *[Slang]*, buglehorn†, saxhorn, flugelhorn†, althorn†, helicanhorn†, posthorn†; sackbut, euphonium, bombardon tuba†.

[Vibrating surfaces] cymbal, bell, gong; tambour†, tambourine, tamborine†; drum, tom-tom; tabor, tabret†, tabourine†, taborin†; side drum, kettle drum; timpani, tympani†; tymbal†, timbrel†, castanet, bones; musical glasses, musical stones; harmonica, sounding-board, rattle; tam-tam, zambomba†.

[Vibrating bars] reed, tuning fork, triangle, Jew's harp, musical box, harmonicon†, xylophone.

sordine†, sordet†; sourdine†, sourdet†; mute.

(iv) PERCEPTION OF SOUND

418. *[Sense of sound.]* **Hearing** -- N. hearing &c v.; audition, auscultation; eavesdropping; audibility.

acute ear, nice ear, delicate ear, quick ear, sharp ear, correct ear, musical ear; ear for music.

ear, auricle, lug, acoustic organs, auditory apparatus; eardrum, tympanum, tympanic membrane.

[devices to aid human hearing by amplifying sound] ear trumpet, speaking trumpet, hearing aid, stethoscope.

[distance within which direct hearing is possible] earshot, hearing distance, hearing, hearing range, sound, carrying distance.

[devices for talking beyond hearing distance: list] telephone, phone, telephone booth, intercom, house phone, radiotelephone, radiophone, wireless, wireless telephone, mobile telephone, car radio, police radio, two-way radio, walkie-talkie *[Mil.]*, handie-talkie, citizen's band, CB, amateur radio, ham radio, short-wave radio, police band, ship-to-shore

radio, airplane radio, control tower communication; *(communication)* 525, 527, 529, 531, 532; electronic devices *[devices for recording and reproducing recorded sound]*, phonograph, gramophone, megaphone, phonorganon†.

[device to convert sound to electrical signals] microphone, directional microphone, mike, hand mike, lapel microphone.

[devices to convert recorded sound to electronic signals] phonograph needle, stylus, diamond stylus, pickup; reading head (electronic devices).

hearer, auditor, listener, eavesdropper, listener-in.

auditory, audience.

[science of hearing] otology, otorhinolaryngology.

[physicians specializing in hearing] otologist, otorhinolaryngologist.

V. hear, overhear; hark, harken; list, listen, pay attention, take heed; give an ear, lend an ear, bend an ear; catch, catch a sound, prick up one's ears; give ear, give a hearing, give audience to.

hang upon the lips of, be all ears, listen with both ears.

become audible; meet the ear, fall upon the ear, catch the ear, reach the ear; be heard; ring in the ear &c *(resound)* 408.

Adj. hearing &c *v.;* auditory, auricular, acoustic; phonic.

Adv. arrectis auribus *[Lat.]*.

Int. hark, hark ye!, hear!, list, listen!, O yes!, Oyez!, listen up *[Coll.]*; listen here!, hear ye!, attention!, achtung *[G.]*.

419. Deafness -- **N.** deafness, hardness of hearing, surdity†; inaudibility, inaudibleness†.

V. be deaf &c *adj.;* have no ear; shut one's ears, stop one's ears, close one's ears; turn a deaf ear to.

render deaf, stun, deafen.

Adj. deaf, earless†, surd; hard of hearing, dull of hearing; deaf-mute, stunned, deafened; stone deaf; deaf as a post, deaf as an adder, deaf as a beetle, deaf as a trunkmaker†.

inaudible, out of hearing.

Phr. hear no evil.

(6) Light

(i) LIGHT IN GENERAL

420. Light -- N. light, ray, beam, stream, gleam, streak, pencil; sunbeam, moonbeam; aurora.

day; sunshine; light of day, light of heaven; moonlight, starlight, sunlight &c *(luminary)* 432; daylight, broad daylight, noontide light; noontide, noonday, noonday sun.

glow &c *v.;* glimmering &c *v.;* glint; play of light, flood of light; phosphorescence, lambent flame.

flush, halo, glory, nimbus, aureola.

spark, scintilla; facula; sparkling &c *v.;* emication[†], scintillation, flash, blaze, coruscation, fulguration[†]; flame &c *(fire)* 382; lightning, levin[†], ignis fatuus *[Lat.]*, &c *(luminary)* 423.

luster, sheen, shimmer, reflexion *[Brit.]*, reflection; gloss, tinsel, spangle, brightness, brilliancy, splendor; effulgence, refulgence; fulgor[†], fulgidity[†]; dazzlement[†], resplendence, transplendency[†]; luminousness &c *adj.;* luminosity; lucidity; renitency[†], nitency[†]; radiance, radiation; irradiation, illumination.

actinic rays, actinism; Roentgen-ray, Xray; photography, heliography; photometer &c 445.

[Science of light] optics; photology†, photometry; dioptrics†, catoptrics†.

[Distribution of light] chiaroscuro, clairobscur†, clear obscure, breadth, light and shade, black and white, tonality.

reflection, refraction, dispersion; refractivity.

V. shine, glow, glitter; glister, glisten; twinkle, gleam; flare, flare up; glare, beam, shimmer, glimmer, flicker, sparkle, scintillate, coruscate, flash, blaze; be bright &c *adj.;* reflect light, daze, dazzle, bedazzle, radiate, shoot out beams; fulgurate.

clear up, brighten.

lighten, enlighten; levin†; light, light up; irradiate, shine upon; give out a light, hang out a light; cast light upon, cast light in, throw light upon, throw light in, shed light upon, shed luster upon; illume†, illumine, illuminate; relume†, strike a light; kindle &c *(set fire to)* 384.

Adj. shining &c *v.;* luminous, luminiferous†; lucid, lucent, luculent†, lucific†, luciferous; light, lightsome; bright, vivid, splendent†, nitid†, lustrous, shiny, beamy†, scintillant†, radiant, lambent; sheen, sheeny; glossy, burnished, glassy, sunny, orient, meridian; noonday, tide; cloudless, clear; unclouded, unobscured†.

gairish†, garish; resplendent, transplendent†; refulgent, effulgent; fulgid†, fulgent†; relucent†, splendid, blazing, in a blaze, ablaze, rutilant†, meteoric, phosphorescent; aglow.

bright as silver; light as day, bright as day, light as noonday, bright as noonday, bright as the sun at noonday.

actinic; photogenic, graphic; heliographic; heliophagous†.

Phr. a day for gods to stoop and men to soar [Tennyson]; dark with excessive bright [Milton].

421. Darkness -- N. darkness &c *adj.*, absence of light; blackness &c *(dark color)* 431; obscurity, gloom, murk; dusk &c *(dimness)* 422.

Cimmerian darkness†, Stygian darkness, Egyptian darkness; night; midnight; dead of night, witching hour of night, witching time of night; blind man's holiday; darkness visible, darkness that can be felt; palpable obscure; Erebus *[Lat.]*; the jaws of darkness [Midsummer Night's Dream]; sablevested night [Milton].

shade, shadow, umbra, penumbra; sciagraphy†.

obscuration; occultation, adumbration, obumbration†; obtenebration†, offuscation†, caligation†; extinction; eclipse, total eclipse; gathering of the clouds.

shading; distribution of shade; chiaroscuro &c *(light)* 420.

noctivagation†.

[perfectly black objects] black body; hohlraum *[Phys.]*; black hole; dark star; dark matter, cold dark matter.

V. be dark &c *adj..* darken, obscure, shade; dim; tone down, lower; overcast, overshadow; eclipse; obfuscate, offuscate†; obumbrate†, adumbrate; cast into the shade becloud, bedim†, bedarken†; cast a shade, throw a shade, spread a shade, cast a shadow, cast a gloom, throw a shadow, spread a shadow, cast gloom, throw gloom, spread gloom.

extinguish; put out, blow out, snuff out; doubt.

turn out the lights, douse the lights, dim the lights, turn off the lights, switch off the lights.

Adj. dark, darksome†, darkling; obscure, tenebrious†, sombrous†, pitch dark, pitchy, pitch black; caliginous†; black &c *(in color)* 431.

sunless, lightless &c *(sun) (light),* &c 423; somber, dusky; unilluminated &c *(illuminate)* &c 420 [Obs.]; nocturnal; dingy, lurid, gloomy; murky, murksome†; shady, umbrageous; overcast &c *(dim)* 422; cloudy

&c *(opaque)* 426; darkened; &c v.. dark as pitch, dark as a pit, dark as Erebus *[Lat.]*.

benighted; noctivagant†, noctivagous†.

Adv. in the dark, in the shade.

Phr. brief as the lightning in the collied night [M. N. D.]; eldest Night and Chaos, ancestors of Nature [Paradise Lost]; the blackness of the noonday night [Longfellow]; the prayer of Ajax was for light [Longfellow].

422. Dimness -- **N.** dimness &c *adj.;* darkness &c 421; paleness &c *(light color)* 429.

half light, demi-jour; partial shadow, partial eclipse; shadow of a shade; glimmer, gliming†; nebulosity; cloud &c 353; eclipse.

aurora, dusk, twilight, shades of evening, crepuscule, cockshut time†; break of day, daybreak, dawn.

moonlight, moonbeam, moonglade†, moonshine; starlight, owl's light, candlelight, rushlight, firelight; farthing candle.

V. be dim, grow dim &c *adj.;* flicker, twinkle, glimmer; loom, lower; fade; pale, pale its ineffectual fire [Hamlet].

render dim &c *adj.;* dim, bedim†, obscure; darken, tone down.

Adj. dim, dull, lackluster, dingy, darkish, shorn of its beams, dark 421.

faint, shadowed forth; glassy; cloudy; misty &c *(opaque)* 426; blear; muggy†, fuliginous†; nebulous, nebular; obnubilated†, overcast, crepuscular, muddy, lurid, leaden, dun, dirty; looming &c *v.*. pale &c *(colorless)* 429; confused &c *(invisible)* 447.

423. *[Source of light, self-luminous body.]* **Luminary** -- **N.** luminary; light &c 420; flame &c *(fire)* 382.

spark, scintilla; phosphorescence, fluorescence.

sun, orb of day, Phoebus, Apollo†, Aurora; star, orb; meteor, falling star, shooting star; blazing star, dog star, Sirius; canicula, Aldebaran†; constellation, galaxy; zodiacal light; anthelion†; day star, morning star; Lucifer; mock sun, parhelion; phosphor, phosphorus; sun dog†; Venus.

aurora, polar lights; northern lights, aurora borealis; southern lights, aurora australis.

lightning; chain lightning, fork lightning, sheet lightning, summer lightning; ball lightning, kugelblitz *[G.]*; *[chemical substances giving off light without burning]* phosphorus, yellow phosphorus; scintillator, phosphor; firefly luminescence.

ignis fatuus *[Lat.]*; Jack o'lantern, Friar's lantern; will-o'-the-wisp, firedrake†, Fata Morgana *[Lat.]*; Saint Elmo's fire.

[luminous insects] glowworm, firefly, June bug, lightning bug.

[luminous fish] anglerfish.

[Artificial light] gas; gas light, lime light, lantern, lanthorn†; dark lantern, bull's-eye; candle, bougie *[Fr.]*, taper, rushlight; oil &c *(grease)* 356; wick, burner; Argand†, moderator, duplex; torch, flambeau, link, brand; gaselier†, chandelier, electrolier†, candelabrum, candelabra, girandole†, sconce, luster, candlestick.

[non-combustion based light sources] lamp, light; incandescent lamp, tungsten bulb, light bulb; flashlight, torch *[Brit.]*; arc light; laser; *[microwave radiation];* maser neon bulb, neon sign; fluorescent lamp.

[parts of a light bulb] filament; socket; contacts; filler gas.

firework, fizgig†; pyrotechnics; rocket, lighthouse &c *(signal)* 550.

V. illuminate &c *(light)* 420.

Adj. self-luminous, glowing; phosphoric†, phosphorescent, fluorescent; incandescent; luminescent, chemiluminescent; radiant &c *(light)* 420.

Phr. blossomed the lovely stars, the forget-me-nots of the angels [Longfellow]; the sentinel stars set their watch in the sky [Campbell]; the planets in their station list'ning stood [Paradise Lost]; the Scriptures of the skies [Bailey]; that orbed continent, the fire that severs day from night [Twelfth Night].

424. Shade -- **N.** shade; awning &c *(cover)* 223; parasol, sunshade, umbrella; chick; portiere; screen, curtain, shutter, blind, gauze, veil, chador, mantle, mask; cloud, mist, gathering.

of clouds.

umbrage, glade; shadow &c 421.

beach umbrella, folding umbrella.

V. draw a curtain; put up a shutter, close a shutter; veil &c *v.;* cast a shadow &c *(darken)* 421.

Adj. shady, umbrageous.

Phr. welcome ye shades! ye bowery thickets hail [Thomson].

425. Transparency -- **N.** transparence, transparency; clarity; translucence, translucency; diaphaneity†; lucidity, pellucidity†, limpidity; fluorescence; transillumination, translumination†.

transparent medium, glass, crystal, lymph, vitrite†, water.

V. be transparent &c *adj.;* transmit light.

Adj. transparent, pellucid, lucid, diaphanous, translucent, tralucent†, relucent†; limpid, clear, serene, crystalline, clear as crystal, vitreous, transpicuous†, glassy, hyaline; hyaloid *[Med.]*, vitreform†.

426. Opacity -- **N.** opacity; opaqueness &c *adj.*. film; cloud &c 353.

V. be opaque &c *adj.;* obstruct the passage of light; obfuscate, offuscate†.

Adj. opaque, impervious to light; adiaphanous†; dim &c 422; turbid, thick, muddy, opacous†, obfuscated, fuliginous†, cloud, hazy, misty, foggy, vaporous, nubiferous†, muggy† &c *(turbidity)* 426.1.

smoky, fumid†, murky, dirty.

426a. Turbidity -- **N.** turbidity, cloudiness, fog, haze, muddiness, haziness, obscurity.

nephelometer *[instrument to measure turbidity]*.

Adj. turbid, thick, muddy, obfuscated, fuliginous†, hazy, misty, foggy, vaporous, nubiferous†; cloudy *(cloud)* 353.

smoky, fumid†, murky, dirty.

427. Semitransparency -- **N.** semitransparency, translucency, semiopacity; opalescence, milkiness, pearliness†; gauze, muslin; film; mica, mother-of-pearl, nacre; mist &c *(cloud)* 353.

[opalescent jewel] opal.

turbidity &c 426.1.

Adj. semitransparent, translucent, semipellucid†, semidiaphanous†, semiopacous†, semiopaque;

opalescent, opaline†; pearly, milky; frosted, nacreous.

V. opalesce.

(ii) SPECIFIC LIGHT

428. Color -- **N.** color, hue, tint, tinge, dye, complexion, shade, tincture, cast, livery, coloration, glow, flush; tone, key.

pure color, positive color, primary color, primitive complementary color; three primaries; spectrum, chromatic dispersion; broken color, secondary color, tertiary color.

local color, coloring, keeping, tone, value, aerial perspective.

[Science of color] chromatics, spectrum analysis, spectroscopy; chromatism†, chromatography†, chromatology†.

[instruments to measure color] prism, spectroscope, spectrograph, spectrometer, colorimeter *(optical instruments)* 445.

pigment, coloring matter, paint, dye, wash, distemper, stain; medium; mordant; oil paint &c (painting) 556.

white as a sheet, white as driven snow, white as a lily, white as silver; like ivory &c *n..*

431. Blackness -- N. blackness, &c *adj.;* darkness, &c *(want of light)..* 421; swartliness†, lividity, dark color, tone, color; chiaroscuro &c 420.

nigrification†, infuscation†.

jet, ink, ebony, coal pitch, soot, charcoal, sloe, smut, raven, crow.

[derogatory terms for black-skinned people] negro, blackamoor, man of color, nigger, darkie, Ethiop, black; buck, nigger *[U.S.]*; coon *[U.S.]*, sambo.

[Pigments] lampblack, ivory black, blueblack; writing ink, printing ink, printer's ink, Indian ink, India ink.

V. be black &c *adj.;* render black &c *adj..* blacken, infuscate†, denigrate; blot, blotch; smutch†; smirch; darken &c 421.

black, sable, swarthy, somber, dark, inky, ebony, ebon, atramentous†, jetty; coal-black, jet-black; fuliginous†, pitchy, sooty, swart, dusky, dingy, murky, Ethiopic; low-toned, low in tone; of the deepest dye.

black as jet &c *n.,* black as my hat, black as a shoe, black as a tinker's pot, black as November, black as thunder, black as midnight; nocturnal &c *(dark)* 421; nigrescent†; gray &c 432; obscure &c 421.

Adv. in mourning.

432. Gray -- **N.** gray &c *adj.;* neutral tint, silver, pepper and salt, chiaroscuro, grisaille *[Fr.]*.

[Pigments] Payne's gray; black &c 431.

Adj. gray, grey; iron-gray, dun, drab, dingy, leaden, livid, somber, sad, pearly, russet, roan; calcareous, limy, favillous†; silver, silvery, silvered; ashen, ashy; cinereous†, cineritious†; grizzly, grizzled; slate-colored, stone-colored, mouse-colored, ash-colored; cool.

433. Brown -- **N.** brown &c *adj.. [Pigments],,* bister ocher, sepia, Vandyke brown.

V. render brown &c *adj.;* tan, embrown†, bronze.

Adj. brown, bay, dapple, auburn, castaneous†, chestnut, nut-brown, cinnamon, russet, tawny, fuscous†, chocolate, maroon, foxy, tan, brunette, whitey brown†; fawn-colored, snuff-colored, liver-colored; brown as a berry, brown as mahogany, brown as the oak leaves; khaki.

sun-burnt; tanned &c *v.*.

Primitive Colors

434. Redness -- **N.** red, scarlet, vermilion, carmine, crimson, pink, lake, maroon, carnation, couleur de rose *[Fr.]*, rose du Barry†; magenta, damask, purple; flesh color, flesh tint; color; fresh color, high color; warmth; gules *[Heral.]*.

ruby, carbuncle; rose; rust, iron mold.

[Dyes and pigments] cinnabar, cochineal; fuchsine†; ruddle†, madder; Indian red, light red, Venetian red; red ink, annotto†; annatto†, realgar, minium†, red lead.

redness &c *adj.;* rubescence†, rubicundity, rubification†; erubescence†, blush.

V. be red, become red &c *adj.;* blush, flush, color up, mantle, redden.

render red &c *adj.;* redden, rouge; rubify†, rubricate; incarnadine.; ruddle†.

Adj. red &c *n.,* reddish; rufous, ruddy, florid, incarnadine, sanguine; rosy, roseate; blowzy, blowed†; burnt; rubicund, rubiform†; lurid, stammell blood red†; russet buff, murrey†, carroty†, sorrel, lateritious†; rubineous†, rubricate, rubricose†, rufulous†.

rose-colored, ruby-colored, cherry-colored, claret-colored, flame-colored, flesh-colored, peach-colored, salmon-colored, brick-colored, brick-colored, dust-colored.

blushing &c *v.;* erubescent†; reddened &c *v..* red as fire, red as blood, red as scarlet, red as a turkey cock, red as a lobster; warm, hot; foxy.

Complementary Colors

435. Greenness -- **N.** green &c *adj.;* blue and yellow; vert *[Heral.].*

emerald, verd antique *[Fr.]*, verdigris, malachite, beryl, aquamarine; absinthe, cr=eme de menthe *[Fr.].*

[Pigments] terre verte *[Fr.]*, verditer†, verdine†, copperas.

greenness, verdure; viridity†, viridescence†; verditure†.

[disease of eyes with green tint] glaucoma, rokunaisho *[Jap.Tr.]*.

Adj. green, verdant; glaucous, olive, olive green; green as grass; verdurous.

emerald green, pea green, grass green, apple green, sea green, olive green, bottle green, coke bottle green.

greenish; virent†, virescent†.

green *(learner)* 541, new, inexperienced, novice, *(unskillful)* 699.

green (ill, sick).

Phr. green with envy; the green grass of Ireland; the wearing of the green.

436. Yellowness -- **N.** yellow &c *adj.;* or.

[Pigments] gamboge; cadmium-yellow, chrome-yellow, Indian-yellow king's-yellow, lemonyellow; orpiment†, yellow ocher, Claude tint, aureolin†; xanthein *[Chem]*, xanthin†; zaofulvin†.

crocus, saffron, topaz; xanthite†; yolk.

jaundice; London fog†; yellowness &c *adj.;* icterus†; xantho-cyanopia†, xanthopsia *[Med.]*.

Adj. yellow, aureate, golden, flavous†, citrine, fallow; fulvous†, fulvid†; sallow, luteous†, tawny, creamy, sandy; xanthic†, xanthous†; jaundiced†, auricomous†.

gold-colored, citron-colored, saffron-colored, lemon-colored, lemon yellow, sulphur-colored, amber-colored, straw-colored, primrose-colored, creamcolored; xanthocarpous†, xanthochroid†, xanthopous†.

yellow as a quince, yellow as a guinea, yellow as a crow's foot.

warm, advancing.

437. Purple -- N. purple &c *adj.;* blue and red, bishop's purple; aniline dyes, gridelin†, amethyst; purpure *[Heral.]*; heliotrope.

lividness, lividity.

V. empurple†.

Adj. purple, violet, ultraviolet; plum-colored, lavender, lilac, puce, mauve; livid.

438. Blueness -- **N.** blue &c *adj.;* garter-blue; watchet†.

[Pigments] ultramarine, smalt, cobalt, cyanogen *[Chem]*; Prussian blue, syenite blue†; bice†, indigo; zaffer†.

lapis lazuli, sapphire, turquoise; indicolite†.

blueness, bluishness; bloom.

Adj. blue, azure, cerulean; sky-blue, sky-colored, sky-dyed; cerulescent†; powder blue, bluish; atmospheric, retiring; cold.

439. Orange -- **N.** orange, red and yellow; gold; or; flame color &c *adj.. [Pigments]* ocher, Mars'orange†, cadmium.

cardinal bird, cardinal flower, cardinal grosbeak, cardinal lobelia (a flowering plant).

V. gild, warm.

Adj. orange; ochreous†; orange-colored, gold-colored, flame-colored, copper-colored, brass-colored, apricot-colored; warm, hot, glowing.

440. Variegation -- N. variegation; colors, dichroism, trichroism; iridescence, play of colors, polychrome, maculation, spottiness, striae.

spectrum, rainbow, iris, tulip, peacock, chameleon, butterfly, tortoise shell; mackerel, mackerel sky; zebra, leopard, cheetah, nacre, ocelot, ophite[†], mother-of-pearl, opal, marble.

check, plaid, tartan, patchwork; marquetry-, parquetry; mosaic, tesserae[†], strigae[†]; chessboard, checkers, chequers; harlequin; Joseph's coat; tricolor.

V. be variegated &c *adj.;* variegate, stripe, streak, checker, chequer; bespeckle[†], speckle; besprinkle, sprinkle; stipple, maculate, dot, bespot[†]; tattoo, inlay, damascene; embroider, braid, quilt.

Adj. variegated &c *v.;* many-colored, many-hued; divers-colored, party-colored; dichromatic, polychromatic; bicolor[†], tricolor, versicolor[†]; of all the colors of the rainbow, of all manner of colors; kaleidoscopic.

iridescent; opaline[†], opalescent; prismatic, nacreous, pearly, shot, gorge de pigeon, chatoyant[†]; irisated[†], pavonine[†].

pied, piebald; motley; mottled, marbled; pepper and salt, paned, dappled, clouded, cymophanous[†].

mosaic, tesselated, plaid; tortoise shell &c *n.*. spotted, spotty; punctated[†], powdered;

speckled &c v.; freckled, flea-bitten, studded; flecked, fleckered†; striated, barred, veined; brinded†, brindled; tabby; watered; grizzled; listed; embroidered &c v.; daedal†; naevose†, stipiform†; strigose†, striolate†.

(iii) PERCEPTIONS OF LIGHT

441. Vision -- N. vision, sight, optics, eyesight.

view, look, espial†, glance, ken *[Scot.]*, coup d'oeil *[Fr.]*; glimpse, glint, peep; gaze, stare, leer; perlustration†, contemplation; conspection†, conspectuity†; regard, survey; introspection; reconnaissance, speculation, watch, espionage, espionnage *[Fr.]*, autopsy; ocular inspection, ocular demonstration; sight-seeing.

point of view; gazebo, loophole, belvedere, watchtower.

field of view; theater, amphitheater, arena, vista, horizon; commanding view, bird's eye view; periscope.

visual organ, organ of vision; eye; naked eye, unassisted eye; retina, pupil, iris, cornea, white; optics, orbs; saucer eyes, goggle eyes, gooseberry eyes.

short sight &c 443; clear sight, sharp sight, quick sight, eagle sight, piercing sight, penetrating sight, clear glance, sharp glance, quick glance, eagle glance, piercing glance, penetrating glance, clear eye, sharp eye, quick eye, eagle eye, piercing eye, penetrating eye; perspicacity, discernment; catopsis[†].

eagle, hawk; cat, lynx; Argus[†].

evil eye; basilisk, cockatrice *[Myth.]*.

V. see, behold, discern, perceive, have in sight, descry, sight, make out, discover, distinguish, recognize, spy, espy, ken *[Scot.]*; get a sight of, have a sight of, catch a sight of, get a glimpse of, have a glimpse of, catch a glimpse of; command a view of; witness, contemplate, speculate; cast the eyes on, set the eyes on; be a spectator of &c 444; look on &c *(be present)* 186; see sights &c *(curiosity)* 455; see at a glance &c *(intelligence)* 498.

look, view, eye; lift up the eyes, open one's eye; look at, look on, look upon, look over, look about one, look round; survey, scan, inspect; run the eye over, run the eye through; reconnoiter, glance round, glance on, glance over turn one's looks upon, bend one's looks upon; direct the eyes to, turn the eyes on, cast a glance.

observe &c *(attend to)* 457; watch &c *(care)* 459; see with one's own eyes; watch for &c *(expect)* 507; peep, peer, pry, take a peep; play at bopeep[†].

look full in the face, look hard at, look intently; strain one's eyes; fix the eyes upon, rivet the eyes upon; stare, gaze; pore over, gloat on; leer, ogle, glare; goggle; cock the eye, squint, gloat, look askance.

Adj. seeing &c *v.;* visual, ocular; optic, optical; ophthalmic.

clear-eyesighted &c *n.;* eagle-eyed, hawk-eyed, lynx-eyed, keen-eyed, Argus-eyed.

visible &c 446.

Adv. visibly &c 446; in sight of, with one's eyes open at sight, at first sight, at a glance, at the first blush; prima facie *[Lat.]*.

Int. look!, &c *(attention)* 457.

Phr. the scales falling from one's eyes; an eye like Mars to threaten or command [Hamlet]; her eyes are homes of silent prayer [Tennyson]; looking before and after [Hamlet]; thy rapt soul sitting in thine eyes [Milton].

442. Blindness -- N. blindness, cecity[†], execation[†], amaurosis[†], cataract, ablepsy[†], ablepsia[†], prestriction[†]; dim-sightedness &c 443; Braille, Braille-type; guttaserena (drop serene), noctograph[†], teichopsia[†].

V. be blind &c *adj.;* not see; lose sight of; have the eyes bandaged; grope in the dark.

not look; close the eyes, shut the eyes-, turn away the eyes, avert the eyes; look another way; wink &c *(limited vision)* 443; shut the eyes to, be blind to, wink at, blink at.

render blind &c *adj.;* blind, blindfold; hoodwink, dazzle, put one's eyes out; throw dust into one's eyes, pull the wool over one's eyes; jeter de la poudre aux yeux *[Fr.]*; screen from sight &c*(hide)* 528.

Adj. blind; eyeless, sightless, visionless; dark; stone-blind, sand-blind, stark-blind; undiscerning[†]; dimsighted &c 443.

blind as a bat, blind as a buzzard, blind as a beetle, blind as a mole, blind as an owl; wall-eyed.

blinded &c *v..*

Adv. blindly, blindfold, blindfolded; darkly.

Phr. O dark, dark, dark, amid the blaze of noon [Milton].

443. *[Imperfect vision.]* **Dimsightedness** *[Fallacies of vision.]* -- **N.** dim sight, dull sight half sight, short sight, near sight, long sight, double sight, astigmatic sight, failing sight; dimsightedness

&c.; purblindness, lippitude†; myopia, presbyopia†; confusion of vision; astigmatism; color blindness, chromato pseudo blepsis†, Daltonism; nyctalopia†; strabismus, strabism†, squint; blearedness†, day blindness, hemeralopia†, nystagmus; xanthocyanopia†, xanthopsia *[Med.]*; cast in the eye, swivel eye, goggle-eyes; obliquity of vision.

winking &c *v.;* nictitation; blinkard†, albino.

dizziness, swimming, scotomy†; cataract; ophthalmia.

[Limitation of vision] blinker; screen &c *(hider)* 530.

[Fallacies of vision] deceptio visus *[Lat.]*; refraction, distortion, illusion, false light, anamorphosis†, virtual image, spectrum, mirage, looming, phasma†; phantasm, phantasma†, phantom; vision; specter, apparition, ghost; ignis fatuus *[Lat.]* &c *(luminary)* 423; specter of the Brocken; magic mirror; magic lantern &c *(show)* 448; mirror lens &c *(instrument)* 445.

V. be dimsighted &c *n.;* see double; have a mote in the eye, have a mist before the eyes, have a film over the eyes; see through a prism, see through a glass darkly; wink, blink, nictitate; squint; look askant†, askant askance†; screw up the eyes, glare, glower; nictate†.

dazzle, loom.

Adj. dim-sighted &c *n.;* myopic, presbyopic†; astigmatic, moon-eyed, mope-eyed, blear-eyed, goggle-eyed, gooseberry-eyed, one-eyed; blind of one eye, monoculous†; half-blind, purblind; cock-eyed, dim-eyed, mole-eyed; dichroic.

blind as a bat &c *(blind)* 442; winking &c *v..*

444. Spectator -- **N.** spectator, beholder, observer, looker-on, onlooker, witness, eyewitness, bystander, passer by; sightseer; rubberneck, rubbernecker *[U.S.]*.

spy; sentinel &c *(warning)* 668.

V. witness, behold &c *(see)* 441; look on &c *(be present)* 186; gawk, rubber *[Slang]*, rubberneck *[U.S.]*.

445. Optical Instruments -- **N.** optical instruments; lens, meniscus, magnifier, sunglass, magnifying glass, hand lens; microscope, megascope†, tienoscope†.

spectacles, specs *[Coll.]*, glasses, barnacles, goggles, eyeglass, pince-nez, monocle, reading glasses, bifocals; contact lenses, soft lenses, hard lenses; sunglasses, shades *[Coll.]*.

periscopic lens[†]; telescope, glass, lorgnette; spyglass, opera glass, binocular, binoculars, field glass; burning glass, convex lens, concave lens, convexo-concave lens[†], coated lens, multiple lens, compound lens, lens system, telephoto lens, wide-angle lens, fish-eye lens, zoom lens; optical bench.

astronomical telescope, reflecting telescope, reflector, refracting telescope, refractor, Newtonian telescope, folded-path telescope, finder telescope, chromatoscope; X-ray telescope; radiotelescope, phased-array telescope, Very Large Array radiotelescope; ultraviolet telescope; infrared telescope; star spectroscope; space telescope.

[telescope mounts] altazimuth mount, equatorial mount.

refractometer, circular dichroism spectrometer.

interferometer.

phase-contrast microscope, fluorescence microscope, dissecting microscope; electron microscope, transmission electron microscope; scanning electron microscope, SEM; scanning tunneling electron microscope.

[microscope components] objective lens, eyepiece, barrel, platform, focusing knob; slide, slide glass, cover glass, counting chamber; illuminator, light source, polarizer, *[component parts of telescopes]* reticle, cross-hairs.

light pipe, fiber optics mirror, reflector, speculum; looking-glass, pier-glass, cheval-glass, rear-view mirror, hand mirror, one-way mirror, magnifying mirror.

[room with distorting mirrors] fun house.

prism, diffraction grating; beam splitter, half-wave plate, quarter-wave plate.

camera lucida *[Lat.]*, camera obscura *[Lat.]*; magic lantern &c *(show)* 448; stereopticon; chromatrope†, thaumatrope†; stereoscope, pseudoscope†, polyscope†, kaleidoscope.

photometer, eriometer†, actinometer†, lucimeter†, radiometer; ligth detector, photodiode, photomultiplier, photodiode array, photocell.

X-ray diffractometer, goniometer.

spectrometer, monochromer, UV spectrometer, visible spectrometer, Infrared spectrometer, Fourier transform infrared spectrometer, recording spectrometer; densitometer, scanning densitometer, two-dimensional densitometer.

abdominoscope†, gastroscope *[Med.]*, helioscope†, polariscope†, polemoscope†, spectroscope.

abdominoscopy†; gastroscopy *[Med.]*; microscopy, microscopist.

446. Visibility -- **N.** visibility, perceptibility; conspicuousness, distinctness &c *adj.;* conspicuity[†], conspicuousness; appearance &c 448; bassetting[†]; exposure; manifestation &c 525; ocular proof, ocular evidence, ocular demonstration; field of view &c *(vision)* 441; periscopism[†].

V. be become visible &c *adj.;* appear, open to the view; meet the eye, catch the eye; basset; present itself, show manifest itself, produce itself, discover itself, reveal itself, expose itself, betray itself; stand forth, stand out; materialize; show; arise; peep out, peer out, crop out; start up, spring up, show up, turn up, crop up; glimmer, loom; glare; burst forth; burst upon the view, burst upon the sight; heave in sight; come in sight, come into view, come out, come forth, come forward; see the light of day; break through the clouds; make its appearance, show its face, appear to one's eyes, come upon the stage, float before the eyes, speak for itself &c *(manifest)* 525; attract the attention &c 457; reappear; live in a glass house.

expose to view &c 525.

Adj. visible, perceptible, perceivable, discernible, apparent; in view, in full view, in sight; exposed to view, en vidence; unclouded, unobscured[†], in the foreground.

obvious &c *(manifest)* 525; plain, clear, distinct, definite; well defined, well marked; in focus; recognizable, palpable, autoptical†; glaring, staring, conspicuous; stereoscopic; in bold, in strong relief.

periscopic†, panoramic.

before one's eyes, under one's eyes; before one, +a vue d'oeil *[Fr.]*, in one's eye, oculis subjecta fidelibus *[Lat.]*.

Adv. visibly &c *adj.;* in sight of; before one's eyes &c *adj.;* veluti in speculum *[Lat.]*.

447. Invisibility -- N. invisibility, invisibleness, nonappearance, imperceptibility; indistinctness &c *adj.;* mystery, delitescence†.

concealment &c 528; latency &c 526.

V. be invisible &c *adj.;* be hidden &c *(hide)* 528; lurk &c *(lie hidden)* 526; escape notice.

render invisible &c *adj.;* conceal &c 528; put out of sight.

not see &c *(be blind)* 442; lose sight of.

Adj. invisible, imperceptible; undiscernible†, indiscernible; unapparent, non-apparent; out of sight, not in sight; a perte de vue *[Fr.]*; behind the scenes, behind the curtain; viewless, sightless; inconspicuous, unconspicuous†; unseen &c *(see)* &c 441; covert &c *(latent)* 526; eclipsed, under an eclipse.

dim &c *(faint)* 422; mysterious, dark, obscure, confused; indistinct, indistinguishable; shadowy, indefinite, undefined; ill-defined, ill-marked; blurred, fuzzy, out of focus; misty &c *(opaque)* 426; delitescent†.

hidden, obscured, covered, veiled *(concealed)* 528.

Phr. full many a flower is born to blush unseen [Gray].

448. Appearance -- **N.** appearance, phenomenon, sight, spectacle, show, premonstration†, scene, species, view, coup d'oeil *[Fr.]*; lookout, outlook, prospect, vista, perspective, bird's-eye view, scenery, landscape, picture, tableau; display, exposure, mise en sc ne *[Fr.]*; rising of the curtain.

phantasm, phantom &c *(fallacy of vision)* 443.

pageant, spectacle; peep-show, raree-show, gallanty-show; ombres chinoises *[Sp.]*; magic lantern, phantasmagoria, dissolving views; biograph†, cinematograph, moving pictures; panorama, diorama, cosmorama†, georama†; coup de theatre, jeu de theatre *[Fr.]*; pageantry &c *(ostentation)* 882; insignia &c *(indication)* 550.

aspect, angle, phase, phasis†, seeming; shape &c *(form)* 240; guise, look, complexion, color, image, mien, air, cast, carriage, port, demeanor; presence, expression, first blush, face of the thing; point of view, light.

lineament feature trait lines; outline, outside; contour, face, countenance, physiognomy, visage, phiz., cast of countenance, profile, tournure†, cut of one s jib, metoposcopy†; outside &c 220.

V. appear; be visible, become visible &c 446; seem, look, show; present the appearance of, wear the appearance of, carry the appearance of, have the appearance of, bear the appearance of, exhibit the appearance of, take the appearance of, take on the appearance of, assume the appearance, present the semblance of, wear the semblance of, carry the semblance of, have the semblance of, bear the semblance of, exhibit the semblance of, take the semblance of, take on the semblance of, assume the semblance of; look like; cut a figure, figure; present to the view; show &c *(make manifest)* 525.

Adj. apparent, seeming, ostensible; on view.

Adv. apparently; to all seeming, to all appearance; ostensibly, seemingly, as it seems, on the face of it, prima facie *[Lat.]*; at the first blush, at first sight; in the eyes of; to the eye.

Phr. editio princeps *[Lat.]*.

449. Disappearance -- **N.** disappearance, evanescence, eclipse, occultation.

departure &c 293; exit; vanishing point; dissolving views.

V. disappear, vanish, dissolve, fade, melt away, pass, go, avaunt†, evaporate, vaporize; be gone &c *adj.;* leave no trace, leave 'not a rack behind' [Tempest]; go off the stage &c *(depart)* 293; suffer an eclipse, undergo an eclipse; retire from sight; be lost to view, pass out of sight.

lose sight of.

efface &c 552.

Adj. disappearing &c *v.;* evanescent; missing, lost; lost to sight, lost to view; gone.

Int. vanish!, disappear!, avaunt!†, get lost!, get out of here &c *(ejection)* 297.

CLASS IV

WORDS RELATING TO THE INTELLECTUAL FACULTIES

DIVISION I

FORMATION OF IDEAS

SECTION I.

OPERATIONS OF INTELLECT IN GENERAL

450. Intellect -- N. intellect, mind, understanding, reason, thinking principle; rationality; cogitative faculties, cognitive faculties, discursive faculties, reasoning faculties, intellectual faculties; faculties, senses, consciousness, observation, percipience, intelligence, intellection, intuition, association of ideas, instinct, conception, judgment, wits, parts, capacity, intellectuality, genius; brain

Copyright: Distributed in the United States

By Peter Mark Roget

Published in 29 April 1852

Copyright ©. No part of this publication may be reproduced, stored in a system, pulled in any form or by any means electronic, mechanical, photocopying, recording or otherwise sent without the written permission of the publisher. Please do not participate in or support copyright infringement of this content in any way. You must not rotate this book in any form Darin Saelee Do not control or control users directly '